Worlds of Wonder: Readings in Canadian Science Fiction and Fantasy Literature

26

REAPPRAISALS:
CANADIAN
WRITERS

Worlds of Wonder: Readings in Canadian Science Fiction and Fantasy Literature

Edited by
Jean-François Leroux and
Camille R. La Bossière

University of Ottawa Press

REAPPRAISALS
Canadian Writers

Gerald Lynch
General Editor

National Library of Canada Cataloguing in Publication

Worlds of wonder : readings in Canadian science fiction and fantasy literature / edited by Jean-François Leroux and Camille La Bossière.

(Reappraisals, Canadian writers ; 26)
Includes bibliographical references.
ISBN 0-7766-0570-4

1. Science fiction, Canadian (English) – History and criticism.
2. Fantastic fiction, Canadian (English) – History and criticism.
3. Canadian fiction, (English) – 20th century – History and criticism.
I. Leroux, Jean-François II. La Bossière, Camille R. III. Series.

PS8191.S34W67 2004 C813'.087609054 C2003-905901-4

University of Ottawa Press gratefully acknowledges the support extended to its publishing programme by the Canada Council and the University of Ottawa.

We acknowledge the financial support of the Government of Canada through the Book Publishing Industry Development Program (BPIDP) for our publishing activities.

UNIVERSITY OF OTTAWA
UNIVERSITÉ D'OTTAWA

Cover illustration: Hourglass Nebula. Courtesy of NASA/JPL/Caltech.
Cover design by Laura Brady
Copyedited by Käthe Roth
Proofreading by Joan Irving

ISBN 0-7766-0570-4
ISSN 1189-6787

542 King Edward, Ottawa, Ont. Canada K1N 6N5
press@uottawa.ca http://www.uopress.uottawa.ca

Printed and bound in Canada

Contents

Introduction

JEAN-FRANÇOIS LEROUX

> Nous disions le contraire de ce que nous voulions puis le contraire encore... Malgré ce cauchemar, je me suis obstiné. Sur mon tourne-disques, pour rêver que je revenais sur terre, j'ai mis 'la nuit' de Vivaldi. Mes hauts parleurs on craché, grondé, toussé puis jeté à pleins flots du Wagner. Bon joueur, j'ai lancé Wagner à la conquête du Graal. Progrès: ça m'a donné 'chu t'un homme ordinaire' de Robert Charlebois. Très bien: j'ai fait appel aux 'ancêtres' de Georges Dor mais les ai retrouvés en pleins 'nuit et brouillard' de Jean Ferrat. Puis cela s'est transformé en rafales d'orage électrique, aussitôt interrompues par d'immenses éclats de rire de nez. Puis tout s'est tu.
>
> – Jacques Brossard, *Le Métamorfaux* (1988)

> The interface is where the action is. No need to move or follow, but only to tune the perceptions on the spot.
>
> – Marshall McLuhan, "Canada: The Borderline Case" (1977)

> The sky above the port was the color of television, tuned to a dead channel.
>
> – William Gibson, *Neuromancer* (1984)

NORTHROP FRYE ONCE FAMOUSLY observed that the question nagging much of Canadian literature is not "Who am I?" but "Where is here?" Preoccupied as it is (in the popular conception, at least) with brains in jars on Mars and similarly fabulous fairyland fare, science fiction and fantasy would seem singularly unsuited to answering such a question. However, the very title of "master gatherer," John Robert Colombo's 1979 collection of Canadian SF and fantasy, the first-ever such collection—*Other Canadas*—suggests the contrary.

In their introduction to a compendium of scholarly essays on the *topos* commissioned by the National Library, *Out of This World: Canadian Science Fiction and Fantasy Literature* (1995), Allan Weiss and Hugh Spencer took up the challenge implicit in Colombo's designation by directing their attention to the "distinctly Canadian" theme of the "search for identity" (14). Naturally coming from thence to resolve Frye's question, the authors provide as their tentative answer the following: in contradistinction to British and American SF, the Canadian subset of the genre is "political as opposed to ... technological" in its "focus" (15). In other words, just as American SF from 1925 to 1965 rehearses "versions of the fable of America"—as the lead essay by John Clute in *Out of This World* goes on to elaborate—so, too, does SF this side of the border rhyme nicely with the rest of "Can Lit," notably in its adaptations of the "fable of survival" and the related themes treated by Colombo in the following essay (Clute 22, 26). Canadian SF, Clute concludes from an analysis of A. E. van Vogt's work, emphatically does not share the dominant SF "ethos" epitomized by the "patriotic populist positivism" of American SF, with its ostensible "trust in reason" sometimes merely amounting, as in the fiction of Robert A. Heinlein, to jingoistic boosterism (23).

Predictably, then, defining by opposition exactly what the Canadian ethos is, has become a major preoccupation of scholars in the field. In his otherwise pioneering study of the genre, *Canadian Science Fiction and Fantasy* (1992), David Ketterer ends on a prudent note, predicting the continuation of "an SF and fantasy that, at its best and typified by de Mille's *Strange Manuscript*, is open-minded, tentative, considered, tolerant, critical, subversive, and richly ambiguous" (167). To their credit, collectively and individually, all of the contributors to this volume, themselves mental travellers in a land at once uncanny and homely, valiantly strive to describe just such an ethos—and so, by extension, to answer the question "Where is here?"

Though by nature impossible to pinpoint on any map, the area of this concern can be circumscribed by a series of indirections. It can be perceived first, at a distance, by way of the attention that many of the contributors pay to narrative modes, emplotment being, since Aristotle, a means to communicate universal or cultural knowledge of human action and character—the domain of ethics and politics. Allusions to such theorists of "grand narratives" as Northrop Frye, Margaret Atwood, Frank Kermode, Jean-François Lyotard, and Fredric Jameson attest, again distantly, to this attention. Canadian SF and fantasy once broadly and usefully located in such a continuum with "international and historical developments in the genre" (Weiss)—as in the lead piece by Ketterer and the surveys of the genre, its evolution, and its subgenres by Allan Weiss and Judith Saltman—its "deeply moral and philosophical expressions in mythopoeic form" (Saltman) are further pressed into the service of local struggles for survival and identity, be they feminist-utopian (Amy J. Ransom), racial (Sherry Vint), post-colonial (Laurence Steven and Ceri Morgan), scientific-humanist (Raywat Deonandan and Ruby S. Ramraj), or national-cultural (Helen Siourbas). That these issues are also putatively issues of global concern is what Veronica Hollinger's envoi "On Being Canadian," over which hovers the (unsummoned) ghost of Marshall McLuhan, reminds us.[1] They are so because they are fundamentally ethical issues, having to do with the treatment of the other, the definition of the self, and their possible reconciliation. The exploration of an unsettled borderland between self and other, not only in Hollinger's envoi but in the contributions of Ransom, Steven, David J. Jarraway, and Dominick M. Grace, is evidence of this.

How, then, to return to our original question: can we define the place of this possible meeting? Many of the present contributors, following Frye, locate (our) virtue in the classical *via mediocritatis,* or golden mean between vices; others, such as Hollinger (and McLuhan), in (our) very "being-borderless."[2] Not surprisingly, given the ambiguity built into that act of self-definition, in this conspectus of Canadian SF and fantasy the utopian impulse toward reconciliation is repeatedly accompanied and challenged by a dystopian critique of the methods used to achieve it, sometimes even in the same piece. At the limit, as in the critiques of the colonial-romantic and utopian-romantic imaginary conducted by Colleen Franklin and myself, respectively, this impulse can be said to land the self in a hell of its own making. In fact, one of the major contributions of this study is suggested by the fact that discussions thus dovetail into each other.

Speculatively, in the fashion of Canadian SF and fantasy itself, the contributors tend to betray that "generous reticence" (71) characteristic of Canadian writing as a whole, according to Robert Kroetsch's "Beyond Nationalism: A Prologue" (1981). The nebula of contradictory intentions and theses so charted might consequently be read, with similar generosity, as a form of adequation. That is, it mimics in small the ironies that Ketterer has remarked in such leading Canadian SF and fantasy writers as William Gibson and van Vogt, Clute's representative author. In the works of these, Ketterer finds a preponderance of the colour grey suggestive of "a moral indeterminacy and a blurring of all realities": here, as in de Mille, "simple black-and-white oppositions [would] mask the truth" (144, 46). Ketterer finds the same "duality" and "ambivalence" in "the leading figure in Québec SF today," Élisabeth Vonarburg, figured this time in the shape of a Janus made to "embod[y] the mission of [Canadian] SF" (157, 83, 157). Fittingly, then, that figure is reduplicated both on the cover of Ketterer's book and in his conclusion: "SF depends largely on an appreciation of contexts and fantasy largely on deconstructive inversions of inner and outer. That appreciation and that deconstructive experience are very much Canadian. What should result—and I believe has resulted," as Ketterer signs off, looking forward and back, "is an SF and fantasy that ... is open-minded, tentative, considered, balanced, tolerant, critical, subversive, and richly ambiguous"(167). To that ethos the present collection is emphatically dedicated.

NOTES

1. See, for example, McLuhan's "Canada: The Borderline Case," in which he argues that Canada's state of "between-ness" can be made to serve, paradoxically, as a form of self-definition (233).
2. "Canada might well be described as the Switzerland of the world," writes Ketterer (167), rehearsing a theme familiar to students of McLuhan and Frye.

WORKS CITED

Clute, John. "Fables of Transcendence: The Challenge of Canadian Science Fiction." In Andrea Paradis, ed., *Out of this World: Canadian Science Fiction and Fantasy Literature*, 20–27. Kingston: Quarry Press and National Library of Canada, 1995.

Colombo, John Robert. "Four Hundred Years of Fantastic Literature in Canada." In Andrea Paradis, ed., *Out of this World: Canadian Science Fiction and Fantasy Literature*, 28–40. Kingston: Quarry Press and National Library of Canada, 1995.

Colombo, John Robert, ed. *Other Canadas: An Anthology of Science Fiction and Fantasy.* Toronto: McGraw-Hill Ryerson, 1979.

Ketterer, David. *Canadian Science Fiction and Fantasy.* Bloomington and Indianapolis: Indiana University Press, 1992.

Kroetsch, Robert. "Beyond Nationalism: A Prologue." In *The Lovely Treachery of Words: Essays Selected and New*, 64–72. Oxford: Oxford University Press, 1989.

McLuhan, Marshall. "Canada: The Borderline Case." In David Staines, ed., *The Canadian Imagination: Dimensions of a Literary Culture*, 226–48. Cambridge: Harvard University Press, 1977.

Weiss, Allan, and Hugh Spencer. "Introduction." In Andrea Paradis, ed., *Out of this World: Canadian Science Fiction and Fantasy Literature*, 12–19. Kingston: Quarry Press and National Library of Canada, 1995.

"Another Dimension of Space": Canadian Science Fiction and Fantasy and Atwood's *Blind Assassin*

DAVID KETTERER

AFTER THE 1974 PUBLICATION of my *New Worlds for Old: The Apocalyptic Imagination, Science Fiction, and American Literature*, I began teaching a survey course entitled "Science Fiction and Allied Literature." When I gave that course for a second time, in 1975–76, its content was much the same—no Canadian titles were included—but a student enrolled in that class told me that he thought the time was ripe for a first anthology of Canadian SF. I agreed and set about reading what was available and assembling a list of likely contents. I quickly discovered that what was available and that list of contents would have pretty much to coincide: an anthology would have to consist mainly of short stories, but Canadian SF short stories were in very short supply. I drafted an introduction and mailed it with a proposed list to the Canadian publisher Peter Martin Associates, which had recently published the SF collection *North by 2000: An Anthology of Canadian Science Fiction* (1975) by the American-born Canadian H. A. Hargreaves. Around the same time, I discovered that "master gatherer" John Robert Colombo was at work on a similar project. I was planning a trip to Toronto and arranged to visit Colombo at his Toronto home. There was little point in our both proceeding with anthologies the contents of which would significantly overlap. The upshot was that I sank my anthology into Colombo's. What was written as my introduction, "Canadian Science Fiction: A Survey," would figure as an essay in Colombo's *Other Canadas: An Anthology of Science Fiction and Fantasy* (1979).

Before long, I received a letter from William Toye, who was editing the *Oxford Companion to Canadian Literature*: Would I be willing to furnish an entry on Canadian SF and fantasy? My entry "Science Fiction and Fantasy in English and French" appeared in 1983 in the first edition of *The Oxford Companion to Canadian Literature*. In March of that year, an extended version was published in *Science-Fiction Studies* under the title "An Historical Survey of Canadian SF."

After editing the *Oxford Companion*, William Toye turned to editing a series of volumes on Canadian literary and cultural topics, and asked me to write one on Canadian SF and fantasy. Unfortunately (or fortunately), however, the field grew at such a rate during the 1980s that the manuscript that I finally submitted around 1990 was three times too long for the modest series for which it had been commissioned. In some desperation, I queried a number of Canadian publishers. There was some interest from McGill-Queen's University Press, but publication there would involve a lengthy process of grant-seeking. Because Indiana University Press had published the hardback edition of *New Worlds for Old*, I tried that press as well. And so it was that my *Canadian Science Fiction and Fantasy* was published by an American university press in 1992.

By 1992, the field of Canadian SF and fantasy was solidly established and boasted two international "stars," writers acclaimed both within the genres of SF and fantasy and within the parameters of mainstream literature. William Gibson achieved this acceptance with *Neuromancer* (1982), the novel that limned cyberspace and launched cyberpunk; and Margaret Atwood, with *The Handmaid's Tale* (1985), a feminist contribution to the dystopian tradition of Zamyatin and Orwell. While some might question Gibson's Canadian credentials, Atwood's are in no doubt. In the genre or field of Canadian fantasy, perhaps Guy Gavriel Kay comes closest to occupying the same space.

Margaret Atwood's recent novel, *The Blind Assassin* (2000), is not itself SF or fantasy, but it includes among its characters a writer of SF and fantasy, and instalments of a science-fantasy saga by that writer are ostensibly at the heart of Atwood's novel. The fact that many readers are likely to be puzzled (and perhaps irritated) by Atwood's SF-and-fantasy emphasis in this novel encourages me to attempt a variety of explanations by way of apology.

It is in *The Blind Assassin* that Atwood's own long-term interest in SF and fantasy comes to weigh in. Her survey of Canadian fantasy in Colombo's *Other Canadas* focuses on Canadian supernatural monsters, notably the Wendigo.[1] The Wendigo is also the subject of the third of four lectures that Atwood delivered at Oxford University in 1991, which were published as *Strange Things: The Malevolent North in Canadian Literature* (1995). Phantom monsters, prehistoric dinosaurs, it might be additionally noted, flit in and out of Atwood's 1979 novel *Life Before Man.*

Atwood first signalled her interest in the fantastic by her choice of topic for a doctoral dissertation at Harvard, the work of the three most famous Victorian Gothic romancers: H. Rider Haggard, author of *She* (1887); George Macdonald, author of *Phantastes* (1858) and *Lilith* (1895); and W. H. Hudson, author of *The Purple Land* (1885) and *The Crystal Age* (1885). Atwood did not complete her dissertation, but an offshoot was published in 1965 as "Superwoman Drawn and Quartered: The Early Forms of *She.*"[2]

Canadian poet Al Purdy seems to have been the first to note a science-fictional frisson in Atwood's poetry. In a 1971 review of her collection *The Journals of Susanna Moodie* (1970), Purdy claims that the poems "make a strange, slightly-off-from-reality impression on the reader, as if Atwood were from Mars. ... And Atwood is not talking to a possible reader; she is an entirely subjective Martian" (81). The Canadian academic and Hugo Award-winning SF fan Susan Wood Glicksohn usefully elaborated on Purdy's insight in her 1974 article "The Martian Point of View," in which she claims that Atwood's "double voice, this stance of a stranger and a native in a strange land gives [her] poetry its science fiction quality" (163). Poetry titles such as *Speeches for Doctor Frankenstein* (1966) and *Interlunar* (1984) further signpost her SF interest.[3]

The Gothic novel *Lady Oracle* in Atwood's 1976 novel *Lady Oracle* anticipates the science-fantasy novel about a blind assassin in *The Blind Assassin.* Joan Foster, the heroine of the earlier novel, finally decides, "I won't write any more Costume Gothic ... maybe I'll try some science fiction" (345). As Margaret Ann Doody notes, Joan's decision here is "prophetic of her creator's career. Atwood was to become a world success in 1985 with *The Handmaid's Tale,* a science-fiction-like horror story ... a dystopia" (27). That novel—a "contextual dystopia"—won the Governor General's Award for fiction and, within the world of SF, the first Arthur C. Clarke Award. According to John Updike, "Atwood, as she showed in the futuristic 'Handmaid's Tale,' is a dab hand at science fiction" (142). In John Clute's concurrent testimony, "*The Handmaid's Tale* soon gained a reputation as the best sf novel ever produced by a Canadian" (70), evincing a complexity which the 1990 film version, in spite of a script by Harold Pinter, regrettably failed to convey.[4]

While the fragmented, incomplete science-fantasy story told in alternating sections in *The Blind Assassin* has important elements in common with *The Handmaid's Tale*—an upper class, the Snilfards, brutally oppresses an underclass, the Ygnirods, the males of which are almost as badly treated as the females—the former is not, technically speaking, a work of SF or fantasy, but an SF tale within a love story within a family saga. And so it is necessary to begin with an interpretive synopsis of the entire plot: such is its dazzling complexity, and so subtle are its sleights-of-hand, that even after reading this fictional Rubik's Cube time and again, it is difficult to be sure what exactly has gone on.

The term "blind assassin" has multiple referents—Atwood's *Blind Assassin* contains the recollections of Iris Chase Griffen, a widow who is eighty-two years old in 1999, the year that she completes her memoir; the text of her sister's 1947 novel; and various newspaper and other clippings. Atwood, it would seem, has performed a silent editorial function. Iris is recalling her life and that of her family during and between the two world wars, particularly her younger sister Laura's experience in twentieth-century Ontario. Her desired addressee is Sabrina Griffen, the granddaughter somewhere in India whom Iris hardly knows. Iris's death at the novel's end, in May 1999, coincides more or less with the end of the century. In this millennial fiction looking back over the twentieth century, Iris is anticipating and linking herself to the twenty-first century, which, thankfully, she will not live to experience. An old temporal world is about to be exchanged for a new one. And this is what gives *The Blind Assassin* an overall science-fictional feel: SF is all about new worlds for old.

Obviously enough, though, Atwood's novel is not itself SF; it is a realistic family saga and love story centred on the Chase family of the fictional Ontario town of Port Ticonderoga and the more dangerous Griffen family of Toronto into which Iris Chase reluctantly marries. Iris and Laura are the daughters of a prosperous Port Ticonderoga button manufacturer, Norval Chase. He inherited The Button Factory, a Victorian enterprise, from his father, Benjamin, who founded it in the early 1870s. Iris's memoir begins with what seems to have been Laura's suicide at age twenty-five in May 1945, the subject of the novel's first sentence: "Ten days after the war ended, my sister drove a car off a bridge" (1). In the penultimate section of the book, an item from *The Port Ticonderoga Herald and Banner* reports the May 1999 death of Iris, aged eighty-three. This is a novel in which all the major characters die.

World War I, in which Iris's father's two brothers died (and her father was seriously injured), was good for buttons. But a decline set in after the war, along with increased numbers of communist sympathizers and growing unionization among workers. At an annual Saturday-before-Labour-Day Button Factory picnic in 1934, Laura and Iris meet for the first time an attractive, mysterious stranger born somewhere in Europe—a fellow-traveller and union activist—named Alex Thomas.[5] Laura falls in love with him. Because of a strike, a murdered night watchman, and suspected arson at The Button Factory in December 1934, Alex, on the run, is hidden by Laura and Iris in the cellar and later the attic of their grand home, Avilion. The story of the lovers Laura and Alex would seem gnomically to be told in the book *The Blind Assassin* by Laura Chase, published posthumously in 1947. Iris, on the other hand, goes along with her father's despairing idea that she marry a wealthy Toronto owner of a firm called Royal Classic Knitwear, a would-be politician and something of a Nazi sympathizer named Richard E. Griffen. Only by this marriage and the absorption of The Button Factory into Griffen-Chase Royal Consolidated Industries Ltd. will Iris and, much more importantly, the impractical Laura be able to continue living in the style to which they been accustomed.[6] Their father drinks himself to death shortly after the marriage.

Laura's novel *The Blind Assassin* has become a feminist cult classic and Laura herself a "feminist icon a bit like Elizabeth Smart" (Sage 22). It was originally published two years after her 1945 death by the New York firm of Reingold, Janes & Moreau (the last a possible reference to an Atwood ancestor, Cornwallis Moreau, who was born in Halifax in 1749, the son of an ex-monk [see Sullivan 18–19]).[7] In 1999 it is being republished in England by "Artemisia Press" (283), presumably an equivalent of the feminist press Virago.[8] The novel describes an affair, conducted in borrowed or rented rooms, between an unnamed wealthy young woman and an unnamed man who is hiding from the authorities. The reader assumes that these lovers correspond to Laura and Alex. Atwood's novel comes in fifteen untitled chapters (three sets of five), each with a variable number of titled sections. Sections from Laura Chase's *Blind Assassin* appear in chapters I, II, IV, VI, VIII, X, XII, and XIV.

The male fugitive makes some money by writing pulp SF and fantasy. During the assignations, he entertains the young woman by telling her such stories, the most important and sustained one involving a young man on the planet Zycron who is a blind assassin. The science part of this Conan-the-Barbarian-style science fantasy is confined to the setting: Zycron "has seven seas, five moons, and three suns of varying strengths and colours." Events take place mainly in its major city, the doomed "Sakiel-Norn, roughly translatable as The Pearl of Destiny ..." (15). The fugitive begins his tale with a description of a ruined city: Sakiel-Norn is destined to be "destroyed in a battle ..." (11). The city's power and grandeur depend upon the labour of slaves, particularly the children who weave luxury carpets: "[T]he incessant close labour demanded of these children caused them to go blind by the age of eight or nine. ..." A carpet was valued by the number of children blinded in its creation. Once blind, the children—both boys and girls—were sold to brothel keepers. Some, adept at picking locks, escaped, "took up the profession of cutting throats in the dark, [and] were greatly in demand as hired assassins" (22). Sakiel-Norn is also famous for its practice of sacrificing children—both boys and girls. Nine girls are sacrificed each year by the Snilfard ruling class "to the Goddess of the Five Moons" (27). Three months before a ritual sacrifice, the girl's tongue would be cut out so that the celebrants would not be disturbed by any cries of distress during the ritual, which included defloration the night prior to the girl's death by a courtier playing the Lord of the Underworld.

Our hero, a young blind assassin, is hired by a power-hungry faction to kill the king of Sakiel-Norn. X (his code name, the only one given) is to disguise himself as the to-be-sacrificed girl and, as "she" is about to be killed, stab the king "who serve[s] as High Priest on these occasions" (29). This involves the previous killing of a guard, the "Lord of the Underworld" courtier (after he has had his way with the girl), and the girl. The dead girl is to supply the necessary ceremonial clothing. But, as things turn out, X arrives before the "Lord of the Underworld," and it is X who takes the girl's virginity because they have fallen in love on the spot. Now they must escape together.

So what exactly, the reader might reasonably ask, is the point of this science fantasy story and the other SF and fantasy elements in Atwood's novel? As the reader reads on, he or she may (or may not) become aware of parallels between the planet Zycron story and the realistic stories of Iris, Laura, and world history. Iris's arranged marriage and a sacrificed girl on Zycron obviously have something in common: "You might say she looked like a pampered society bride" (29), says Xycron's fugitive creator. But with this example of the essentializing, literalizing, and estranging values of SF I am anticipating my argument. The first point to make about the pulp SF and fantasy material is its temporal appropriateness.

Pulp SF and modern fantasy were born and came to fruition in the years between the two world wars. It is with these years, particularly the 1930s and the World War II years that followed, that *The Blind Assassin* is most concerned. Pulp SF, or what Hugo Gernsback originally called "scientifiction," is usually taken as beginning with Gernsback's founding of the American magazine *Amazing Stories* in April 1926. Given the fugitive's need to make some money as a hack writer in the 1930s, it is certainly plausible that he would turn to SF and fantasy. Genre or pulp SF and fantasy were a novelty of the times.[9] These genres appealed mainly to males; but Iris and, to a lesser extent, Laura were fans: "We preferred—or I preferred, and Laura tagged along—[the 'pulpy, trashy' magazines (smuggled into Canada by a servant's brother)] with stories about other lands or even other planets. Spaceships from the future, where women would wear very short skirts made of shiny fabric and everything would gleam ..." (152–53).

Although the fugitive focuses on the blind assassin, there are other aspects of life on Zycron that he also turns to fictional account. West of "a range of mountains" is an area "said to be roamed after sunset by the voracious inhabitants of the crumbling tombs located there" (10). Vampires are always popular, and the examples that we are given of the fugitive's futuristic stories more or less run the gamut of fantastic pulp plots of the time. A later section introduces the warlike Lizard Men of the planet Xenor who attack Zycron. For a while the competing classes and warring groups on Zycron are united against this common enemy, which turns out to be susceptible to hurled "balls of burning pitch," the Zycronians having "discovered that the Xenorians' metal pants are inflammable at high temperatures." But the Xenorians "develop a gas that will render the Zycronians unconscious" (401). Earth is also at war with the Xenorians and, in a connected story, after being attacked in space by "a Xenorian zorch-craft" (351), two space pilots from Earth inexplicably find themselves "on the planet of Aa'A" (353), home "of the peachiest women they had ever seen" (352). Grown on trees and plucked when ripe, these Peach Women seem to inhabit a utopia of the mindless narcotic type.

A couple of the fugitive's SF stories have no links with Zycron. The first of them is too cerebral to complete. A group of crystalline extraterrestrials explore Earth and attempt "communications with those Earth beings they assume are like themselves: eyeglasses, windowpanes" (250), and so on. The story described in the "Alien on Ice" section, about a dangerous, tentacle-headed, light-green alien thawed out after being encased in a glacier, owes something to that pulp classic by John Campbell first published in *Astounding Science Fiction* in 1938, "Who Goes There?" It has been twice filmed as *The Thing*.

In her acknowledgments, Atwood thanks "Lorna Toolis and her staff at the Toronto Public Library's Merril Collection of Science Fiction, Speculation, and Fantasy" (523). According to Lorna Toolis, Atwood and her assistant "went through every fantasy pulp the Merril Collection holds" over three separate visits beginning on 23 November 1999 (e-mail communications, 29 January 2001 and 1 February 2001). Atwood's assistant, Jennifer Osti, tells me, "The book was largely written by fall 1999 and most visits to the Merril Collection were in search of a cover image" (letter to Ketterer, 6 April 2001).[10] It is very useful to know that at one point Atwood was thinking in terms of a science fantasy or sci-fi illustration for her cover. But finally no such image was used.[11] And it might reasonably be assumed that the fugitive's stories, generally representative pastiches of the pulp SF and fantasy field of the 1930s, derive from Atwood's knowledge of that field long *before* her trawling visits to the Merril Collection.

The explosion of genre SF between the wars had a good deal to do with the relationship between war and SF. The condition of war forces an escalation of invention, of technical and medical advances. Inventions were the stock-in-trade of the genre that Gernsback named. But there is also the anticipatory frame of mind that the possibility of war encourages. I. F. Clarke's *Voices Prophesying War* (1966, 1992) establishes the link between such warning texts as George Chesney's 1871 bestseller *The Battle of Dorking*, a pseudo-documentary illustrating the ease with which an invading German army might reach London, and H. G. Wells's *War of the Worlds* (1898). In his entry "War" in *The Encyclopedia of Science Fiction*, Brian Stableford observes, "One of the principal imaginative stimuli to futuristic and scientific speculation has been the possibility of war, and the possibility that new TECHNOLOGY might transform war" (1296). He goes on to point out that "future-war stories enjoyed a second heyday in the UK between the wars, when the actual example of WWI caused many writers to believe that a new war might mean the end of civilization ..." (1297). One example was Neil Bell's *The Gas War of 1946* (published in 1931 as by "Miles"; republished in 1934 under the author's name and the title *Valient Clay*).

As it happens, I. F. Clarke's title phrase, "voices prophesying war," from Coleridge's "Kubla Khan," figures in Iris's description of the 1936 "Xanadu" Beaux Arts Ball at Toronto's Royal York Hotel: "We did not hear any 'ancestral voices prophesying war'..." (273). Later, Iris asks, regarding "Kubla Khan," "Why were the ancestral voices prophesying war?" (334). And later yet, after watching a TV news report of a war somewhere, Iris comments, "They have a generic look to them, these wars ..." (477). They are a "pulp" genre in the grimmest sense of the word.

The young woman in Laura's novel comes across one of her lover's stories in one of the SF or fantasy pulps—*Wonder Stories*, *Weird Tales*, or *Astounding*, we are not told which one; its title is "*Lizard Men of Xenor. First Thrilling Episode in the Annals of the Zycronian Wars*" (399). We know that the blind assassin story that the fugitive is telling his lover will culminate in a battle and that a barbarian horde (the Children of Joy or the Children of Desolation, depending on your perspective) will destroy the famous city of Sakiel-Norn. Clearly, the fugitive conceived this battle as a climax to not just one war. His account of the overcome city may owe something to one of the books he apparently owns—Gustave Flaubert's *Salammbô* (1862)—a story set against the historical revolt of mercenaries against Carthage in 240–237 BC. (A Carthaginian funerary urn inscription is the second of Atwood's three epigraphs to her novel.) The fugitive also writes of "the Xenorian Wars" (350) involving the Lizard Men. In the real world, he is implying World War II; today's reader might well extrapolate a World War III.

I have not mentioned what may be the main reason for the fugitive's being drawn to SF, given that the fugitive appears to be based on Alex. As a communist and revolutionary socialist, Alex naturally lives in anticipation of a socialist utopia. Various theoreticians, notably Darko Suvin, have argued that SF has an obligation to provide blueprints for something approaching a utopian future. There is a tradition of socialist utopias—Bellamy's *Looking Backwards* being the best known—that can be viewed as SF or SF-related. For many people the present real world, in Alex's case the 1930s world, might well be understood as a dystopia. The affinity between the dystopian literary tradition and SF has long been recognized. Kingsley Amis's pioneering survey *New Maps of Hell* (1963) treats the terms "dystopia" and "science fiction" as synonymous. Alex's version of the fugitive's tale of the blind assassin falls into the category of dystopian SF. Consequently, there are interesting relationships between *The Blind Assassin* and Atwood's dystopia *The Handmaid's Tale*.[12]

Port Ticonderoga will seem an unlikely name for an Ontario town to any reader who knows something about American history. But perhaps only Canadian readers will immediately recognize that the name is a fabrication. Port Ticonderoga, the place and the name, is an invention, a fiction, a fantasy. Iris gives a fictifact account of how it came to be: "Colonel Parker, a veteran of the last decisive battle fought in the American Revolution, that of Ticonderoga ... upped stakes, crossed the border, and named our town, thus perversely commemorating a battle in which he'd lost" (144–45).

Ticonderoga (Iroquois for "between two waters") is a village in Essex County, New York, on a neck of land between Lake George and Lake Champlain. The fort there, built by the French and named Fort Carillon in 1755, has a colourful history. During the French and Indian War, it was captured by General Jeffrey Amherst in 1759 and renamed Fort Ticonderoga. On 10 May 1775, at the beginning of the Revolutionary War, the fort was captured in a surprise attack by Ethan Allen and his Green Mountain Boys. But in 1777 British troops under General Burgoyne retook it. Later that year, the fort was surrendered at the Convention of Saratoga. The British abandoned it after setting fire to its buildings. Its fortifications restored in 1909, Fort Ticonderoga is now a tourist attraction.

Given the battle-scarred history of the fort, the fictional name Port Ticonderoga (a one-letter change) provides a link with the war theme in both twentieth-century history and in SF. But no doubt also relevant are the references to Fort Ticonderoga in Hawthorne's "The Custom-House—Introductory to 'The Scarlet Letter.'" There, the Collector, who customarily sits by the fireplace, is compared to "an old fortress, like Ticonderoga, from a view of its gray and broken ruins" (22)—and its survival. The old Collector and "Old Ticonderoga" share "the features of stubborn and ponderous endurance ..." (32). In this regard, the survivor Iris might be viewed as a female Old Ticonderoga. The ability to endure, to balance past, present, and future, is a part of the balancing act that constitutes what Hawthorne, later in his Custom-House sketch, describes as the firelit, moonlit balancing act of writing romances—that is, of creating that "neutral territory, somewhere between the real world and fairy-land, where the Actual and the Imaginary may meet, and each imbue itself with the nature of the other" (36). I believe that, via Fort/Port Ticonderoga, Atwood is, in effect, yoking the aesthetic licence of Hawthornesque romance to her own balancing of the real world and fairyland, fairyland in her case including the SF, fantasy, and mythic material. Atwood puts a good deal of effort into imbuing the real world of her novel with the qualities of fairyland. For example, an 1899 Montreal newspaper report describes how, "Standing at sunset on the graceful new Jubilee Bridge ... one views an enchanting faeryland as the lights of the Chase button factory wink on, and are reflected in the sparkling waters [of the Louveteau River]" (51). And parallels with *The Scarlet Letter* itself become particularly apparent toward the conclusion of *The Blind Assassin*. But links between Iris, Hawthorne's Hester embroidering, and the moonlight of Hawthornesque romance are suggested early on: Iris, for example, persists with her writing, "hunched over as if sewing by moonlight" (43). *The Scarlet Letter* is also hinted at by Winifred's talk of "girls who'd got themselves in trouble" and Iris's imagining them writing in blood, "in such red, red letters" (325). "An old story" is her comment on the next line.[13]

Although *The Blind Assassin* can be classified as a Hawthornesque romance, it actually incorporates a variety of genres. Reviewer Alex Clark types it as "a family saga" (covering five generations) that includes "pulp sci-fi, clue-strewn detective novel, newspaper reportage and tragic confessional romance," and finally "a mystery novel whose chief character is absent" (10). Anita Brookner's review adds "melodrama" to this list (51). An often handy solution in such mixed genre cases is to invoke Northrop

Frye's concept of the "anatomy"—"A form of prose fiction, traditionally known as the Menippean or Varronian satire ... characterized by a great variety of subject matter and a strong interest in ideas" (*Anatomy* 365). Given the quasi-encyclopaedic scope of *The Blind Assassin*—its desire to tell a love story in the context of the ideological cross-currents of the entire twentieth century and world-shaking historical events—Frye's term is as good an encompassing description as any.

But the impact of Northrop Frye on *The Blind Assassin* goes rather beyond the anatomy genre or mode. *The Blind Assassin* makes the most sense if it is viewed as a practical illustration or dramatization of the mythic displacement theory outlined in Frye's *Anatomy of Criticism*. Frye argues that the season-inspired stories of mythology (including the Bible) form the basis of all literature. Depending on how realistic their displacement is, these archetypal stories are relatively obvious in the romance forms of literature, less so in the case of the realistic novel. So SF, at bottom an apocalyptic romance form, is easily related to "the Flood archetype" (203). The importance of the romance to Frye's theory is further explored in *The Secular Scripture: A Study of the Structure of Romance* (1979), which deals with the Lady of Pain figure and the themes of descent and ascent; and the work of Rider Haggard, one of Atwood's doctoral dissertation subjects, is singled out repeatedly as especially representative (57, 114, 169, 173). For Haggard, "A real story had to 'have a heart,' that is, a focus or centre implying a total shape with a beginning and an end" (169). The "total story or romance" constitutes a "cycle" (173).

In a general sense, Frye applies his four basic *mythoi*—those of tragedy, romance, comedy, and irony—to human history; but Hayden White takes that tack further in *Tropics of Discourse: Essays in Cultural Criticism* (1976). White develops Frye's distinction between story and plot structure. Given that "pre-generic plot structures are interpreted as the 'displaced' forms of the *mythoi* that supposedly give to different poetic fictions one among others of their specific emotive effects I invoke the distinction in order to suggest its utility as a way of identifying the specifically 'fictive' element in historical accounts of the world" (61). Putting Frye and White together involves a layering conception of history atop realistic fiction, realistic fiction atop romance fiction, and romance fiction atop mythology. The ascending levels tell the same story, but in increasingly realistic ways.

Surely, the parallel between this hierarchy and the overlaying scheme of *The Blind Assassin* is readily apparent. Atwood overlays twentieth-century Canadian and world history, in its economic, political, and cultural dimensions, atop the realistic family saga and love story, and the realistic family saga and love story atop the science-fantasy romance of the blind assassin of Zycron. The mythological base might seem to be missing, but the Zycron story is largely compounded of myth, and mythic details frequently surface in the overall text. In Atwood's novel, what recurs on all three levels are the constants of human behaviour, the constants of the human condition.[14] The constants are oppression, injustice, envy, competition, love, betrayal, sacrifice, birth, death, and war. And, of course, the Blind Assassin. A literal figure in the Zycron story, the Blind Assassin is a metaphor for Eros, Justice (the other blind god), History, and Time. Iris herself overlays the three key moments in the tragic/ironic mythos that constitutes *The Blind Assassin*: "The knife stab, the shell-burst, the plummet of the car from the bridge" (418)—that is, the blind assassin at work on Zycron, the explosive destruction of the world wars, the death of Laura. We have yet to discover that, with regard to Laura, Iris performed the role of Blind Assassin. No one gets through life without injuring someone else.[15]

Atwood also uses a simpler strategy to knit her science fantasy and family saga stories together—the refrain "another dimension of space," repeated some ten times (9, 10, 15, 350, 351, 355, 428, 465, 469, 500). It first appears at the very beginning of chapter 2 in the second instalment of Laura's novel and its relationship to the immediately preceding first-instalment description of a photograph should be readily apparent; the fugitive asks the young woman what kind of story she wants him to tell: "You can have your pick: jungles, tropical islands, mountains. Or another dimension of space—that's what I'm best at" (9). Zycron exists in another dimension of space, but so, too, does the world depicted in the photograph in the first instalment of Laura's *Blind Assassin*: "She has a single photograph of him." They're sitting under a tree at a picnic (presumably the same picnic at which Iris and Laura first met Alex): "He's holding up his hand, as if ... to protect himself from those in the future who might be looking at him ... through this square, lighted window of glazed paper" (4). The photograph is a portal to another dimension of space: "She ... stares down into it, as if she's peering into a well or pool—searching beyond her own reflection for something else, something else she must have dropped or lost, out of reach but still visible, shimmering like a jewel on sand" (5); or, it might be added, like Sakiel-Norn, the Pearl of Destiny, on Zycron. A third picnicker on one side of the photo has been "scissored off" except for a hand (5). This edited photo will be re-described in the last instalment of Laura's *Blind Assassin*, "Epilogue: The other hand." The severed hand, "resting on the grass," belonged to Iris—"The hand that will set things down" (517). The "other dimension of space" captured by the photo is the past, the dimension of memory. And missing bits—holes in time—are always filled in by fantasy.

Clearly, the very elastic, catholic phrase "another dimension of space" can apply to any conceivable location. Like the fictional Zycron, the fictional Port Ticonderoga exists in "another dimension of space." So does twentieth-century Canada. So does the Earth of the twentieth century. Any historical event can exist at all only in "another dimension of space." Increasingly it will become apparent that the formula "another dimension of space" applies ultimately to the flatland of the page. It is the dimension of imagination, of fiction, of writing.

This handy conception goes back at least as far as Atwood's time at the University of Toronto. In her final undergraduate year, she wrote an essay for Jay Macpherson entitled "The Uses of the Supernatural in the Novel," which includes this statement: "The supernatural may extend the levels of human consciousness into a fourth dimension that has its possibilities for existence within the human imagination" (quoted in Sullivan, *The Red Shoes* 170). This conception finally collapses all distinctions that might be posited between all literary worlds and so justifies the presence of SF and fantasy realms in what seems to be a realistic novel.

I can only briefly describe the many touches of fantasy, fairytale, and mythology that fleck *The Blind Assassin* as they fleck Atwood's other novels. Everything in *The Blind Assassin*, not just the "faeryland" (51) button factory previously noted, is edged with the fantastic: Mackenzie King's "Kingsmere" (14); "the Sybil in her bottle" (42); Iris and Laura on "our thorn-encircled island, waiting for rescue" (43); and finally, "the scale-shaped seeds" of milkweed pods "overlapping like the skin of a dragon" (140). These fantastic touches partake of both truth and illusion. In Chapter III, a section entitled "The Button Factory" is immediately followed by a section entitled "Avilion," the name of the impressive Chase family home in Port Ticonderoga. Thus the mundane is placed alongside the magical, the real world alongside fairyland. Taken from Tennyson's *Idylls of the King*, "Avilion was where King Arthur went to die" (61). The names of the three Chase sons, Norval, Edgar, and Percival, imply "Arthurian revival with a hint of Wagner" (62). A section set in "the Imperial Room of the Royal York Hotel" (225) in Toronto is immediately followed by one set in the ersatz "Arcadian Court," a lunch spot "at the top of Simpson's department store" in Toronto (230).[16]

Like a wolf (see 344), the ice cold of winter is also a blind assassin. Coleridge's "Kubla Khan" supplies the "caves of ice" image which links the frozen, death-dealing alien of the aborted Campbellian SF story with Canada in winter: "The snow fell, softly at first, then in hard pellets that stung the skin like needles" (334). The unidentified "he," with "flashing eyes" and "floating hair" (quoted 335), who is feared in Coleridge's poem, becomes Alex, the exotic alien in Atwood's novel.[17]

So reality and history are underwritten by fantasy and fable, by fiction and imagination. Of course, obliterating the distinction between reality and fantasy is a typically postmodern move.[18] Atwood's postmodern, extreme relativist ideology, however, is combined with an alternative compounded of Jung, Spengler, and Frye.[19]

Iris's compilation of memoir and other material (the equivalent of Atwood's novel) is intended for one reader, her granddaughter Sabrina Griffen. Aimee Griffen (Iris's long disaffected daughter and Sabrina's mother) died of a drug overdose. Iris wants Sabrina (whose father is unknown) to know what Iris conceives to be the truth about her grandparents' lives and their antecedents. But Iris is not an altogether reliable narrator. She withholds until near the end of the narrative (as she is anticipating her own death and the dawning twenty-first century and new millennium) a number of surprising revelations, which I have also withheld and must now (with apologies) give away. It seems that it was Iris and not Laura who wrote the cult novel *The Blind Assassin* and arranged for it to be published under Laura's name in the hope of perpetuating her memory (and perhaps righting wrongs).[20] It was Iris, not Laura, who had the relationship with Alex, although it was Laura who was in love with him.[21] Alex was Aimee Griffen's father, not Richard Griffen. So the early comparison of the sewing-by-moonlight Iris and Hawthorne's Hester Prynne is directly appropriate. This has been a story of adultery with Alex in the Arthur

Dimmesdale role, and Richard in that of Roger Chillingworth.[22] (A displaced Pearl has become a doomed city—Sakiel-Norn, the Pearl of Destiny.[23]) Richard, it seems, forced himself on Laura and got her pregnant; but the embryo was aborted.

It seems very likely that Iris, in the role of Blind Assassin, was responsible for her sister's suicide. Laura's suicide followed Iris's telling her of Alex's death in the war and of her, Iris's, relationship with Alex. Laura reacted to all this in silence: "She looked right through me. Lord knows what she saw. A sinking ship [i.e., Alex's death in World War II], a city in flames [i.e., the destruction of Sakiel-Norn], a knife in the back [i.e., Iris stabbing Laura]" (488). Like *The Scarlet Letter, The Blind Assassin* is a story of guilt, and of love both adulterous and incestuous (with love between sisters in place of that between daughter and father).

The effect of these end-of-novel revelations is to turn *The Blind Assassin* into something like the formulaic detective or mystery novel, in which the solutions have the effect of dramatically revising and even obliterating much of the previous narrative. That narrative is replaced by a sketchily corrected version.[24] (An analogous turnaround is affected by the "Historical Notes" conclusion to *The Handmaid's Tale.*) This was a risky strategy on Atwood's part. It explains reviewer Alex Clark's criticism that the novel "falls short of making the emotional impact that its suggestive and slippery plot at times promises" (10), and the anonymous *Economist* reviewer's similar complaint of a "dispersed" impact (158). But Atwood's shock about-turns do serve to underscore the fact that Iris's twentieth-century world, like ours, has gone. Today, in 2001, we are incontestably no longer in the twentieth century. One or two years ago it was real; we were still *in* it. Now the twentieth century is history, merely "another dimension of space." Drained of immediate reality, it is now subject to endless revision and fabrication.

For Iris, the past lost its reality after World War II—at that point, there was no yesterday, "yesterday ... had vanished," there was only "a tomorrow" (507), the threshold of science fiction. "The Threshold" titles the last chapter of the novel, which follows a newspaper account of Iris's death in May 1999. There is an actual threshold, but the title recalls the beginning and end setting in *The Scarlet Letter* and implies, among other things, the threshold of the future, the twenty-first century. Iris describes a daydream of a future meeting with Sabrina. She imagines Sabrina "crossing the threshold of" her "fossilized cottage."[25] By the time Sabrina has finished reading Iris's account, Iris herself will exist only in another dimension of space—on the page "is the only place I will be" (521):

Iris has already equated the twenty-first century with the tense future imperative of SF:

> ... there's a far-off roaring, like a tidal wave racing inshore. Here comes the twenty-first century, sweeping overhead like a spaceship filled with ruthless lizard-like aliens or a metal pterodactyl. Sooner or later it will sniff us out, it will tear the roofs off our flimsy little burrows with its iron claws. (477)

Indulging "apocalyptic visions" (478), Iris is imagining a World War III that is a Wellsian war of the worlds.[26] Fantastic maybe, but SF *is* the realism of the twenty-first century.

In spite of her visions, Iris wants to leave Sabrina with the impression that she has the freedom to start from scratch:

> Your real grandfather was Alex Thomas, and as to who his own father was, well, the sky's the limit. Rich man, poor man, beggar-man, saint, a score of countries of origin, a dozen cancelled maps, a hundred levelled villages—take your pick. Your legacy from him is the realm of infinite speculation. You're free to reinvent yourself at will. (513)

But is the last line true? Omitting to take account of Sabrina's maternal inheritance, isn't it a non sequitur? The "realm of infinite speculation" would seem to be the realm of SF and fantasy, but that realm, as represented in *The Blind Assassin,* is a Frygian romance form that serves to make particularly clear those aspects of the human condition (including DNA) that are endlessly repeated. Sabrina will have inherited *something* from Iris Chase Griffin; and her grandfather, Alex Thomas, whatever his background may have been, did have a genetic inheritance to pass on.

Atwood's true position is most succinctly expressed in her SF story "Homelanding." The woman-from-Earth narrator explains to the aliens of an unnamed planet something of her birthplace. "Much of Canada," she says, "is covered with water; that accounts for our interest in reflections, sudden vanishings, the dissolution of one thing into another. Much of it however is rock, which accounts for our belief in Fate" (85). The importance of Fate is accentuated, given that in Canada, if it's cold enough, water can rapidly become rock-like. "Homelanding" is included in Atwood's 1992 collection *Good Bones*, a title that suggests a correlation between bones and rock on the one hand, and flesh and water on the other. Atwood, it would seem, believes in a combination of the fixed and the mutable, or, if you like, a combination of rock-hard science and fluid fiction.

The fixed, fated, or destined bone or rock is signalled by the implied rock of Fort Ticonderoga; by Medusa imagery with its threat of petrification; and finally, by the "Norn" part (more obviously than the "Sakiel" part) of the city name "Sakiel-Norn" (presumably the "Destiny" part of "The Pearl of Destiny" translation). The three female "norns" (representing past, present, and future) are the Scandinavian equivalent of the three classical Fates.[27] This seems apparent enough from the repeated themes of love, sacrifice, betrayal, war, birth, death, and such that connect the historical, the mundane fictional, and the science-fictional/fantastic planes of *The Blind Assassin*. Nowhere in Atwood's text is there an explanation for the prologue title of the cult novel supposedly by Laura Chase—"Perennials for the Rock Garden"—beyond the fact that the edited photograph of the picnickers is kept between the pages of a book of that title. But in the light of the description of Canada in "Homelanding," it makes some sense to identify the "Rock Garden" with the rock of Canada and the perennials with the themes that repeat in this as in Atwood's other novels.

Looking at the photograph is like "peering into a well or pool" in which the past, or the truth, is "Drowned, but shining" (5). Imagery of dissolution in water intrudes early. Laura's car ends up in a "shallow creek" at the bottom of a ravine (1). There was an earlier occasion when Laura "could've drowned" in the Louveteau River (150). When Iris looks in a mirror, sometimes she sees her "young girl's face ... drowned and floating just beneath my present face ..." (43). "Water is nebulous ... yet it can kill you" (270), says the narrator of Zycron. It is like time and history. "Time," says Iris, is "like silt in a pond" (299), and perhaps like the foot of the stair "pool of darkness ... wet as a real pool" that she later describes (367). "Avilion had once had an air of stability ... a large, dumpy boulder plunked down in the middle of the stream of time ..." (382). Like much SF, Atwood's novel is fundamentally about extended time, and time considered as "another dimension of space." At one point, the hero of Laura's novel is "like a reflection in a shivering pool" (412). For Iris, Richard becomes another evanescent reflection, blurred "like the face in some wet, discarded newspaper" (479), or like "oil on a puddle" (510). The association of "sudden vanishings" with water might be related to a particularly perceptive review of *The Blind Assassin* entitled "Vanishing Act: Alex Clark on Atwood's ambiguous magic." The object of the vanishing act in question is Laura: "What we have, at the end, is a mystery novel whose chief character is absent" (10).

It would seem that while Atwood views many aspects of the twenty-first century future as fixed, imagination and/or the magic mirror of watery art can effect fantastic transformations. As I have noted, Iris writing "as if sewing by moonlight" is akin to Hester Prynne (43); in my present context she is particularly akin to Hester embroidering her letter "A." Iris is also a stand-in for Margaret *A*twood as *a*uthor. Like Hester embroidering those fixed lines, Atwood, a not-so-blind *a*ssassin writing fiction that is by turns mundane, science-fictional, and fantastic, is able, within limitations, to modify the often grim fixities of life by elaborating their meanings, by new reflections (reflections reversing right and left).

Finally, if bone is to rock as flesh is to water, then water and flesh might both be categorized as variable coverings, and such coverings (albeit of an artificial rather than natural kind) are much in evidence in *The Blind Assassin*. Artificial coverings, or clothing and other manufactured fabrics, are directly named or implicit in the following section titles: "The carpets"; "The Button Factory"; "The trousseau"; "Black ribbons"; "The chenille spread"; "The fur coat"; "Hand-tinting"; "The houndstooth suit"; "Red brocade"; "The eggshell hat"; "The Top Hat Grill"; "The laundry"; "Yellow curtains"; and "Gloves." The fictitious covering of fancy dress is, of course, essential to the Xanadu ball.

It is a short step, via the link between fabric and fabrication,[28] to relate the notion of coverings protecting or embellishing the surfaces of humans, animals, and things to fictions woven around thematic or story kernels which are also the kernels of life. Realism, romance, SF, fantasy, fairytale, and mythology are all merely different coverings. Thus, in *The Blind Assassin*, realism, which seems best represented by Richard Griffen's Royal Classic Knitwear, can be displayed alongside the flashy, alternative coverings of SF and fantasy, which seem best represented by those extraordinary, exotic, horrifically expensive carpets of Sakiel-Norn. "Sakiel" contains the word "silk" (s-i-el-ka); and, from Atwood's very poetic description, the reader must surely imagine pearly silk carpets like water. Sakiel-Norn, we are told, was "renowned ... for its weaving. ... [I]ts cloth shone like liquid honey, like crushed purple grapes, like a cup of bull's blood poured out in the sun. ... [I]ts carpets were so soft and fine you would think you were walking on air, an air made to resemble flowers [the perennials of art?] and flowing water" (21–22).

NOTES

1. In order to allow my long-ago colleague Margaret Atwood to check over the use I had made of her answers to six questions I had asked her, I sent her a copy of a near-finalized state of this essay as an e-mail attachment. She responded by e-mail on 10 July 2001 with a list of "error corrections & comments." I made the necessary corrections/adjustments and have recorded her comments (preceded by the title "Comments" to distinguish them from her answers) in these sometimes dissenting Atwood endnotes. I am most grateful to Margaret Atwood for her time and trouble, and for permission to publish her answers and comments.

"Comments": "'Canadian Monsters' came out of thinking what ELSE I might have covered in *Survival*—that, humour, war stories were some of the things I thought about. As for the things I cited, didn't have to look, had already read them ... e.g. Brown Waters (Wendigo story) was lying around the house."

2. "Comments": "Reaney invited me to write it cause he knew I was interested in Haggard. Who, like much else, I did not seek out but merely read as a child, when I was also reading a lot of sci fi, comic books with the same themes (Flash Gordon, Captain Marvel) Boys' Own Annual adventure stories and so forth. ... [*She*] was ... a horribly influential book. For its kind of fin de siecle femme fatale, see also *Icons of Perversity*, an enjoyable book about Victorian painting."

3. "Comments": "Interlunar—a lovely word meaning the dark of the moon. Milton uses it among others.... For other sf allusions, see short story 'The Man from Mars' [in *Dancing Girls*, 1977], and 'Snake Poems' [in *Interlunar*]."

4. Atwood has also twice contributed to the *Tesseracts* series of Canadian SF and fantasy anthologies. Her SF story "Freeforall" in *Tesseracts²* (1987) is related to *The Handmaid's Tale* as a dystopian response to the AIDS crisis. In the year 2026, because of a raft of sexual plagues, a group called the Mothers carry out a genetic programme by marrying off selected teenage boys and girls who will procreate

without sex—turkey basters are used instead. Outside this arrangement, areas of unsafe, total sexual licence—Freeforalls—are encouraged for culling purposes. "Homelanding" appears in *Tesseracts*[3]. Escaping from domination by machines, the female narrator has landed on a planet where she hopes to regain contact with nature. She explains her world to the alien natives; what she calls the "prong people" are, of course, human males, as distinct from the female "cavern people." Atwood thought enough of this story to include it in her 1992 collection *Good Bones.*

5. "Comments": "Alex's origins—from away, yes. But raised after early childhood in Canada ... He would not by that time have had a foreign accent. Most likely provenance for him is Armenia, viz the massacres & genocide that went on there during WWI. A number of orphans were brought to Canada before Armenians were declared Orientals or some such and barred from Canada for a couple of decades. That would certainly explain why he was interested in cities now rubble, vanished races etc. He does refer to this, though does not name the country. How do I know ... went to school with several children of survivors."

6. "Comments": Iris "marries for the sake of Laura, realistically realizing that the two of them wouldn't have much hope in the world of work. See conversation with father before engagement."

7. On 21 February 2001 I wrote to Margaret Atwood and asked her six questions about *The Blind Assassin.* Atwood responded by e-mail on 26 April 2001 following her return from a promotional tour of "Australia, Japan, etc." By that date I had completed this essay so the six endnotes here, which quote my questions and Atwood's answers, were, like Atwood's "Comments," a late addition.

Ketterer, re the publisher of *The Blind Assassin* by Laura Chase: "I wondered if your ancestor Cornwallis Moreau rather than a more obvious possibility, H. G. Wells' doctor, was the particular third allusion."

Atwood: "Moreau—ancestor, yes, that too. The word comes from 'moor,' I'm told. Anyway I wanted a French presence in the small-publishing scene. ... Then there are Reingold and Jaynes. NB bad words—despite the general belief that you couldn't publish these—Mailer being the usual example—you could & did, if slipped—but not on the first page—in small numbers by smaller publishers into literary texts of the Elizabeth Smart (the C-word, the B-word, more) and the Cyril Connolly *Unquiet Grave* (the C word) kind. *Unquiet Grave* was pub in the US by Harper's in—I think—1944. The nipple snipping *Reflections in a Golden Eye* (Carson McCullers) by the way was early 40s. A surprise to remember that!" In this answer Atwood appears to have segued, at least in part, into responding to John Updike's objection that Laura's 1947 novel contains words that could not have been published in 1947 (144).

8. "Comments": "The small press—Virago too mainstream. Something smaller

& more esoteric. Virago in its earlier incarnation, perhaps. But not a direct reference."

9. Ketterer: "Why did you make Alex a writer of pulp science fiction/fantasy rather than some other kind of writer?"

Atwood: "Why is Alex a pulp writer—a) major market of the 30s b) about the only thing of the kind he could do for quick returns, and under a batch of pseudonyms. Note he writes other pulp stuff too—romances, etc—he gives her a choice of genres & that's the one she picks.

"Anyway the form allowed and still allows for the kind of parallel social commentary that has been inherent in it from the beginning, the beginning being Plato's *Republic*, Atlantis, and the Book of Revelations, eh?

"In any case I knew the form well, from days of old. (My thesis—never finished, but mostly—was on 19th C English fantasies, from George Macdonald through *She*, etc. etc., leading to Lewis & Tolkein. ... I searched through US stuff in period, up through the 30s, looking for anything comparable ... oh those undead women. ..."

10. Ketterer: "I gather from Lorna Toolis that late in 1999 you and your assistant made three visits to the TPL Merril Collection and went through every fantasy/sf pulp magazine in that library. ["Comments": "Didn't go through all."] Were you looking for anything specific?"

Atwood: "Visit to Merril library—looking for covers, period @ 1933 to 1936–7. Didn't find one we could use but it was fun looking. Also pinpointing the exact magazines available for that sort of (Conan-type) writing. Amazing who published in those things, and how many adjectives the stories contained."

11. "Comments": "England (Bloomsbury) found the cover cause they needed it first. It happens to be a Sat Eve Post cover of 1934, which fits the period exactly. The dress is pretty strange, one-armed as it is. ... Ultimately we wanted something that would play against the title. We looked at a blonde in a doorway, but she was too late and also too plump."

12. At least two reviewers have drawn attention to the connection: Margaret Anne Doody observes that both novels involve "sexual slavery, sacrifice and cruelty" (28); Elaine Showalter, that Atwood's *The Blind Assassin* "recalls her most celebrated novel, *The Handmaid's Tale*, turned inside out" (53).

13. Ketterer: "You must be frequently asked about the place name 'Port Ticonderoga.' The association that I have (apart from the historical/mythic references to the fortress) is with the Fort Ticonderoga references in Hawthorne's 'Custom House' sketch. Was that at all in your mind?" (This was the only one of my questions that Atwood dodged—at least initially.)

Atwood: "Port Ticonderoga—Fort Ticonderoga is a real place, changed hands a large number of times; also nobody can say quite what the name means."

"Comments": "Banal to point it out, but one chooses fictional names for small towns so the people in real small towns won't think they are in the book and then sue one.... The Collector is interesting—I doubtless read it ["The Custom-House" sketch] at some point—took Perry Miller's American Romantics course at Harvard—but, not to duck the question, the direct answer is No. It was not in my mind. [But for the likelihood of an unconscious or mediated Hawthorne influence, see the here omitted next paragraph continuation of Atwood's Ticonderoga comment in notes 22 and 27 below.]

"Chose Ticonderoga for the war-relation reasons plus its final destruction, plus as usual I looked at map & chose plausible location and name that would not be out of the question." For the Chase button factory as an "enchanted faeryland" (51), see note 27 below.

Atwood and I both taught American literature courses at Sir George Williams University in 1967–68. She is knowledgeable about that field, as *The Handmaid's Tale* (which most definitely draws on *The Scarlet Letter*) also indicates. And *The Scarlet Letter* is not the only American novel reflected (in however mediated a fashion) in *The Blind Assassin*. Confusion about who was driving a car involved in "a terrible smash-up" (491) and talk of Laura's never being a "good driver" (1), along with reference to "carelessness" (517), invoke *The Great Gatsby*. And there are at least a couple of other American authors who may have contributed to Atwood's novel in more general ways. The humorous Kilgore Trout SF stories in such Kurt Vonnegut novels as *Slaughterhouse-Five* (1968) and the reprinted invented novel *The Smugglers of Lost Soul's Rock* in Gardner's *October Light* (1976) both variously parallel the functions of the SF stories and Laura's novel in *The Blind Assassin*.

14. Since these constants amount to Tarot-like distillations, or kernels, of life, it should be noted that Atwood is a skilled Tarot-card reader (see Sullivan, *The Red Shoes* 179, 183, 186, 214, 246–47, 255, 321).

15. "Comments": "Why is everyone so fixated on Frye? Why not McLuhan, equally present at the time? (*Mechanical Bride*) It's as if I had never read anything before 1958! And had not won the Sunday School prize in Bible Studies ... or read the full Andrew Lang collection, Greek mythology, etc. quite long before that time! I read *Gulliver's Travels*, full text including the wacky scientific experiments and the flying island, as a child. Talk about your dystopias and Utopias! Such books were just lying around the house ... plus a lot of rather high-class sci fi like *Penguin Island* and *RUR* and *The War with the Newts*. And *1984* and *Brave New World*. And *War of the Worlds*, plus all the Wells short stories—he invented a great many themes. And Jules Verne of course. My dad liked them. Fun for you to play around with Frye, but really my evil tendencies were already formed. I only took a half course with him, after all! For dead

women, see Pierre Berton's piece in his recent collection of short pieces—can't remember the name but the one about the sci fi writer who works as a short order cook is the first one—written in the 40s sometime I think. (The guy improvises Cinderella as a pulp fantasy, and has the undead women—who of course owe their descent to both *Dracula* and *She*.)

"The seed story of Sakiel-Norn's destruction can be found right after the battle of Jericho—the city of Ai is destroyed, and named for that destruction—Ai means pile of stones or heap of rubble. For 'rubble,' see also Alice Munro—end of her story 'Meneseteung'—also about writing and its futilities."

Atwood's lengthy response above to my Frye argument would seem to indicate that she had understood or intuited Frye's theory of romance and realistic forms as displacements of mythic/biblical stories long before her encounters with Frye. It would seem that Andrew Lang (1844–1912) deserves most of the credit. Titles such as *Myth, Ritual and Religion* (1887) and *Modern Mythology* (1897) and his argument that folklore laid the foundation for literary mythology must have struck Atwood as anticipatory of Frye's theory. See also note 24 below.

16. "Comments": "Arcadian Court and Imperial Room real places. I longed to get the Honeydew (a chain eatery) in as well—see 'Kubla Khan' ['For he on honey-dew hath fed']—but used Diana Sweets instead. The Honeydews did serve something called Honey Dew, but no Milk of Paradise. Toronto's commercial establishments mythologized themselves then, as they do today—the costume ball stuff was all real too. They just loved dressing up as exotics."

17. "Comments": "The flashing-eyed one is a poet, of course, so the most obvious equivalent would be—eventually—Iris."

18. "Comments": "postmodern? How about plain old modern? Don't forget one cut one's teeth on the 'modernists'—a ton of them really. Beckett and Kafka spring to mind, hot writers in 1959, and Joyce of course. How about *Ulysses* and *The Waste Land* for mix of genres and intertextuality? Donnez moi un break, as we used to say in French class, in high school, thus mixing our genres before we'd ever heard of such a thing."

19. "Comments": "NB although Spengler's *Decline of the West* was another of those books lying around the house, I never actually—ahem—got through it. Shaming to confess, but there you are."

20. "Comments": "writing of novel—revenge! She does it to get at Richard. Among other reasons. And among other ways of getting at Richard."

21. "Comments": "Laura was in love with Alex. No evidence for vice versa, though he takes an interest at one point, possibly he idealizes her."

22. "Comments": "but Chillingworth KNOWS. Richard doesn't."

23. "Comments" (omitted from note 13 above and continued here and in note 27 below): "For Pearl, see *Night of the Hunter* [1955], a film that riveted me in—was it—1956. The little girl's name is Pearl, whereas the older girl who flirts with

men is Ruby. (Oh that red colour.) I'd say both novel & screenplay are highly Hawthorne-influenced—have written about this if you're interested."

24. I had originally written "That narrative is drained of its truth and replaced...."

"Comments": "preceding part of novel not 'drained of its truth.' Iris has never lied to us, the readers, although—as she herself has pointed out—she hasn't put everything in. Perceptive readers got it pretty early on that Iris is the author—there are many clues, one of them being that Laura has never been interested in clothes, but whoever wrote the BA obviously was. So for such readers there is no jack in the box surprise ... As for 'emotional impact,' that obviously varies from reader to reader. It may have something to do with how old one is. Want all the letters describing helpless weeping? Hey—the publisher cried! (The man publisher.)

"Mortality is au fond Iris' subject, which is the point too of *The Peach Women of A'aa*. And of Swift's *Struldbrugs*, as far as that goes. Can't live with it, can't really LIVE without it ... See also 'Happy Endings,' in [Atwood's] *Murder in the Dark* [1994], as a fantasy title."

25. "Comments": "for thresholds, see threshold ceremonies in *The Gift*, by Lewis Hyde. One threshold ceremony is the funeral. Over thresholds, the spirit steps from one stage of life into another. But the crossing of spirits can go two ways—who is it that really comes calling on Iris?"

In response to this question, I e-mailed Atwood on 11 July 2001: "I must admit I had totally missed the possibility that it may be the shade of Laura who crosses Iris' threshold at the end of your novel! And should I relate the event to Little Red Riding Hood and the wolf given the italicized '*Grandmother*'? Intertextuality is a bottomless pit."

Atwood replied on 12 July 2001: "I wasn't thinking of Laura per se but of threshold-crossing in general—life to death etc. Iris has waited the whole book for a knock upon her door that she hopes will be Sabrina's ... but it isn't. And she has seen a number of pseudo-Sabrina's throughout, all of them dressed in black, the first one in 'The Presentation.' So who IS that young woman in black with the sparkling raindrops who appears in the last chapter? In Iris' 'future tense' monologue?

"Let's call it that knock on the door that resounds throughout our literature, and was heard (for instance) at the end of *The Seventh Seal*. ... Whether one crossed the threshold in the direction of death, or whether death crosses the threshold in the direction of one, amounts to the same thing. But it's a threshold.

"Threshold ceremonies are evident too in the Scottish First Footings ceremony, in the groom carrying the bride across the threshold ...

"Hex signs used to be placed on thresholds to keep the evil spirits out. Witches couldn't cross thresholds unless invited. How long have I known all this? Ever since Andrew Lang et al. ..."

In the context of this essay, Atwood's comments serve to emphasize that the recurring female fetch or ghost dressed in black (another undead woman—see note 9 above) is an important fantasy element in *The Blind Assassin*. They serve also to distance the concluding threshold scene in *The Blind Assassin* from those in *The Scarlet Letter* (much as Hester's embroidered letter distances, by enrichment rather than adulteration, its meaning from "adulteress").

26. "Comments": "Iris does have a rock garden, of course. Winifred makes her do it. It is rather a failure—see p. 296 Bloomsbury version—and is certainly another heap of rubble or 'jumbled pile of stone' [see note 15 above]. Which would explain why she has a book on rock gardens at her disposal."

27. Ketterer: "'Sakiel-Norn' is the kind of name that teases academic interpreters. I can see that 'Norn,' presumably one of those past, present, or future Norse Fates, fits with the 'Destiny' part of 'The Pearl of Destiny' but what of 'Sakiel'? Is the inclusion of 'Saki' or 'saki' relevant? You must have had something in mind and, if you are willing to divulge what is was, I would be most interested."

Atwood: "Sakiel: see Omar, so moving-fingerly featured. Saki is the wine-bearer exhorted to turn down the empty cup, etc. [For] iel—see Ariel, Ezekiel, Emmanuel—el being a God word. Norn is fate-ish but also has that forlorn, lost & gone, French horn sound to it."

28. "Comments" (omitted from note 13 above and continued directly from note 22 above): "And NB—fabric and fabrication in piece I wrote about Matt Cohen, and the Scarlet Letter A meaning Author & Artist in my Cambridge lectures, coming out in 2002 spring—so, interesting correspondences. But I didn't have the textile connection directly in my head. These were just the kinds of things they made in small factories in small towns at that time, see *Going to Town* by K. Ashenberg [...] cited in Acknowledgements. The town I used as a template for this was Paris, Ontario. Where you will also find something very close to the faeryland bit of writing. That's how people wrote then! It ain't just author making it up."

WORKS CITED

Anonymous. "Hand-and-I Co-ordination." [Review of *The Blind Assassin*]. *The Economist* (23 September 2000): 157–58.

Atwood, Margaret. *The Blind Assassin*. London: Bloomsbury, 2000.

——. "Canadian Monsters: Some Aspects of the Supernatural in Canadian Fiction." In John Robert Colombo, ed., *Other Canadas: An Anthology of Canadian Science Fiction and Fantasy*. Toronto: McGraw-Hill Ryerson, 1979.

——. "Freeforall." In Phyllis Gotlieb and Douglas Barbour, eds., *Tesseracts^2*, 130–38. Victoria: Porcépic, 1990. Reprinted in David G. Hartwell and Glenn

Grant, eds., *Northern Suns: The New Anthology of Canadian Science Fiction*, 17–24. New York: Tor, 1999.

——. "Homelanding." In Candas Jane Dorsey, ed., *Tesseracts³*, 83–86. Victoria: Porcépic, 1990. Reprinted in Atwood, *Good Bones*, 121–28. London: Bloomsbury, 1992.

——. *Lady Oracle*. Toronto: McClelland and Stewart, 1976.

——. "Superwoman Drawn and Quartered: The Early Forms of *She*," *Alphabet* 10 (July 1965).

——. *Survival: A Thematic Guide to Canadian Literature*. Toronto: Anansi, 1972.

Brookner, Anita. "Artfully administered shocks." [Review of *The Blind Assassin*]. *The Spectator* 285 (7 October 2000): 50–51.

Clark, Alex. "Vanishing Act: Alex Clark on Atwood's ambiguous magic." [Review of *The Blind Assassin*]. *The Guardian* (30 September 2000): 10.

Clarke, I. F. *Voices Prophesying War, 1763–1984*. Oxford: Oxford University Press, 1966.

Clute, John. "Atwood, Margaret (Eleanor)." In John Clute and Peter Nicholls, eds., *The Encyclopedia of Science Fiction*, 69–70. London: Orbit, 1993.

Doody, Margaret Ann. "Royal Classic Knitwear." [Review of *The Blind Assassin*]. *London Review of Books* 22 (5 October 2000): 27–29.

Frye, Northrop. *Anatomy of Criticism*. Princeton: Princeton University Press, 1957.

——. *The Secular Scripture: A Study of the Structure of Romance*. Cambridge: Harvard University Press, 1976, 1992.

Glicksohn, Susan Wood. "The Martian Point of View." *Extrapolation* 16 (May 1974): 161–73.

Hawthorne, Nathaniel. *The Scarlet Letter*. Vol. 1 in the Centenary Edition of the *Works of Nathaniel Hawthorne*. 20 volumes. Edited by William Charvat et al. Columbus: Ohio State University Press, 1962–88.

Ketterer, David. "Canadian Science Fiction: A Survey." *Canadian Children's Literature* 10 (Spring 1978): 18–23. Reprinted in John Robert Colombo, ed., *Other Canadas: An Anthology of Canadian Science Fiction and Fantasy*, 326–33. Toronto: McGraw-Hill Ryerson, 1979.

——. "An Historical Survey of Canadian SF." *Science-Fiction Studies* 10 (March 1983): 87–100.

——. "Science Fiction and Fantasy in English and French." In William Toye, ed., *The Oxford Companion to Canadian Literature*, 730–39. Toronto: Oxford University Press, 1983.

Purdy, Al. "Atwood's Moodie." *Canadian Literature* 47 (Winter 1971): 81.

Sage, Lorna. "Sisterly sentiments." [Review of *The Blind Assassin*]. *Times Literary Supplement* 5087 (29 September 2000): 22.

Showalter, Elaine. "Virgin Suicide." [Review of *The Blind Assassin*]. *New Statesman* (2 October 2000): 53.

Stableford, Brain. "WAR." In John Clute and Peter Nicholls, eds., *The Encyclopedia of Science Fiction*, 1296–98. London: Orbit, 1993.

Sullivan, Rosemary. "Atwood, Margaret." In William Toye, ed., *The Oxford Companion to Canadian Literature.* Toronto: Oxford University Press, 1983. Revised in Eugene Benson and William Toye, eds., *The Oxford Companion to Canadian Literature*, 2nd ed., 63–66. Toronto: Oxford University Press, 1997.

——. *The Red Shoes: Margaret Atwood Starting Out.* Toronto: HarperFlamingo, 1988.

Teidelbaum, Sheldon. "The Handmaid's Tale." *Cinefantastique* 20 (March 1990): 16–17, 19–20, 22, 24.

——. "*The Handmaid's Tale*: Costumes." *Cinefantastique* 20 (March 1990): 25, 61.

——. "*The Handmaid's Tale*: Design." *Cinefantastique* 20 (March 1990): 23, 57.

——. "*The Handmaid's Tale*: Directing Dystopia." *Cinefantastique* 20 (March 1990): 21, 61.

Updike, John. "Love and Loss on Zycron." [Review of *The Blind Assassin*]. *New Yorker* (18 September 2000): 142–45.

White, Hayden. *Tropics of Discourse: Essays in Cultural Criticism.* Baltimore: Johns Hopkins University Press, 1978.

The Canadian Apocalypse

ALLAN WEISS

HISTORIES OF SCIENCE FICTION often trace the genre's roots as far back as ancient times and the works of Greek and Roman authors. Such efforts at seeking classical precursors are occasionally controversial. But there is one subgenre whose ancient roots are not in doubt: apocalyptic science fiction. Science fiction that portrays the end of the world, however the term may be defined by various authors, shows clearly the influence of St. John's text; in its symbols, images, structures, and themes, apocalyptic science fiction is a direct descendant of this Ur-Apocalypse.

Yet science fiction is also, and above all, a reflection of its own time and place. However much it may portray the future or the distant past, it mainly speaks out of and to its historical context. By portraying the end, apocalyptic literature reveals much about a culture's concept of time, and about how it sees its relationship to the universe; as Frank Kermode has shown, the nature of the end has implications for everything that comes before it. Apocalyptic science fiction can best be understood, then, by considering both its long-established tropes and its particular social and political contexts.

Not surprisingly, Canadian science-fiction authors—English and French—have worked within the conventions of the subgenre, producing works that are easily comparable with end-of-the-world narratives from Britain, the United States, and France. Their works exhibit both the familiar tropes that we associate with such fiction and the historical situations that shaped how the apocalypse has been repeatedly (re)conceived. Each era produced its own vision of what will produce the end, and of how humanity will cope (if it manages to cope at all) with global disaster. Of course, individual authors portray the apocalypse in distinctive ways, but the tropes of the sub-genre and the preoccupations of each age seem to play a greater role than does the individual voice in shaping the fiction.

It would be useful, then, as a foundation to a study of Canadian works of this type, first to distinguish apocalyptic science fiction from other forms of apocalyptic writing, and then to delineate its major tropes. What differentiates apocalyptic science fiction from other apocalyptic literature is, obviously, the role of scientific and technological principles in producing the end. Whereas St. John and the medieval apocalyptic writers emphasized the role of God, science-fiction writers stress that the end will come due to natural or human-made catastrophes. In very broad terms, much nineteenth- and early-twentieth-century apocalyptic science fiction predicts that time alone, or some astronomical event, will destroy humanity and even Earth itself. Comets, asteroids, and even planets strike our planet, wiping out human life or reducing it to a few scattered remnants. In short stories and novels such as Edgar Allan Poe's "The Conversation of Eiros and Charmion" (1839), H.G. Wells's "The Star" (1897), and Philip Wylie and Edwin Balmer's *When Worlds Collide* (1933), the end of the world comes because of an object hurtling down from the sky. An even earlier natural source of doom appears in Lord Byron's "Darkness" (1816), which traces the possible effects of the extinguishing of the sun. In Wells's *The Time Machine* (1895), the end is the natural result of the process of evolution, and the Time Traveler's viewing of the heat-death of the sun is one of the most famous endings—in every sense of the word—in all of science fiction.

As humanity developed more effective ways of fighting wars and manipulating the environment, and particularly as Western society's optimism concerning the power of science and technology declined after the First and Second World Wars, the source of apocalypse became less often natural and more often artificial. Even a work as early as Stephen Vincent Benét's "By the Waters of Babylon" (1937) shows military technology reaching the point where it could entirely destroy Western civilization; in this story, the United States has been laid waste by incendiary bombs and chemical and biological weapons. In E. M. Forster's "The Machine Stops" (1909), the human world is entirely technological, and the society portrayed faces a kind of apocalypse when the machine that takes care of it breaks down. Of course, the most important development in this context was the invention of the atom bomb and the arms race that followed the Second World War. Throughout the postwar period came countless visions of the end coming through humankind's irresponsible handling of its unsurpassed power to destroy. From Walter M. Miller Jr.'s *A Canticle for Leibowitz* (1959) to James Morrow's *This Is the Way the World Ends* (1986), nuclear weapons became the primary means by which we bring on the apocalypse ourselves. On the other hand, during the 1960s we saw the rise of ecological disasters in literature, beginning with such works as John Brunner's *The Sheep Look Up* (1972). More recently, as we shall see, the definition of "apocalypse" has been extended to include the conceptual apocalypse—the end of the world as we know it—and what we might describe as the postmodern apocalypse, in which the nature of the end and, therefore, of all that has produced it are difficult if not impossible to define.

Because of its origins in religious writings and its particular historical development, apocalyptic science fiction exhibits a number of key tropes. An important subset of apocalyptic SF is post-holocaust SF, those works that portray the world after a disaster—usually nuclear—has wiped out most of humanity. Since its Jewish beginnings, apocalyptic literature has been visionary literature; traditionally, an apocalyptic work recounts the vision of a prophet who receives a message from God and is directed to convey this message to the world. Indeed, "apocalypse" is from a Greek word meaning "revelation." In keeping with this tradition, much apocalyptic SF emphasizes the role of the narrator as one who has seen a vision of the end—whether natural or man-made—and who feels compelled to share it as a moral lesson to us all. What this means in technical terms is a stress on point of view, with the role of the narrator foregrounded to a remarkable degree. In fact, recent apocalyptic works such as Doris Lessing's *Memoirs of a Survivor* (1974) and Morrow's *This Is the Way the World Ends* are at least partially metafictional since the conveying of the story and therefore the message constitute the prime focus. Apocalyptic SF also shows its biblical roots in its imagery of fire (notably falling from the sky), earthquakes, particular colours such as red and black, and beasts (mutants and others), as well as in its division of society into the enlightened—those who know (science or God)—and the unenlightened. The world may end in light, an ending that usually implies some sort of spiritual transcendence, or in darkness, which usually implies a more nihilist vision.

Other major tropes include social and physical devolution, especially the regression of urban, "civilized" societies into tribal, "primitive" ones; anarchy; scarce resources, sometimes resulting in cannibalism; mythologizing of the past, including the rise of new religions; the sanctification and/or demonization of knowledge, above all scientific knowledge; a cyclical view of history, implying the possible repetition of the disaster; and the question of rebirth. Depending on the author's philosophy and purposes, apocalyptic SF may show humanity being redeemed by the apocalypse or demonstrating that we are fundamentally flawed and therefore doomed.

As we might expect, Canadian apocalyptic SF has followed international trends in the way it has portrayed the end and beyond. Perhaps the first apocalyptic work in Canadian literature is Archibald Lampman's poem "The City of the End of Things" (1894), a nihilistic vision of the industrial city as hell. The poem portrays a simultaneously physical and spiritual destruction as the forces of modernity swallow humanity until no one is left but the "grim Idiot at the gate." The poem is comparable to Byron's "Darkness"—and, perhaps more obviously, James B. V. Thomson's "The City of Dreadful Night"—in its use of apocalyptic images that must be read symbolically rather than in conventionally science-fictional terms. Lampman's focus, like Byron's and Thomson's, is on spiritual rather than physical annihilation.

Early Canadian works of true science fiction stress the role of natural catastrophes in destroying the world and exhibit a much greater optimism concerning our ability to cope with, or even overcome, the disaster. For example, in Emmanuel Desrosiers's *La Fin de la terre* (1931) the world is suffering a mysterious series of geological crises. These may be triggered in part by overpopulation and overuse of resources, or perhaps the world has simply reached the end of its life and God is ending it. While humanity is not directly responsible for, and cannot stop, what is happening, people can flee the planet and build a new world on Mars—with the unlikely assistance of the natives there. The novel provides a classic 1930s vision of the future, featuring huge cities dominated by large, pristine buildings, and transportation via bigger and better airplanes—including ones that can fly to other planets. The novel, moreover, contains a trope that seems pervasive in French-Canadian apocalyptic and post-holocaust works: geological catastrophe. In many of the works mentioned below, Earth is convulsed by earthquakes and volcanoes, and humans take refuge in underground cities—or, as in Jacques Brossard's "L'engloutissement" (1983), the underground city is itself the world being destroyed by earthquakes.

Few apocalyptic works appeared before the Second World War. And so such natural disasters are comparatively rare, while, as one might expect, the prospect of nuclear holocaust obsessed writers in both English and French Canada during the postwar period. Visions of the end through nuclear war can be seen in Yves Thériault's *Si la bombe m'était contée* (1962), a collection of short stories on the theme. In "Akua nuten: le vent du sud," for example, Kakatso, a Montagnais hunter and trapper, sees a flash far to the south; not long afterward, an airplane lands, carrying whites fleeing from the holocaust. He refuses to help them, feeling instead that the whites have gotten what they deserved and that now the land will be freed from their colonization and domination. But the wind carries radiation to his land, and he shares the fate of the rest of the world. Jean Simard's "L'abri" (1964) is about Mr. Harris, a man pragmatic and prudent to a fault. He constructs a bomb shelter, ensuring that it is built, armed, and equipped beyond specifications. But when he sees the destruction produced by a nuclear strike and the futility of his rational efforts to save his family from a thoroughly irrational event, in utter despair he turns his machine gun on his wife and children. Jean Tétreau presents a well-realized apocalyptic setting in *Les Nomades* (1967), in which a young Italian girl moves through a Europe destroyed by what appears to be an accidental nuclear war triggered (again) by geological events. Her journey fits well into the post-holocaust fiction pattern of the "journey through the wasteland" and "settlement and establishment of a community" described by critic Gary K. Wolfe in his essay "The Remaking of Zero" (10–11). Tétreau's Silvana enjoys a brief Edenic relationship with a Danish man named Niels, as the land restores itself around them; but ultimately she must find her way "home"—or at least what is left of it—on her own. The novel is a coming-of-age narrative in which the protagonist grows not merely into an adult but also into a matriarch. Maurice Gagnon's *Les Tours de Babylone* (1972) is a post-holocaust novel about a world divided into a dystopic city-state and the barbarian tribes that live in the wasteland surrounding it. The narrator, Severe, eventually chooses to side with the tribes, who represent freedom, and to betray the oppressive masters of Babylon.

Post-nuclear-holocaust stories dominated the postwar period up to and even into the nineties: in Heather Spears's *Moonfall* trilogy (1991–96), for example, it appears that nuclear weapons created the wasteland and the genetic mutations that resulted in bicephalic humans becoming the norm. Classic images of the world after a nuclear holocaust appear in René Beaulieu's *Légendes de Virnie* (1981) and in stories such as Jean Ferguson's "Ker le tueur de Dieu" (1974), in which humanity has been returned to a quasi-medieval existence by an ancient, now-forgotten nuclear war.

Among the many developments in military nuclear technology that inspired yet other stories bitterly attacking the insanity of such weapons, that of the neutron bomb, with its ability to kill people while leaving buildings intact, seems to have provoked particular animosity over its ironically "clean" effects. Claire Dé's "Le 2 juin," for example, portrays how the residents of the Notre-Dame-de-Grâce district of Montréal cope with the after-effects of the dropping of an N-bomb.

William C. Heine's *The Last Canadian* (1974) portrays the destruction of North America through the release of a deadly virus by an insane Russian scientist. Only a few thousand survivors are left, to become dangerous carriers of the disease (why they are not killed by the virus is never explained). One of them, a Korean War veteran named Gene Arnprior, is the novel's hero. He survives more than just the biological weapon; he also manages to withstand Soviet small-arms, landmines, and nuclear attacks while travelling through the devastated landscapes of Canada and the United States. His luck runs out only when he threatens to infect Asia and Europe by flying to the Soviet Union in revenge for the Russian treachery.

With the coming of the seventies, we see more and more examples of apocalypse through environmental degradation. André-Jean Bonelli's *Loona: ou Autrefois le ciel était bleu* (1974) is a post-holocaust narrative about a future Earth that is no longer able to sustain human life—or any life that has not radically mutated—because of humanity's ecological damage; the protagonists, Lars and Loona, escape the megalomaniacal villain, Polsen, and quest to find some unpolluted sky. Margaret Atwood's *The Handmaid's Tale* (1985) may be seen as a post-holocaust work in which North America's population, at least, is suffering the effects of toxic and nuclear wastes, which have led to sterility and the rise of the theocratic dystopia, Gilead. Similar nuclear and non-nuclear environmental damage forms the basis of the post-holocaust world in Élisabeth Vonarburg's *Le Silence de la cité* (1981) and *Chroniques du pays des mères* (1992). Through pollution and nuclear waste, we have destroyed the world in Daniel Sernine's "Le monde malade de l'humanité" (1981). We learn that the main character, Gil Behrer, is an alien launching the Atropos Project: because of its behaviour humanity has become a cancer on the planet that must be excised so that Earth can heal, and the aliens are in the process of performing the surgery. The story features classic post-holocaust images of new quasi-religions and anarchic behaviour, particularly on the part of groups such as a suicidal cult and the Crazies ("Dements"). An ecological catastrophe looms in Peter Watts's *Starfish* (1999), about a deadly micro-organism released by researchers penetrating the depths of the ocean.

The works surveyed thus far involve a physical apocalypse in the conventional sense: the world is actually destroyed, or nearly so, and humanity suffers mass death. But in more recent years authors have explored variations on the apocalypse that do not involve actual slaughter on a large scale. What occurs instead is a fundamental change, one whose implications are uncertain. Such works can be classified as "postmodern" apocalypses, a term that may in some ways be a contradiction in terms. An apocalypse, as we have seen, is an ending that makes sense of what has gone before; the twilight of Earth that we see in *The Time Machine* reinforces the truth of evolutionary change, while the nuclear and environmental disasters we see in much twentieth-century science fiction didactically point to the need for humans to modify their behaviour or pay the ultimate price. In such cases, the ending is clearly defined, and, consequently, so is the route that takes us there. But in the postmodern apocalypse, the "ending" is tentative and open to doubt, so that perhaps we are seeing not an ending so much as another step in an undirected process: apocalypse without closure.

One excellent example of a postmodern apocalypse is Robert Charles

Wilson's *The Harvest* (1992). Aliens arrive on Earth offering humanity immortality; the process of transformation is entirely voluntary, and there is no catch—except of course for the fact that it would entail a massive shift in how we define "human." We define ourselves as human in part by our mortality, so that characters must decide whether they are willing to surrender their humanity in favour of a form of transcendence. Most accept the offer, but a small band of humans, including the protagonist Matt Wheeler, resist, at least at first. Wilson frequently refers to "the end of the world," but of course no physical destruction is taking place—quite the contrary, in fact. Yet it *is* the end of humanity as we know it, and whether the ending constitutes a death, a rebirth, or merely a transition is open to debate.

Hugh A. D. Spencer's "Icarus Down/Bear Rising" (1992) presents a similarly conceptual apocalypse. Military officers and an anthropologist travel to northern Canada to discover why a satellite has mysteriously crashed there. As becomes clear to the anthropologist, what is happening is a paradigm shift: the Native worldview is beginning to replace the European, scientific one, and the laws of physics no longer apply. A helicopter stops functioning and drops straight down; other equipment ceases to work. Once again, it is the end of the world as we have defined it, without the need for mass destruction or death. Although Spencer is not himself Aboriginal, the story can be read as a postcolonial narrative; it is unquestionably a challenge to the European worldview, and thus the depiction of a radical but non-physical and perhaps non-final ending.

In the postmodern apocalypse, it is frequently unclear what is causing the world to end and how we are to take it. An excellent example of a truly uncertain apocalypse is P. K. Page's "'Unless the Eye Catch Fire ...'" (1979). For unexplained reasons, Earth is heating up, and the sun becomes a constant, burning presence whose effects can be felt even when it is shining on the other side of the world. At the same time, however, the narrator and many other people see strange colours, suggesting that they are gaining a new vision in spiritual as well as physical terms. The story contains many of the familiar tropes of more conventional disaster narratives—anarchy, shortages of food and water, and so on—and physical destruction is definitely at hand. Yet those who can see the colours gain a higher knowledge and, with that, a higher unity. At the end, the narrator says, "We are together now. United, indissoluble. Bonded" (86).

Much like Page's story, the film *Last Night* (1998), directed by Don McKellar, ends in light. Once again, we never learn why or how the world is ending, but for McKellar explanation is not the point. His focus is on how individual characters cope with their final hours; most engage in meaningless but familiar and comforting rituals. Patrick, the main character, has been scarred by the death of his wife and seeks solitude, but a woman named Sandra who enlists his help to return to her husband forces him out of his shell. The mysterious nature of the apocalypse reinforces the meaninglessness of contemporary life, since the world is ending in a meaningless mass death. Yet a kind of personal transcendence is possible. One hallmark of postmodern works is their self-reflexivity; and there are hints in the film that the ending these characters are facing is nothing more or less than the end of one movie.

The Canadian apocalypse thus reflects international and historical developments in the genre. Over time, as our culture, our obsessions, our hopes, and our fears have changed, so have our visions of the end. Whether the end comes through natural means, through our own careless, irresponsible actions, or through something tentative and indefinable, Canadian science-fiction authors have used the end of the world to explore vast global and personal themes. We can therefore learn much about our view of the world by examining how we have prophesied its destruction, and what sort of rebirth, if any, we predict will follow.

WORKS CITED

Atwood, Margaret. *The Handmaid's Tale*. Toronto: McClelland and Stewart, 1985.

Beaulieu, René. *Légendes de Virnie*. Montréal: Le Préambule, 1981.

Benét, Stephen Vincent. "By the Waters of Babylon." 1937. In *Beyond Armageddon: Twenty-One Sermons to the Dead*, 240–60. New York: Donald I. Fine, 1985.

Brossard, Jacques. "L'engloutissement." In André Carpentier, ed., *Dix contes et nouvelles fantastiques par dix auteurs québécois*, 89–115. Montréal: Quinze, 1983.

Brunner, John. *The Sheep Look Up*. New York: Harper & Row, 1972.

Byron, Lord. "Darkness." 1816. *Lord Byron: Selected Poems and Letters*. Ed. William H. Marshall, 219–21. Boston: Houghton Mifflin, 1968.

Dé, Claire. "Un 2 juin." In *La Louve garou*, 131–37. Montréal: Éditions de la Pleine Lune, 1982.

Desrosiers, Emmanuel. *La Fin de la terre*. Montréal: Librarie d'Action Canadienne-Française, 1931.

Ferguson, Jean. "Ker, le tueur de Dieu." In *Contes ardents du pays mauve*, 80–94. Montréal: Leméac, 1974.

Forster, E. M. "The Machine Stops." 1909. In Ben Bova, ed., *The Science Fiction Hall of Fame*, vol. 2B, 228–58. Garden City: Doubleday,1973.

Heine, William C. *The Last Canadian*. Markham: Simon & Schuster, 1974.

Kermode, Frank. *Sense of an Ending: Studies in the Theory of Fiction*. New York: Oxford University Press, 1967.

Lampman, Archibald. "The City of the End of Things." 1894. In *The Poems of Archibald Lampman (Including At the Long Sault)*, 179–82. Ed. Margaret Coulby. Whitridge. Toronto: University of Toronto Press, 1974.

Last Night. Dir. Don McKellar. Perf. Don McKellar, Sandra Oh, David Cronenberg, Callum Keith Rennie, Genevieve Bujold, and Sarah Polley. McKellar, 1998.

Lessing, Doris. *Memoirs of a Survivor*. London: Octagon, 1974.

Morrow, James. *This Is the Way the World Ends*. New York: Harcourt Brace, 1986.

Page, P. K. "'Unless the Eye Catch Fire....'" *Malahat Review* 50 (1979): 65–86.

Poe, Edgar Allan. "The Conversation of Eiros and Charmion." 1839. In *The Science Fiction of Edgar Allan Poe*, 65–71. Harmondsworth: Penguin, 1976.

——. "La monde malade d'humanité." In *Le Vieil homme et l'espace*, 103–45. Montréal: Le Préambule, 1981.

Simard, Jean. "Un abri." In *13 récits*, 33–55. Montréal: Éditions HMH, 1964.

Spears, Heather. *The Children of Atwar*. Victoria: Beach Holme, 1993.

——. *Moonfall*. Victoria: Beach Holme, 1991.

——. *The Taming*. Edmonton: Tesseract Books, 1996.

Spencer, Hugh. "Icarus Down/Bear Rising." *On Spec* 4, no. 1 (1992): 11–22.

Tétreau, Jean. *Les Nomades*. Montréal: Éditions du Jour, 1967.

Thériault, Yves. *Si la bombe m'était contée*. Montréal: Éditions du Jour, 1962.

Vonarburg, Élisabeth. *Chroniques du pays des mères*. Montréal: Québec/Amérique, 1992.

——. *Le Silence de la cité*. Paris: Éditions Denoël, 1981.

Watts, Peter. *Starfish*. New York: Tor, 1999.

Wells, H. G. "The Star." 1897. In Donald L. Lawlor, ed., *Approaches to Science Fiction*, 86–95. Boston: Houghton Mifflin, 1978.

——. *The Time Machine*. 1895. New York: Tor, 1986.

Wilson, Robert Charles. *The Harvest*. New York: Bantam, 1992.

Wolfe, Gary K. "The Remaking of Zero: Beginning at the End." In Eric S. Rabkin, Martin H. Greenberg, and Joseph D. Olander, eds., *The End of the World*, 1–19. Carbondale: Southern Illinois University Press, 1983.

Wylie, Philip, and Edwin Balmer. *When Worlds Collide*. New York: Frederick A. Stokes, 1933.

Notes on the Contemporary Apocalyptic Imagination: William Gibson's *Neuromancer* and Douglas Coupland's *Girlfriend in a Coma*

VERONICA HOLLINGER

"The Year 2000 Has Already Happened."

– Jean Baudrillard (1987)

I WANT TO SET UP A DIALOGUE between two very different novels that demonstrate features of the apocalyptic imagination. William Gibson's classic cyberpunk novel *Neuromancer* is a mid-eighties refutation of apocalyptic anxieties, a manifesto for cool anti-apocalypticism. Douglas Coupland's neo-conservative salvation story, *Girlfriend in a Coma*, is a late-nineties expression of apocalyptic wish-fulfilment, a Generation-X fantasy of (re)creating the world. *Neuromancer* is one of the most widely read science fiction novels of the past fifty years, and it was almost single-handedly responsible for the turn toward postmodernism of science fiction theory and criticism in the nineties. Among its various challenges to the conventions of genre SF is its attempt to rewrite some of the thematic implications of apocalyptic plot elements. Coupland's novel, published just before the turn of the millennium, is a post-generic fiction, drawing freely on a variety of realist, science fictional, and fantasy plot elements to create a hybrid narrative that looks hardly anything like science fiction. In spite of this, it also self-consciously recalls science fiction's Golden Age apocalypticism, specifically through its intertextual borrowings from Arthur C. Clarke's 1953 novel *Childhood's End.*

Anti-Apocalyptic

> Things aren't different. Things are things.
>
> – William Gibson, *Neuromancer*

The mid-eighties generated a variety of critical-theoretical reports on the contemporary "condition" that, taken together, influenced most subsequent mappings of the postmodern as a more-or-less new, more-or-less different, more-or-less transformed moment in historical consciousness. At the same time, many of these reports from the edge were careful to discourage any investment in scenarios of radical catastrophe and transformation; for the most part, they argued strongly against the seductions of apocalyptic logic and rhetoric. One exemplary statement is Jean-François Lyotard's by-now classic definition of postmodernism as "incredulity toward metanarratives" (xxiv), suggesting, as it does, an intellectual refusal of the logic of apocalypse, which is nothing if not the logic of a totalizing master narrative.[1] Equally discouraging of attempts to characterize the present in terms of apocalyptic endings and beginnings is Jacques Derrida's deconstructive (anti)philosophy, which challenges deep-seated anxieties about—and desires for—originary moments and revelatory closures in human history; deconstruction convincingly argues that the movements of history are more accurately characterized by terms such as "free play" and "infinite deferral."[2]

At this same moment in the mid-eighties, science fiction took one of its most significant turns with the publication of *Neuromancer*, which virtually established cyberpunk as its own SF subgenre. *Neuromancer* simultaneously relies upon and dismisses genre SF's long-standing fascination with apocalyptic scenarios. After hundreds of pages of non-stop suspense and narrative action, the final scene in Gibson's novel appears to be an anti-climactic throwaway. The text here concentrates on Wintermute, a vastly powerful artificial intelligence (AI), which, through its union with the Neuromancer AI, is now integrated into a coherent subject/self of awesome proportions and capacity. As Wintermute announces to Gibson's protagonist, Case, "I'm the sum total of the works, the whole show." If any SF situation were ever set up for apocalyptic revelation, this would seem to be it, but when Case asks, in suitably world-weary-hacker tones, "So what's the score? How are things different? You running the world now? You

God?," the AI replies only, "Things aren't different. Things are things" (269–70). The AI also informs Case that it is now in communication with another vast intelligence like itself in the Centauri system; to this potentially world-shaking piece of interstellar news, Case responds merely with, "Oh ... Yeah? No shit?" "No shit," affirms the AI: "And then the screen was blank" (270).

For all intents and purposes, this is the concluding scene of *Neuromancer*, an action novel that provides its fair share of climactic moments but rarely fails to undercut them when their significance threatens to get out of hand. Although the text certainly mobilizes the imagery of apocalypse to build narrative tension, it ultimately dismisses the apparent significance of these images. The Rastafarian inhabitants of the Zion-habitat, for example, believe themselves to be living in "the Final Days" (110), engaged in an all-or-nothing spiritual struggle with the forces of "Babylon." Like most of the central human characters in *Neuromancer*, however, they have been recruited by the Wintermute entity and serve non-human interests.

Keeping in mind that the apocalypse promises not only ending but also revelation, it is significant that the final scenes in *Neuromancer* provide neither conclusions nor disclosures. One crucial feature of Gibson's plot is that Wintermute cannot know the "true name," which, when spoken, will fuse Wintermute and Neuromancer into one vast virtual entity. Here is how Gibson presents the climactic moment when Case hacks this information from the Villa Straylight's computers:

> – *now*
> and his voice the cry of a bird
> unknown,
> 3Jane answering in song, three
> notes, high and pure.
> A true name. (262)

The moment of apocalyptic revelation remains "unspoken" in the text; consequently, the text is incapable of imparting the apocalyptic revelation to its own readers.

Earlier in the novel, at the climax of its central action sequence—the Straylight run—an obviously much less world-weary Case has demanded the password that would unite the divided selves of the AI, and his demand is couched in terms of a passionate desire for the radical transformation of his fictional world: "Give us the fucking code.... If you don't, what'll change? What'll ever fucking change for you?... I got no idea at all what'll happen if Wintermute wins, but it'll *change* something!" (260). When Wintermute wins, it certainly does change *something*, but not for Case or for any of the other central human characters, whose lives remain untouched by either catastrophe or revelation. This is Case's "happy ending":

> He spent the bulk of his Swiss account on a new pancreas and liver, the rest on a new Ono-Sendai and a ticket back to the Sprawl.
>
> He found work.
> He found a girl who called herself Michael. (270)

In his 1986 introduction to *Burning Chrome*, Gibson's first collection of short stories, editor Bruce Sterling—well known for his own fiery millennial prophecies about the death of old-guard science fiction—identifies "boredom with the Apocalypse" as a "distinguishing mark of the emergent new school of Eighties SF [that is, of cyberpunk]" (xi). Cyberpunk, at least in Gibson's original version, demonstrated a kind of postmodern ennui toward SF's long tradition of radical endings-and-beginnings. In part, of course, this is because of the dissipation of the Cold War anxieties that produced novels such as Walter M. Miller's *A Canticle for Leibowitz* and films such as Stanley Kubrick's *Dr. Strangelove*. But it is also the result of the anti-climactic nature of an over-hyped end-of-the-millennium, an ending that we were poised to experience for what seemed like the entire second half of the twentieth century.

Apocalyptic

> She closes her eyes and she sees things—images of blood and soil mixed together like the center of a Black Forest cake; Grand Canyons of silent office towers. Houses, coffins, babies, cars, brooms, and bottle caps all burning and draining into the sea and dissolving like candies.
>
> – Douglas Coupland, *Girlfriend in a Coma*

The cool anti-apocalypticism of cyberpunk SF not only challenged the deep-seated apocalyptic tendencies of SF as a whole, but, as the official end of the millennium approached, served as a continuing site of resistance to the growing tide of eschatological sentiment in both genre fiction and mainstream cultural analyses. The dizzying lack of boundaries and the devastating disavowal of metaphysical significance embodied in both the writings of Lyotard and Derrida and in cyberpunk reflect only one side of the critical-historical coin. In fact, given the ambivalence built into past and contemporary debates over the imminence or immanence of the end, most theoretical reports from the edge have been less than completely successful in resisting the lure of apocalyptic rhetoric. (We might recall, for instance, Foucault's prophecies of "the end of man," Derrida's commitment to the idea of "the end of metaphysics," and, of course, Baudrillard's continuing assessment of the overtaking of the "real" by its "simulation.")

Coupland's *Girlfriend in a Coma* enacts a quite precise repudiation of the Derridean universe of absolute futility and freedom, and a particularly contemporary (re)turn to the anxious comforts of apocalyptic logic. In his novel, the end of the world provides a genuine salvation for disaffected characters who find themselves trapped in the unending and meaningless stream of time-in-technoculture. While the novel's plot is relatively unencumbered by the technologically inflected discourse of conventional science fiction, its focus is very specifically the anomie of Western technoculture in the two decades leading up to the end of the millennium. If *Neuromancer* was *the* speculative fiction for the mid-eighties, *Girlfriend in a Coma* demonstrates the distance between that moment of relative cultural confidence and its own moment in the late nineties.

As has been frequently noted, Gibson's novel is populated by a wide variety of artificial intelligences and technologically enhanced humans; *Neuromancer* celebrates a post-humanist acceptance of the fusion of the human and the technological. In contrast, Coupland's novel constructs such a merging in terms of loss and dehumanization: when one character asks whether the new technologies have made human beings "new and improved and faster and better," another wearily tells her, "You'll get used to them.... It's not up for debate. We lost. Machines won" (143). If a defining feature of the central human characters in *Neuromancer* is their ability to adapt to a constantly changing technological environment, that same environment has rendered Coupland's GenXers "stunted" and "lacking" (143).

Coupland's novel is set in the affluent middle-class suburbs of Vancouver, and his main characters are a group of childhood friends for whom the promise of the seventies has been betrayed by the increasingly banal realities of the eighties and nineties. As adults, they inhabit, in Coupland's terms, a wasteland of North American commodification and addiction. They are also the unlikely survivors of the end of the world. On November 28, 1999, every single human being in the world, except for these six friends (and Richard's teenaged daughter, Meaghan), falls into a deep sleep and dies. Human time and human history, which have become reduced to insignificance, simply stop. The world will remain asleep for a year, until these characters come to accept their roles as the neo-apostles of a re-created reality.

Reading *Girlfriend in a Coma* is like reading a fictional affirmation of Fredric Jameson's observation, in essays such as "Postmodernism and Consumer Society" (1983) and "Postmodernism, or The Cultural Logic of Late Capitalism" (1984), that contemporary Western culture can be defined, in part, through its loss of the sense of a viable future, concomitant with its loss of a sense of history. According to Jameson, history has been transformed into nostalgia, and the past has been reduced to a series of glossy images available to us in endless circulation through electronic media; at the same time, the failure of the utopian imagination in the context of commodity capitalism spells the failure of our ability to imagine better futures, if indeed we can still imagine any futures at all. It is this version of the postmodern loss of both past *and* future that we can read in *Girlfriend in a Coma*, a novel whose characters hover between dreams of a golden past forever lost in time and a future that is at once banal and dreadful.

In 1979, when the novel opens, seventeen-year-old Karen Ann McNeil, the eponymous girlfriend, leaves a sealed letter with her boyfriend Richard and then proceeds to fall into a coma that lasts until 1997, thus prefiguring the sleep that will eventually overtake all of humanity. In her letter to Richard, Karen expresses, in typical contemporary youth-speak, her extreme anxiety about time-future:

> I've been having these visions this week. ... [T]hese voices are arguing while I get to see bits of (this sounds so bad) the Future!

> It's dark there—in the Future, I mean. It's not a good place. Everybody looks so old and the neighborhood looks like shit (pardon my French!!)
>
> I'm writing this note because I'm scared.... I feel like sleeping for a thousand years—that way I'll never have to be around for this weird new future. (28)

Significantly, the sign of her body's failure is its now utter dependence upon technology; as Richard notes, "The machinery of [Karen's] new life was fully set in motion—the IVs, respirator, tubes, and wave monitors" (29). Karen's new cyborg body spells tragedy, not triumph. Contrast the comatose Karen with *Neuromancer*'s central female character, the razor-girl/bodyguard Molly Millions. Endowed by technology with more-than-human speed and strength, Molly too has experienced a coma of sorts: the money for her techno-enhancements has been earned by her work as a "meat puppet," a prostitute who remains unconscious of the work that her body is doing: "Renting the goods, is all," as she describes it (147).

While Karen hides out in her coma, Richard and his friends wander aimlessly through nearly two decades of enervated, coma-like existence before being rescued by the end of the world. The only possible redemption from absolute insignificance is through the absolute destruction of things as they are. So in Coupland's impossible fantasy of salvation, history comes to an end and his characters are transformed into "post-historic" subjects who are then returned to the world in order to "clear the land for a new culture" (275, 274).

Coupland's novel is neoconservative salvation history complete with ritual sacrifice. Karen, who has awakened after eighteen years, is the novel's Christ-figure; she must willingly return to her coma so that the human world can start up again. Richard and his friends will devote the rest of their lives to making that world a more meaningful place. The novel concludes with images of newfound truth, newfound hope, and the potential for a newly recreated world:

> Richard thinks about being alive at this particular juncture in history and he can only marvel—to be alive at this wondrous point—this jumping-off point toward further reaches. ... You'll soon see us walking down your street [he thinks], our backs held proud, our eyes dilated with truth and power.

> ... We'll draw our line in the sand and force the world to cross our line. Every cell in our body explodes with the truth. ... We'll be adults who smash the tired, exhausted system. We'll crawl and chew and dig our way into a radical new world. We will change minds and souls from stone and plastic into linen and gold—that's what I believe. That's what I know. (284)

Coupland's rejection of the hip anti-apocalypticism of texts such as *Neuromancer* is further emphasized by his novel's self-consciously intertextual (re)turn to the paradigmatic Golden Age apocalypticism of Arthur C. Clarke. Early in *Girlfriend*, considering his own dismal moment in time, Richard muses:

> That month I had read a science fiction story, *Childhood's End*. In it, the children of Earth conglomerate to form a master race that dreams together, that collectively moves planets. This made me wonder, what if the children of Earth instead fragmented, checked out, had their dreams erased and became vacant? What if instead of unity, there was atomization and amnesia and comas? (61)

Richard's ultimate vision of the achievement of a long-deferred adulthood goes on to rewrite Clarke's tale of the end of the human race—or, more accurately, of the evolution of the *children* of the human race into a vast psychic organism that triumphantly sets out for the stars. Clarke's final vision in *Childhood's End*, referred to by the one remaining human spectator as "the climax of all history" (214), is one of the most transcendent moments in genre SF. Coupland echoes Clarke's metaphorical appeal to images of infancy and maturity to dramatize the release of his characters from their long childhood within the stifling exigencies of commodity capitalism. As Richard's vision demonstrates, Coupland's characters are also on the verge of experiencing the as-yet-unknown freedoms of a new *adult* mode of being.

Girlfriend in a Coma assures its readers that a new world is attainable: "Haven't you always felt that you live forever on the brink of knowing a great truth? Well, that feeling is true. There *is* the truth. It does exist" (272). Like a textual Moses, however, *Girlfriend* can only point us toward the Promised Land; it cannot itself enter. Although it ends on a note of radical desire, at a "jumping-off point toward further reaches," it nevertheless has nothing to say about the new world toward which it gestures.

In fact, both *Neuromancer* and *Girlfriend in a Coma* fall silent as they approach the edge of apocalyptic revelation. *Neuromancer*'s silence is deliberate and ironic; it confirms that there is nothing to reveal, that "things aren't different. Things are things." It de-emphasizes the potential for (political) change within the historical processes of an increasingly interconnected global order. *Girlfriend*'s silence—equally apolitical—is the text holding its breath on the edge of significance. Unlike *Neuromancer*'s characters, *Girlfriend*'s characters have awakened from their decades-long "coma," and the text leaves them—and its readers—poised for a revelation that is always to come at the end of human history.

On Being Canadian: An Ending, of Sorts

Neuromancer was written by an American writer who has lived in Canada for decades but whose publishing career owes everything to his initial (and continuing) success in the United States; *Girlfriend in a Coma* is by a Canadian writer celebrated as a spokesperson for all of North America's "Generation X." Rather than concluding that these novels "fail" at being adequately "Canadian," however, I want to suggest that they very successfully evoke an authentic feature of contemporary "Canadian-ness," exactly insofar as they address issues of concern to a generalized global techno-culture. They demonstrate something we tend to downplay about our culture, perhaps because it seems to us to be too "American": this being-borderless, this being-trans-national, this being-global.

NOTES

1. *The Postmodern Condition* was translated into English in 1984, the same year that *Neuromancer* was published.
2. Derrida published two very influential essays on apocalyptic themes, "No Apocalypse, Not Now (full speed ahead, seven missiles, seven missives)" and "Of an Apocalyptic Tone Recently Adopted in Philosophy." Their English translations appeared in 1982 and 1984, respectively.

WORKS CITED

Baudrillard, Jean. "The Year 2000 Has Already Happened." In Arthur Kroker and Marilouise Kroker, eds., *Body Invaders: Panic Sex in America*, trans. Nai-Fei Ding and Kuan Hsing Chen, 35–44. Montreal: New World Perspectives, 1987.

Clarke, Arthur C. *Childhood's End.* 1953. New York: Ballantine, 1979.

Coupland, Douglas. *Girlfriend in a Coma.* New York: HarperCollins, 1998.

Derrida, Jacques. "No Apocalypse, Not Now (full speed ahead, seven missiles, seven missives)." Trans. Catherine Porter and Philip Lewis. *Diacritics* 14 (Summer 1984): 20–31.

——. "Of an Apocalyptic Tone Recently Adopted in Philosophy." Trans. John P. Leavey, Jr. *Semeia* 23 (1982): 63–97.

Gibson, William. *Neuromancer.* New York: Ace, 1984.

Jameson, Fredric. "Postmodernism and Consumer Society." In Hal Foster, ed., *The Anti-Aesthetic: Essays on Postmodern Culture*, 111–25. Port Townsend, WA: Bay Press, 1983.

——. "Postmodernism, or, The Cultural Logic of Late Capitalism." *New Left Review* 146 (July/August 1984): 53–94.

Lyotard, Jean-François. *The Postmodern Condition: A Report on Knowledge.* Trans. Geoff Bennington and Brian Massumi. Minneapolis: University of Minnesota Press, 1984.

Sterling, Bruce. "Preface." 1986. In William Gibson, *Burning Chrome*, ix–xii. New York: Ace, 1987.

Welwyn Wilton Katz and Charles de Lint: New Fantasy as a Canadian Post-colonial Genre

LAURENCE STEVEN

THE SITUATIONS OF WELWYN WILTON KATZ, of London, Ontario, an award-winning writer of fantasy for young adults and of Ottawa's Charles de Lint, an internationally known author of over forty books of what has come to be called urban fantasy or mythic fiction, epitomize concerns about voice, cultural appropriation, a national literature, and the creative freedom of writers. Both de Lint's "Afterword" to the 1995 Dark Side Press edition of *Mulengro* and the controversy over Katz's novel *False Face* (1987)—basically, a question of whether a white writer's dealing with Native cultural material is an instance of cultural appropriation—point up a problem that Canadian writers have long faced as they attempt to discover a voice in this country: having no indigenous non-Native culture to draw on, they attempt to graft themselves onto Native material—and the graft does not take.

The nineteenth- and early-twentieth-century depictions of First Nations culture in English-language Canadian literature partook of a fundamental colonial assumption, despite the best intentions of the authors. From Susanna Moodie's characterizing the Indian as nature's "true gentleman"; to Isabella Valancy Crawford's mystical/erotic view of Indianism as expressed in "Malcolm's Katie," "The Camp of Souls," "Said the Canoe," and "The Lily Bed"; Duncan Campbell Scott's romantically elegiac view in "The Onondaga Madonna," "The Forsaken," "On the Way to the Mission"; Archie Belaney's (aka Grey Owl's) gothic view in *The Men of the Last Frontier* (1931); and E. J. Pratt's heroic view in *Brébeuf and His Brethren* (1940)—in all these cases the Indians are in effect exotic beings living in a fantasy land. Indeed, these depictions share one main contour of traditional fantasies: a well-demarcated division between, in J. R. R. Tolkien's terms, the Primary world (ours) and the Secondary (that of fantasy). Belaney goes from England (the Primary world of solid reality) to Canada (the Secondary fantasy realm) where he, as Colin Ross puts it in a trenchant little piece, "played at being an Indian" (257). In Armand Garnet Ruffo's *Grey Owl: The Mystery of Archie Belaney* (1997), the indigenous voice responds to and draws out the implications of such cultural imposition. For her part, Crawford, who lived in Peterborough and Toronto most of her life, never had more than a passing experience of Indians. Despite her much vaunted "mythopoeic imagination" (Frye 148), it remains true that her sensual Indian poems are sublimated fantasies, events in a Secondary world that did not impinge on her Primary one. How imbued she was with traditional European fantasy is clear when one reads her *Fairy Tales* (edited by Penny Petrone and published by Borealis in 1977). Similarly, and perhaps most notably, thanks to significant essays by Flood, Lynch, Titley, and Weis, we are increasingly able to see D. C. Scott, the Confederation poet most renowned for his awareness of Nativeness, as (in his Primary world role as chief bureaucrat of Indian Affairs for the Canadian government) a purveyor of the colonial Secondary world fantasy of Indians as noble savages whose "waning race" needs civilization. He reveals the European provenance of his fantasy most directly in a poem such as "The Piper of Arll."

With the benefit of historical hindsight, post-colonial theory, and the First Nations cultural renaissance since the nineteen-sixties in Canada, the problems associated with the incorporation of Native cultural material into non-Native literature have become more salient. But the fundamental reality remains that a non-Native *Canadian* repository of traditional (mythopoeic/spiritual) cultural lore out of which our writers of fantasy can fashion their worlds simply doesn't exist. When non-Native Canadian writers of fantasy need a lore-hoard out of which to spin a world, they tend to turn away from Canada and draw primarily on the European repository. Sometimes they import the lore to Canada from Europe, as in Perry

Nodelman's *The Same Place But Different* (1993); but usually they go further and base their tales in Europe or the British Isles (as does O. R. Melling in *The Hunter's Moon* [1993]), or go further still and create a Tolkienesque independent imaginary world, peopled and creatured with broadly recognizable European lore (as in Guy Gavriel Kay's *The Fionavar Tapestry* [1984–86]). In effect they replay the difficulty recounted by Dennis Lee in 1974: "The words I knew said Britain, and they said America, but they did not say my home" (399).

Unlike writers in this mainstream of Canadian fantasy, Katz and de Lint choose to incorporate First Nations cultural lore. Both, however, are clearly aware of the dangers of cultural appropriation; they do assiduous research before writing, evidence of their concern to know of what they speak. At the same time, they both apply some slight pressure to the notion of a pure, authentic, proprietary claim to ownership of heritage. Responding to charges of cultural appropriation, Katz says apropos of her Arthurian novel *The Third Magic*, "Despite my Welsh name, I don't think I have any Welsh ancestors. Genetically I am as close to being pure Celt as is possible in the twentieth century, being Irish, Cornish and Highland Scot on both sides of my family. ... Am I stuck with writing things based on my own rather ordinary middle-class experiences?" (32–33). De Lint writes along much the same lines: "My mother's Dutch, my father was born in Sumatra of a mix of Dutch, Spanish and Japanese blood. Does this mean that my literary palette can only be composed of characters with that same genetic background? By such logic, I couldn't even have completely white characters in my writing, little say [*sic*] women, blacks, Native Americans ... or Gypsies ("Afterword"). Beyond the research, though, and the pleas for creative freedom, there is a substantial difference between Katz's and de Lint's treatment of Native material and that of their nineteenth- and early-twentieth-century predecessors. If the earlier undertakings can be seen as impositions of a set of foreign, white, or Western values onto the Native other which is, finally, not understood and only encountered colonially, in Katz's *False Face* (1987) and de Lint's *Moonheart* (1984), there is a tangible relationship between the two worlds, and an accommodation of the one to the other, though accommodation here in no way implies sentimentality and harmony; indeed, encounter often entails shock and violence allied to understanding. Both of these novels represent what might provisionally be called "new fantasy," the characteristic move of which is "the intrusion of the supernatural into the everyday" (Egoff and Saltman, 238).

A teasing out of a working definition of "new fantasy" would now seem to be in order. A specifying of the grounds for associating the work of Katz with de Lint's helps advance that inquiry. While both have written conventional high fantasies with no or minimal crossover from our Primary world of reality, their trademark works mesh elements of realism and fantasy, this and the other world. In fact, for both, the line between fantasy and reality is increasingly porous. While no one is reported to have asked Jack Hodgins if the fantastic party at the end of his magic realist novel *The Invention of the World* (1977) really happened, one of the most frequently asked questions on Charles de Lint's Web site is whether he has seen the other worlds he writes about, or really believes in them. The central premise in de Lint's short story "Uncle Dobbin's Parrot Fair," formally and thematically, is that "we live in a consensual reality where things exist because we want them to exist" (97). De Lint's author of the story within the story, who turns out to be telling the whole thing (or does he?), says that the fantastic things the protagonist encounters really do exist and are not simply "a figment of some fervent writer's imagination—a literary construct, an artistic representation of something that can't possibly exist in the world as we know it" (97). Similarly, for Katz, according to Marianne Micros, "It is difficult ... to pin-point the dividing line between fantasy and reality, or—more to the point—to define what is 'real.' ... Katz believes, as is becoming more and more evident in her work, that fantasy and reality are not separate entities, but constantly blend or interact" (23).

For de Lint's fiction, the main setting is increasingly a modern urban landscape, the fictional city of Newford, which has the characteristics of most North American cities, but which he says grows out of and has affinities with Ottawa. Walking the streets of the city are beings from myth and folklore, both Western and Native American, and the plots revolve around regular folks who get caught up with the otherworldly beings. Sometimes there is a move to a physical otherworld for a time; often, however, the otherworld is here and now, but in "another dimension of space," to borrow Margaret Atwood's phrase.

For Katz, the meshing of fantasy and reality is not so systematic. She is not a writer of mythic fiction; she and her characters are social realists experiencing raids on their articulate space. In most of her new fantasies, the incursions are either fantastic or historical or both. In *False Face*, for example, the Iroquois masks have shamanistic, dangerous power, which we can see as fantasy; yet in the Society of Faces Longhouse on the Six Nations Reserve at Brantford, Ontario, *today*, the masks still *have* that power—so much so that, according to Katz's recounting of the impetus for her novel, the Museum of Indian Archaeology in London, Ontario, removed an authentic mask from display at the request of the Iroquois (*False Face* 153). In *Whalesinger* (1990), Katz has her protagonist talking to a mother whale; she also has Sir Francis Drake's landfall in California come powerfully into the book. In her *Come Like Shadows* (1993) the witches from Macbeth are real in their haunting of a Stratford, Ontario, production; the protagonist meets the historical Macbeth and frees him from their spell (and us from Shakespeare's?). And finally, in her *Out of the Dark* (1995), the meeting of the Vikings with the Skraelings in L'Anse aux Meadows, Newfoundland, is replayed in the newcomer protagonist's relationship with the village kids of nearby Ship Cove.

Tentatively, then, it might be argued that such post-sixties "new" fantasy, where there is an "actual" interpenetration of both worlds, is a post-colonial genre with a particular appropriateness for Canadian writers attempting to "write" this country. If Timothy Brennan is justified in saying that "the rise of the nation state in the late eighteenth and early nineteenth centuries is inseparable from the forms and subjects of imaginative literature" (48), then we in the Canada of two hundred years later, during what many are calling the dissolution of the nation-state in the face of a global culture, will continue to be reflected in our literature. Canada, after all, was confederated in 1867, historically on the cusp between the Enlightenment and postmodernism. We went from being enclaves of French and then English imperialist culture to a national abstraction—in postmodern terms a construction—at the stroke of a pen, and have been looking for our "real" identity ever since. We have never fitted the model of the culturally driven, organicist nation-state. In fact, despite our colonizer roots, we have often found the role of the colonized more amenable. "Can Lit" has settled into Atwood's "victim positions" quite easily.

Of course, there is an irony here. As Linda Hutcheon points out, "When Canadian culture is called post-colonial today the reference is very rarely to the Native culture, which might be the more accurate historical use of the term. ... [A]boriginal writing should be read as standing in ... a counter-discursive relation to the settler literature, just as that settler literature stands counter-discursively against the imperial culture" (156). Canada's stance is, then, a postmodern political ambivalence, at one and the same time a critique of imperialism and complicit with it (161).

Hutcheon surely has a point. It is more than a coincidence that the proto-postmodernist Nietzsche finished his course on rhetoric in Basel and wrote "On Truth and Lies in a Nonmoral Sense" in 1873, only six years after Canada's confederation/construction, and three years before its imperialist imposition of the Indian Act. In an *ex cathedra* statement almost one hundred years later, in *The Bush Garden* (1971), Frye claimed that Canada's "creative schizophrenia" is the result of being "not only a nation but a colony in an empire" (133). But whereas Hutcheon's Canadian postmodern lingers fitfully in the *aporia* of this plurivocal, ambivalent shiftingness (if not schizophrenia)—because to do otherwise is to totalize—both Frye and Atwood want to be whole, to be cured, to answer the question "Where is here?" For Frye, the route is mythic/spiritual and, finally, orthodox; speaking of Canadian poetry, he says, "Here and there we find glints of a vision beyond nature, a refusal to be bullied by space and time, an affirmation of the supremacy of intelligence and humanity over stupid power" (142). An example for Frye is Pratt's depiction of the martyrdom of Brébeuf at the hands of the Iroquois. Articulating an irony that structurally and generically connects the Iroquois directly to the medieval Corpus Christi play soldiers who scourge and crucify Christ, Frye offers a conclusion which echoes that of D. C. Scott: "However frantically they [the Iroquois] may try to beat him off, their way of savagery is doomed; it is doomed in their Nazi descendants; it is doomed even if it lasts to the end of time" (142). Atwood is far more tentative; in her 1972 interview with Graeme Gibson after publishing *Survival*, she hopes wistfully for "a third thing ... the ideal would be somebody who would be neither a killer or a victim, who could achieve some kind of harmony with the world, which is a productive or creative harmony, rather than a destructive relationship towards the world" (27).

Unlike the clear Primary world/Secondary world split of traditional fantasy, or the fusion of the impossible fantastic with prosaic realism, new fantasy offers Katz and de Lint an opportunity to enact this "third thing," to shape a new relationship beyond the dyad of colonizer/colonized, which does not simply reinscribe the traditional values thereof. By creating threshold scenes in whose spaces the characters experience an ethical "placing," new fantasy participates in the "post-colonial search for a way out of the impasse of the endless play of post-modernist difference that mirrors liberalism's cultural pluralism" (Brydon 141). For Homi K. Bhabha, "It is the trope of our times to locate the question of culture in the realm of the *beyond*" (*Location* 1). He refers to the "in-betweenness" (*Location* 1), the "Janus-faced" character of the nation-state, its "hybridity" (*Nation and Narration* 4), and there is a sense in which the "third thing" that new fantasy enacts *is* in between worlds. But Bhabha's terms put the emphasis on stasis or inertia, looking both ways undecidedly, not unlike Hutcheon's postmodern ambivalence; for that reason Tim Wynne-Jones's use of "threshold" to relate fantasy to our country seems preferable: "In an immigrant nation ... Canada, itself, is a threshold. Having crossed a threshold is an integral part of our collective consciousness" (55).

Crossing a threshold entails choice, demands ethical agency. Psychologically considered, a "threshold" is the point below which stimuli are not observable. The following passage by Bhabha indicates more of an awareness of threshold implications:

> Once again, it is the space of intervention emerging in the cultural interstices that introduces creative invention into existence ... the intervention of the "beyond" that establishes a boundary: a bridge, where "presencing" begins because it captures something of the estranging sense of the relocation of the home and the world—the unhomeliness—that is the condition of extra-territorial and cross-cultural initiations. ... The recesses of the domestic space become sites for history's most intricate invasions. In that displacement, the borders between home and world become confused; and, uncannily, the private and the public become part of each other, forcing upon us a vision that is as divided as it is disorienting. (*Location* 9)

"The intervention of the 'beyond' that establishes a boundary: a bridge, where 'presencing' begins"—that might very well be the definition of new fantasy that we seem to need to carry us forward. And "unhomeliness" is surely a fair characterization of the Canadian perpetual search for identity.

False Face

False Face is the story of Laney McIntyre and Tom Walsh. Laney's parents have divorced and she lives with her chillingly efficient and accomplished antique-dealer mother, Alicia, and her preppie/punk/pretty sister, Rosemary. Her father, Ian, is an archaeologist at the University of Western Ontario. Tom is half Iroquois and half white and has moved with his white mother to London from the Six Nations Reserve near Brantford after the death of his father. Laney feels ignored, oppressed, and victimized in her Cinderellaesque home, while Tom feels ripped out of his heritage and home, forced to endure the society of whites. The story concerns the discovery by Laney of a cache of Iroquois artifacts in a bog near her home. A set of false face masks of power—the large Great Doctor mask and the miniature mask used to balance the big one's effect—becomes the centre of contention between Laney, her mother, and Tom. Alicia wants to sell the masks, though Laney feels that she should not, and Tom is adamant that they belong to his people and are extremely dangerous in the wrong hands. Katz adroitly draws us into the power relationships as the masks gradually exert their power. Laney's mother is virtually possessed, and her hatred for her husband becomes focused on Laney. Tom goes to the Six Nations Reserve for help and is rejected by an elder of the Society of Faces. Thrown back on their own resources, Tom and Laney try to get the masks back but fail, though their recognition of and feelings for each other continue to develop. A showdown occurs between Alicia, wearing the big mask, Laney, who owns the little one, her father, and Tom. Alicia directs the power of the mask to kill Ian, and Laney can save him only by willing him possession of the small mask. In doing so, she leaves herself vulnerable, and her mother, through/as the big mask, turns her hatred on her. As Laney is dying, Tom screams at Alicia to see her daughter in Laney and not just her husband. For a moment Alicia does, and gives up the mask, enabling Laney to recover. Tom takes both masks back to the bog and buries them.

The scene on the Six Nations Reserve in which Tom is ignored by the elder illustrates the potential of new fantasy in Katz's hands. Out of an urgent concern for Laney, Tom goes back to the source to get help. From the in-between, postmodern ambivalence of his life in London he has returned home, to authenticity, only to find himself on the outside. Mr. Logan the elder first labels Tom a white, and then says that Tom's problem has "nothing to do with us" (104). To Tom's protests, Logan keeps establishing the racial divide. Yet his doing so both opens a space for the dawning of Tom's understanding, and propels him into it:

> "They're the real thing. And White people own them."
> "White people own everything."
> "You could take them back. It's against the law for them to –"
> "White man's laws!"
> "You don't want them," Tom said, with sudden understanding.
> . . .
> "But the two people who've got those masks don't understand what they have. Those masks will destroy them!"
> "Whites have never understood what they have. They had forests, and they made cities. They had clear streams, and they made cesspools. The Whites take, and so shall they receive."
> "But they're not just Whites! They're people, too!"
> Silence. Shocked, on both sides.
> "And one of them," Tom added slowly, discovering it for the first time, "is my friend."
> "Then it is you who must help them, not we." And he pushed open the cookhouse door, and went inside. (104–05)

In an inversion of Frye's "garrison mentality," the Native elder erects a barricade to keep whites, including Tom, out and the authentic "pure" culture in. Though the masks are "real," they have been contaminated by their journey outside and are no longer of value, no longer authentic, in the eyes of the elder as rendered by Katz. Tom realizes that this claim to authenticity simply does not work, and he appeals to the real culture's "understanding" to help the ignorant outsiders. Again he is rebuffed by the garrison wall. Outsiders, by definition, cannot be helped, cannot be brought inside. Tom's urgency, and the "beyond" that he has found himself rejected into, forces a new thing over the horizon: "a bridge, where 'presencing' begins." First he says the "Whites" are "people" too, which though a bridging concept, is still an abstraction. But the pressure of the ethical place or *topos*, not unrelated to rhetorical ethos, shapes him (and Katz too it seems) into a deeper, newer emerging understanding, a "presencing": one of the people—Laney—is his "friend." Mr. Logan closes the door finally by telling Tom that it is his own responsibility to help his friend. Logan is right, but there is an irony here. Tom is able to help his friend *because* of his Native heritage; he *understands* the masks. The inside comes outside; the garrison wall is breached.

What Katz's threshold scene enacts is two ethics—one which deals with essences and the other with relationships; one which is prescriptive, while the other is responsive; one which is static and absolute, while the other is dynamic, an event. Apropos of this, Derek Attridge says, "To respond fully to the singular otherness of the other person (and thus render that otherness apprehensible) is to creatively refashion the norms whereby we understand persons as a category ..." (24). He goes on: "The other in this situation is therefore not, strictly speaking, a person as conventionally understood in ethics or psychology; it is once again a relation, or a relating, between me, as the same, and that which, in its uniqueness, is heterogeneous to me" (24).

Leaving the longhouse, Tom has crossed a threshold into a new ethic: "He walked and walked, and felt no belonging. Go home, he thought. But there was no home. There was only London, and here" (105). Yet, despite the uncanniness of his space—but also *because* of it—he must, and can, act responsibly and responsively to the singular otherness emerging in the space he once knew as Laney McIntyre, a white girl from London, Ontario. And because he can and does act, so can she. The "third thing" emerges.

The ethical move here is hard to make, and to keep making; it runs the risk of falling into moralism. We see Katz succumbing briefly to that risk as Tom, at his father's grave, reflects on his deceased's nature: "He had not belonged on any Reserve. He had seen people as people, regardless of the colour of their skin. He belonged to a world that didn't yet exist" (105). Surely, the scene, and the novel as a whole, enacts the problem with seeing the other as an abstraction. Yet "people" is just that. But clearly, Tom is not just a *person*, denuded of colour and race and heritage. Far more powerful in the novel than the *concept* of person is the genuine *gesture* of caring by Tom, whose heritage enables it. The gesture proves, *pace* Katz's moralism, that the world of Tom's dad *does* exist. It is not a Secondary world fantasy, but a new fantasy, existing here and now, with us, just across the threshold.

Moonheart

Charles de Lint's *Moonheart* (1984) is a novel of multiple strands—thriller, detective mystery, and otherworld mythic fantasy all in one. Though any attempt briefly to summarize the novel proves daunting, it does have its usefulness; and, surely, the main plotline focuses on Sara Kendall, who lives with her uncle, Jamie Tams, in Tamson House, a wonderful new fantasy invention that sprawls over an entire Ottawa city block. Sara works at her uncle's antique shop, and one day she discovers in a box in storage an Indian medicine bag and a few other artifacts—including a ring, and a painting of a red-haired bard and a Native shaman. The ring, of course, was forged in the Summer Country and holds phenomenal power. It is the object of a search by Thomas Hengwr, a druid from ancient Wales, who had cast the powerful red-haired bard Taliesin adrift on the ocean and had been confined by Taliesin's ring-empowered curse to a standing stone for a thousand years. Taliesin, under the protection of both the Sea Lord and the Forest Lord of the new world, arrived safely on the shores of the manitous, where he later fell in love with the world/time travelling Sara. Eventually, the druid freed himself from the menhir, and lived on through the centuries, finally moving to the new world as well. As we meet him he has taken Kieran Foy, a contemporary of Sara's, as his apprentice in the "Way." The ring is also sought by Mal'ek'a, a monstrous spirit. It turns out that Hengwr and Mal'ek'a were originally one and the same, though Hengwr does not know it. The monster embodies all of the druid's evil pent up over a millennium and can be destroyed only by one of his own blood. Enter Sara, her uncle, and Tamson House: they are all, including the house, descendants of the druid.

Suffice it to say, the evil is finally destroyed, but not before "the world beyond" (which is *our* world in this novel) and the "otherworld" (which is a land of Indians, manitous, Forest Lords from North America and from the British Isles, and trickster Pucks) have been crossed over a number of times—all through the agency of Tamson House. Indeed,

Bhabha's description of "a boundary: a bridge, where 'presencing' begins" fits Tamson House quite literally. It collects the waywards and castoffs and gives them a place, a home—within its confines they have significance:

> "They need some place to be," [Jamie] replied. "Lord knows, the House is big enough. They come for the same reason that you and I and the regulars stay. To get away from the world outside for awhile.
>
> "I can't deny them that. They're like us, Sairey. Different from the norm. And, as this is a place where difference is the norm, they can relax. There's no need to try and fit in because everything fits in here."
>
> That was what Sara liked best about Tamson House: that it didn't seem to be part of the world outside its walls. Stepping over its threshold was like stepping into a place where everything you knew had to be forgotten to make way for new rules. It was here, when the world outside lost all its secrets and seemed to unfold around her, flat and unending, every surprise and wonder ironed out of it, here in the maze of rooms that she could find mystery again and rejuvenate her own sense of wonder. (29)

For de Lint, wonder enables healing and growth—transformation. A significant example is Blue the ex-biker, who through drugs and rage was on his way out of life; once in the house, however, other "Blues" emerge, such as the one who loves cooking: "Sara stifled a grin at the incongruous picture Blue presented at the stove. He stood six two in his boots, wore faded grease-stained jeans with a T-shirt that said 'Harley Davidson' pulled tight around his big shoulders, had a pierced left ear, six o'clock shadow that was about three days old, and long black hair pulled back in a ponytail" (34).

The house, then, offers a place to the unplaced. It is a home, but only by virtue of being *umheimlich*, a threshold into something new. And of course it is so quite literally in the novel; it straddles the worlds, and becomes the portal (from *poros* meaning way through; opposite of *aporia*, dead end) for wonder and terror. As Bhabha puts it, in this bridging locale "[t]he recesses of the domestic space become sites for history's most intricate invasions" (*Location* 9)—intricate here because the house is actually alive, re-presenting the souls of Jamie's father and grandfather. The immortality they have been granted is both a blessing for their descendants, because they can protect them from the invading evil of Mal'ek'a, and a punishment, in that the Mal'ek'a they must overcome is the evil of their "ancestors given a life of its own" (416). They must acknowledge their personal culpability in the evil, and accept responsibility to end it.

The evil haunts the Otherworld as well; known as Mal'ek'a, the Dread-that-Walks-Nameless, it stalks the manitous. De Lint embodies in the Mal'ek'a/Thomas Hengwr plotline the Western infiltration of the new world. A significant subplot involves the trial by combat challenge made by the Quin'on'a war chief Tep'fyl'in to Kieran Foy, whom he sees as an extension of the evil that is Mal'ek'a. The manitou Forest Lord intervenes before Kieran is killed, and Tep'fyl'in is incensed. In his exchange with the Lord we have a rendering of the post-colonial, new fantasy threshold, as in *False Face*:

> "He is not of our people, Father," he said.
>
> "He is more my son this night than you are."
>
> "No!" Tep'fyl'in cried. "He cannot be your son! The stink of evil flows through his veins. He runs with the hare. His acceptance into our Way is a mockery of all we hold true. Because of him and his people, the tribes are gone and we dwindle, forsaken by them. Will you have us wither away into memories?"
>
> "I would have you accept a new Way. Truth wears many faces, Red-Spear. Many paths lead to one destination. It is the spirit that will not accept change that will dwindle and be lost." (384)

Here again is the "third thing." De Lint depicts Tep'fyl'in's violent claim of the authentic "Way" as a garrisoning against the world: "*Left to his own,*" the Forest Lord tells Kieran, "*he would have set as much sorrow into motion as your Mal'ek'a has*" (386; italics in original).

The manitous ultimately join forces with Kieran and go to the aid of the defenders of Tamson House, which is under siege by Mal'ek'a. As the battle rages throughout the vast building, the final confrontation with Mal'ek'a takes place in Sara's bedroom, in the most personal "recess of the domestic space." There, Jamie Tams saves Sara from the brink of death by sacrificing himself to kill the monster. Sara is devastated; she wonders why she lived while Jamie and the others died, and she tells Blue, "I don't know who I am" (427). Yet, just as Tom's responsiveness enables Laney and himself to emerge into a relationship, so Sara acts responsively to the love she feels for (and from) the red-haired bard Taliesin, and wills him back from the afterlife, the Place of Dreaming Thunder: "The moonheart tune thrummed inside her and she willed him to be real, to stay" (435).

New fantasy is an apt genre for a country with a majority multi-culture, which has little or no indigenous folklore and a minority Native culture with a living one. George Grant says that when non-native Canadians go into the Rockies they can sense that Gods are there, but also that they do not speak to them (17). New fantasy, in its intermingling of realism and the other world, in its penchant for allowing both supernatural and psychological interpretations of happenings to co-exist ambiguously, allows writers such as Katz and de Lint to register the voices of the strange Gods, even if they are not finally addressed to them; and it also allows them to speak back, or alongside. It may not be full communion with the Native spirit of place in Canada (seeking such fullness may, according to commentators such as Bhabha and Diana Brydon [141], be a largely white, European prejudice anyway; the fallacy of authenticity), but it is also clearly neither assimilation of Native to Western nor imposition of Western onto Native. It is a third thing, a relationship with a peculiarly Canadian spirit of combined inquisitiveness and tentativeness. The emergence of new fantasy in post-colonial Canada may be an instance of what Jamie MacKinnon calls a "Canadian rhetoric," one "which addresses that middle space *between* universe and homogenous community—between, in Bakhtinian terms, the 'centripetal' forces of sameness, cohesion, and normalization, and the 'centrifugal' forces of diversity, tension and change" (75). It may also be a generic recognition, in light of the fallacy of authenticity, that we are all "creole" (Brydon 141), that we are all E. F. Dyck's "virtual Metis":

> Just as the notion of a unitary "mainstream" writing cracks under pressure ... so too does the concept of (unitary) "aboriginal" writing. This not to say that the label does not serve a useful purpose, nor that the injustice of the historical and contemporary experience of the First Nations Peoples is not real, does not need redress. Quite the contrary: what we call "aboriginal" writing has already made an important contribution to Canadian life and literature, but its greatest contribution is yet to come. For it will teach us, again, that the Other is the bifurcated Self, and that we are all (virtual) Metis.

WORKS CITED

Attridge, Derek. "Innovation, Literature, Ethics: Relating to the Other." *PMLA* 114 (1999): 20–31.

Bhabha, Homi K. *The Location of Culture.* London: Routledge, 1994.

Bhabha, Homi K., ed. *Nation and Narration.* London: Routledge, 1990.

Brennan, Timothy. "The National Longing for Form." In Homi K. Bhabha, ed., *Nation and Narration,* 44–70. London: Routledge, 1990.

Brydon, Diana. "The White Inuit Speaks: Contamination as Literary Strategy." In Bill Ashcroft, Gareth Griffiths, and Helen Tiffin, eds., *The Post Colonial Studies Reader,* 136–42. London: Routledge, 1995.

Crawford, Isabella Valancy. *Fairy Tales of Isabella Valancy Crawford.* Ed. Penny Petrone. Ottawa: Borealis Press, 1977.

De Lint, Charles. "Afterword." *Mulengro.* 1985. Eugene: Dark Side, 1995.

——. *Moonheart.* 1984. New York: Orb, 1994.

——. "Uncle Dobbin's Parrot Fair." In Candas Jane Dorsey and Gerry Truscott, eds., *Tesseracts_,* 87–118. Victoria: Porcépic, 1990.

Dyck, E. F. (Ted). "The Places of Aboriginal Writing 2000 in Canada: The Novel." <http://www.wtc.ccinet.ab.ca/tedyck/abor.00.htm>.

Egoff, Sheila, and Judith Saltman. *The New Republic of Childhood.* Toronto: Oxford, 1990.

Flood, John. "The Duplicity of D. C. Scott and the James Bay Treaty." *Black Moss* 2 (1976): 50–63.

Frye, Northrop. *The Bush Garden.* Toronto: Anansi, 1971.

Gibson, Graeme. *Eleven Canadian Novelists.* Toronto: Anansi, 1973.

Grant, George. *Technology and Empire.* Toronto: Anansi, 1969.

Hutcheon, Linda. "Circling the Downspout of Empire." *Ariel* 20 (1989): 149–75.

Katz, Welwyn Wilton. *False Face.* Toronto: Groundwood, 1987.

——. "My Own Story: Plain and Coloured," *Canadian Children's Literature* 54 (1989): 31–36.

Lee, Dennis. "Writing in Colonial Space." In Bill Ashcroft, Gareth Griffiths, and Helen Tiffin, eds., *The Post Colonial Studies Reader,* 397–410. London: Routledge, 1995.

Lynch, Gerald. "An Endless Flow: D. C. Scott's Indian Poems." *Studies in Canadian Literature* 7 (1982): 27–54.

MacKinnon, Jamie. "Toward a Canadian Rhetoric." *Textual Studies in Canada* 1 (1991): 65–76.

Micros, Marianne. "When is a Book not a Book? The Novels of Welwyn Wilton Katz." *Canadian Children's Literature* 47 (1987): 23–28.

Ross, Colin. "The Story of Grey Owl." In Laurence Steven and Douglas H.

Parker, eds., *From Reading to Writing*, 2nd ed, 254–58. Scarborough: Prentice Hall, 1999.

Titley, Brian. *A Narrow Vision: Duncan Campbell Scott and the Administration of Indian Affairs in Canada*. Vancouver: University of British Columbia Press, 1986.

Weis, L. P. "D. C. Scott's View of History and the Indians." *Canadian Literature* 111 (1986): 27–40.

Wynne-Jones, Tim. "An Eye for Thresholds." In Sheila Egoff et al., eds., *Only Connect*, 3rd ed, 48–61. Toronto: Oxford University Press, 1996.

More Than Just Survival: The Successful Quest for Voice in Guy Gavriel Kay's *Tigana* and Randy Bradshaw's *The Song Spinner*

HELEN SIOURBAS

THE ROOTS OF SPECULATIVE FICTION are often traced back to a time of myth and legend. The enduring appeal of this genre is frequently attributed to its concern with fundamental human emotions. Whether universal or context-specific in scope, speculative fiction allows writers to explore the value systems of their society. Oddly, though, the genre of speculative fiction has usually been neglected by academia, dismissed as children's tales or pulp literature. This neglect is especially ironic with regard to Canadian speculative fiction, which in many cases deals with the same themes as does canonical Canadian literature. As a result, an analysis of Canadian fantasy affords a measure of insight into the evolution of broader Canadian literary issues. In *Survival: A Thematic Guide to Canadian Literature* (1972), Margaret Atwood explains that the main concern of Canadian writing is with the survival of oppressed people. Through their struggles, these people become conscious of their oppression and learn, as Atwood puts it, that "shared knowledge of their place ... is not a luxury but a necessity. Without that knowledge we will not survive" (19). Unfortunately, though, all is not quite so unambiguous as Atwood's thesis, stripped of its irony, might be taken to suggest, since the overall outcome of these quests for cultural survival is often negative: people, as individuals or collectivities, wither in the face of internalized outside forces. Contemporary Canadian fantasy writers have also recognized the importance of survival. But rather than presenting struggles that end in failed collective and self-expression, they imagine struggles that result in triumphant survival of culture and self. There is ironic middle ground as well: Guy Gavriel Kay's 1990 novel *Tigana* and Randy Bradshaw's 1997 film *The Song Spinner* demonstrate that late-twentieth-century Canadian fantasy not only explores the concerns of the broader Canadian literary field, but also depicts the increased confidence in our heritage that has evolved over the last three decades.

Canadian speculative fiction critics (Ketterer 3; Merril 277; Weiss and Spencer 15) have embraced the ideas that Atwood presents in her seminal work of 1972. According to Atwood, an obsession with survival in Canadian literature creates a "superabundance of victims" (39). Though the characters in Canadian literature try to survive oppression in its myriad forms, their attempts result either in failure or in marginal success. As Atwood explains, "The main idea is ... hanging on, staying alive. ... The survivor has no triumph or victory but the fact of his survival; he has little after his ordeal that he did not have before, except gratitude for having escaped with his life" (33). The survivor survives, of course, but remains unfulfilled. This view of survival is shared by many critics of speculative fiction. Judith Merril calls it the "unique sensibility of accepting-and-coping" (284). David Ketterer writes of the "recognition of constraints and the respect-for-superior-powers message" (167). John Clute "translates the fable of survival ... into a fable of lonely transcendence" (26). Survival is thus described as possible but stifling. Contemporary Canadian fantasy, however, moves beyond a pessimistic depiction of survival to show true triumph over oppressive forces: Atwood's "Victor/Victim chain" (101) is established, and broken, and its metal is forged into new glory.

Guy Gavriel Kay's *Tigana* presents the tale of a people robbed of their heritage by a vengeful, grieving sorcerer. The people of Tigana face obstacles to their survival in, as Kay states, the "relationship between history, language, and identity " (qtd in van Belkom 156). When Tigana is ravaged by war with the invading sorcerer Brandin of Ygrath, Prince Valentin is certain that his people, though defeated, will survive: he proclaims, "We leave our children ... who will remember us. Babes in arms our wives and grandfathers will teach when they grow up to know the story.... Brandin of Ygrath can destroy us ... but he cannot take away our name, or the memory of what we have been" (4–5). The sorcerer, however, knowing that history can ensure the survival of identity, uses his power over language to rob his victims of both. To remove all hope of cultural survival from the people of Tigana, he casts a "spell" which strips "its name away ... as if it had never been" (97). Brandin then gives Tigana a new history, identity, and name: "Everyone knew the stories" (451), but the stories of Lower Corte are false. A culture is more thoroughly destroyed when it is replaced by another. The sorcerer's revenge is thus complete: he has obliterated a culture from the minds of all except those who must suffer for their insolence.

Similarly, *The Song Spinner*, the National Film Board of Canada award-winning film directed by Randy Bradshaw, chronicles the story of a people stripped of their heritage by a grieving ruler. The world of Shandrilan no longer knows the joys of music, song, laughter, or sunshine. Upon arriving in Shandrilan, visitors encounter a sign inscribing the Hush Law: "All noise is forbidden. No yelling, no humming, no tap dancing, no music of any kind will be allowed EVER." Squeaky boots are silenced, whole nuts taken off store shelves, and noise-doers sent to the Quiet House. In his despair over lost love, King Frilo, believing that "music ruined [his] life," robs his people of their traditional forms of expression. This silencing has symbolic implications—as the exiled singer Zantalalia explains, "Unless the Sun Watch is performed in the old way with the old songs, the sun will pay no attention to [the] celebration, and [the] children will live a life in darkness." Without music, the dark, dead season of winter will never give way to the rebirth of spring; the people's cultural identity will be lost forever. Like Brandin of Ygrath, King Frilo is biding his time. A generation has passed since his oppressive acts; in another generation, no one alive will remember the past.

Although the people of Tigana and of Shandrilan have been oppressed by seemingly insurmountable forces, they refuse to accept their demise; instead, they fight to regain their heritage and maintain a national identity. Atwood locates the source of this "frantic" struggle in a desire for "group preservation" (112, 132). The people of Tigana cannot help but remember what they have lost; as Alessan tells Devin, the "wound is always open" (Kay 134). They are thus propelled by a frenzied need to fill the cultural void in their lives. Indicative of the wound is Catriana's song of "longing" (32); Dianora's "almost physical pain" at her father's broken statue (176); Baerd's "walk[ing] through a world shaped and reshaped every single moment around the knowledge that Tigana was gone" (279); and finally, Devin's "yearning towards that high note where confusion and pain and love and death and longing could all be left behind him" (568). However, the protagonists know that for memory to ensure a people's survival and not be merely a "blade in the soul" (7), the music and love in which they seek solace must become sources of action. Adreano's impulse is representative of all their emotions as the plots against the tyrant unfold; instead of emptiness, he experiences "a zest, an excitement, that left him unsure whether what he wanted ... was a sword in his hand or a quill and ink to write down the words that were starting to tumble about inside him" (16). Emotions lead to words, which lead to actions. Becoming conscious of oppression is only the first step toward survival.

In Shandrilan, King Frilo has removed all traces of his people's rich cultural heritage; as a result, most have forgotten their past. Even birds "died from longing years ago." The young Aurora, however, represents her people's repressed yearning for their lost heritage. Subconsciously, she feels the loss in dreams of instruments that she has never seen. When she shares these visions, she is mocked by her brother and friends and scolded by her parents, who tell her that the visions will go away as she gets older. Those who live only in the conscious world are unable to understand the yearning for artistic expression. Aurora believes that her visions contain the redemption of her community: "The sounds in my head are so beautiful. I wish everyone could hear them," as she tells her mother. Aurora knows that since "music makes [her] heart feel like dancing ... [it cannot be] evil." Zantalalia encourages her: "Remember what you have learned ... and never let your flame go out." Aurora is the people's dawning consciousness that a society's cultural heritage must not be permanently lost.

Memory of the past traps the people of Tigana and Shandrilan in longing, but their collective pride in their heritage allows them to move beyond hoping for survival to reaching for full gratification. Heritage is neither "decaying" nor a "booby-trap" (Atwood 132), but possibly a means to true success. Because the people of Tigana recognize the value of their cultural identity, they strive to reclaim their place in the world by breaking the sorcerer's spell. Instead of wallowing in sorrow, the people of Tigana find the strength to act through conviction and pride. Although, at the beginning of the conflict, Prince Valentin blames the fall of Tigana on its people's "terrible pride" (Kay 4), at the end their pride saves them. Individually, the people of Tigana may be locked in battles of personal pride, but, collectively, they act to reclaim their heritage. Their actions begin in "[o]ld songs and memories" (34) as the troupe travels the Peninsula of the Palm singing songs, playing music, and writing poems. These travels not only allow them to keep their culture alive, but also allow them to come in contact with like-minded people who will aid them in their quest for survival. In addition, the members of the troupe must convince doubters that their cause is just and worthy. The wizard Erlein's conversion is exemplary in this regard, emblematic of greater social change. When he is first bonded to Alessan, he resents his loss of freedom; though Devin tells him, "You were not free," Erlein believes that he was (292). However, as the struggle against the tyrant nears its climax, Erlein, a "decent man, with the same longing to be free as any of [them]" (609), chooses to help the troupe. Once collective pride in their past replaces individual concerns, success against oppression is within reach.

Similarly, Aurora's desire to free Shandrilan from silence becomes possible only when her longing for sound is transformed into pride for her musical heritage. Zantalalia teaches Aurora about their culture, and they begin a quest to revive the love of music in their people. Zantalalia, who believes that her own "voice is a gift ... that was given to [her] to share with everyone," openly flaunts the laws of Shandrilan. When she first reads the Hush Law, she begins to hum, and even her dress clinks as it moves. When Aurora, fleeing from the Noise Police, stumbles upon a room full of musical instruments, Zantalalia encourages her to play them. The singer also introduces Aurora to both her social and personal history through the girl's late grandfather's song spinner, which produces the "most beautiful noise" Aurora has "ever heard—even better than the songs in [her] head." Although Zantalalia fears that owning the music box may put Aurora in danger, the girl has learned enough to realize that "putting it back in the ground won't help make things better." Instead, she follows her mentor's example and uses the song spinner to teach others about music. She plays school with her brother Tibo, showing him how to use the song spinner. She tells her parents, "I give thanks to Grandfather Gesop, who put the beautiful songs in my head." Eventually, Zantalalia helps Aurora teach her parents by showing them pictures in forgotten books. The singer creates links between past and current beliefs so that the transition from silence to music is less scandalous. As Aurora's parents "remember how life used to be," how "everyone [was] happy," they rediscover pride in their heritage and know that they must "share it with the others." Like the inhabitants of Tigana, the inhabitants of Shandrilan are poised to reclaim their freedom, their heritage, and their happiness.

By sharing the alienated longing inside them with others, the characters of both works turn emotion into positive action, leading to their final triumphs. Unlike the failed views of survival that Atwood uncovers in works in which "[r]omanticism and idealism are usually slapped down fairly hard, by authors as well as characters" (141), the successful views of survival in *Tigana* and *The Song Spinner* do result in joy. Atwood warns that "collective action has been necessary for survival but it may ... stifle individual growth" (173); however, in *Tigana* and *The Song Spinner*, collective action leads to both cultural survival and individual growth. In the end, the people of Tigana succeed, not only in reclaiming their heritage and sharing it with the peninsula, but also in finding fulfillment as human beings. Once they overthrow the tyrant, their past is reclaimed and they can embrace the future with "joy in [their] faces" (Kay 672). Devin's exuberant list of things to accomplish now that Brandin is gone reflects the happiness his companions feel (670). Only those who have no chance of redemption, who have been unable to reconcile personal and collective pride, have poor fates; for instance, Brandin, trapped by grief into inflicting suffering, can only find happiness in another life (656), and Dianora, full of remorse for falling in love with the sorcerer, finds peace in an "odd illumination appearing in the water" (660). These deaths are kept secret from those who are emerging into joy, ensuring that they live free from poisonous vengeance. Devin's final desire to "start chasing down the words and music of all the songs" that his people have lost brings the struggle to reclaim culture and self full circle (670). The people of Tigana have survived, as individuals and as a culture.

The people of Shandrilan also succeed in reclaiming their heritage and finding personal happiness; the quest for the one has actually been a quest for the other. The people, including King Frilo, lead dark, miserable lives without music. With her return, Zantalalia brings "some hope ... [for] the future." King Frilo, who once wanted her "to stop singing in those public places," to marry him and sing only for him, realizes that such an expectation is unrealistic and unfair, both to her and to his people. His epiphany not only allows him to come to terms with his lost love, but also frees his people from oppression; thus his personal enlightenment revives the cultural heritage of his land: the Sun Watch is celebrated with songs, the snowstorm ends, the sun returns, and the people are symbolically reborn as they "sing with [their] hearts." Even the opportunistic Captain Nizzle of the Noise Police, who wants to burn all instruments, gets the "peace and quiet" he has always desired—a cell in the Quiet House. Aurora finds fulfillment in a new purpose, as Zantalalia instructs her to teach her people everything she's learned. The traditional greeting, changed from "good and peaceful day to you" to "biyashitura ... my music goes with you," signals the return of music, song, and happiness to the people of Shandrilan. Like the people of Tigana, the people of Shandrilan have found fulfillment in survival.

In such a way, *Tigana* and *The Song Spinner* show that contemporary Canadian fantasy does not present the "undeniably sombre and negative ... chosen definition of the national sensibility" that Atwood describes (245); rather, it is filled with "rays of light" (41). In the face of horrendous obstacles and oppressive rulers, a people's quest to assert its national identity triumphs. The people, though stripped of their heritage, remember and, by sharing their memories, find the strength to act through a collective pride that leads to their ultimate survival and fulfillment. In the seventies, "voicing" the problem of survival was Atwood's "exploratory plunge," a move which, she argues, "would have been unimaginable twenty years" prior (245). In the nineties, Canadian fantasy shows that the nation's view of itself has evolved since that budding of interest in Canadian literature and nationhood.

WORKS CITED

Atwood, Margaret. *Survival: A Thematic Guide to Canadian Literature.* Toronto: Anansi, 1972.

Clute, John. "Fables of Transcendence: The Challenge of Canadian Science Fiction." In Andrea Paradis, ed., *Out of this World: Canadian Science Fiction and Fantasy Literature,* 20–27. Kingston: Quarry-National Library of Canada, 1995.

Kay, Guy Gavriel. *Tigana.* New York: Penguin, 1990.

Ketterer, David. *Canadian Science Fiction and Fantasy.* Bloomington: Indiana University Press, 1992.

Merril, Judith. "Afterword." In Judith Merril, ed., *Tesseracts,* 274–84. Victoria: Porcépic-Tesseract, 1985.

The Song Spinner. Dir. Randy Bradshaw. Perf. Patti LuPone, John Neville, Brent Carver, David Hemblen, and Meredith Henderson. NFB, 1997.

Van Belkom, Edo. Interview with Guy Gavriel Kay. In *Northern Dreamers: Interviews with Famous Science Fiction, Fantasy, and Horror Writers,* 62–71. Kingston: Quarry, 1998.

Weiss, Allan, and Hugh Spencer. "Introduction." In Andrea Paradis, ed., *Out of this World: Canadian Science Fiction and Fantasy Literature,* 12–19. Kingston: Quarry-National Library of Canada, 1995.

Sublime Objects and Mystic Subjects: Some Lacanian Speculations About Canadian Fantasy Literature Via Barbara Goowdy's *The White Bone*

DAVID R. JARRAWAY

> Thirty years of aligning his every move to what [Tall Time] believed was a world trembling with mystic revelation ... what was it that sustained such a mountainous delusion? [Tall Time] no longer knows.
>
> – Barbara Gowdy, *The White Bone* (1998)

> Like the ancient sphinx, mysticism remains the rendezvous of an enigma.
>
> – Michel de Certeau, "Mysticism" (1968)

JACQUES LACAN'S MORE OR LESS formal introduction of his psychoanalytic theory to North America in the infamous "Languages of Criticism and the Sciences of Man" Symposium at Johns Hopkins University in 1970 seems rather innocuous, if not downright quaint, today. "When I prepared this little talk for you," he observes in "Of Structure as an Inmixing of an Otherness Prerequisite to Any Subject Whatever," "it was early in the morning. I could see Baltimore through the window and it was a very interesting moment because it was not quite daylight ... and I remarked to myself that exactly all that I could see, except for some trees in the distance, was the result of thoughts ... not completely obvious.... The best image to sum up the unconscious is Baltimore in the early morning" (189). But listen now, some thirty years later, to Barbara Gowdy's description of "a vision of the near future" occurring near the end of her recently published fantasy fiction *The White Bone* (1998; hereafter WB):

> Dawn. A smoky yellow light. ... The crocodiles sink down. The separate cries of the queleas attenuate to a single, rapidly fading creak. Mud [the novel's female elephant protagonist] doesn't recognize this place. She doesn't recognize the voice. ... [Later,] the matriarch [of the elephants] starts walking back. "I was dreaming about her," [Mud] says in wonderment, vaguely mystified. (316–17)

If Mud in this passage would appear to be as mystified by the shadowy lineaments of a dreamy pre-dawn unconscious as Lacan, it is perhaps because "from all these psychological or physical 'phenomena,'" in a whole tradition of Western mysticism preceding them, as Michel de Certeau remarks, mystics find themselves in the uncertain throes of "articulating the 'unsayable' ... speaking of 'something' that could no longer be said in words" (15).

De Certeau goes on to write, "The literature placed under the sign of mysticism is very prolific, often even confused and verbose. But it is so in order to speak of what can be neither said nor known" (16). He explains,

> ... those presenting these extraordinary events experienced them as the local and transitory traces of a universal reality, as expressions overflowing with the excess of a presence that could never be possessed ... an object that escapes [which] alternately fascinates and irritates. ... Something is introduced into the consciousness that is not itself consciousness but the annihilation of consciousness, or the spirit of which consciousness seems to be the surface, or an unfathomable law of the universe ... the continuity of a disquieting relationship with the other. (17–18)

In this necessarily brief meditation on a distinct literary genre very much alive in Canada today, I propose a bit later to argue that "the annihilation of consciousness" just described is perhaps one very important—if not the crucial—aspect of the fiction of fantasy. In working toward that argument, however, let me first offer some further Lacanian speculation about the genre that certain of the features of the unspeakable discourse of mysticism just described would appear helpfully to illuminate.[1]

The utterly crucial notion to the mystic thinker and writer of that "something" neither said nor known ("presence that could never be possessed," which is introduced into consciousness, but which has no discernible relation to consciousness itself)—such a notion is perhaps the place to begin in teasing out some of the rhetorical alignments between psychoanalyst and fantasist. For Lacan in his "Structure as an Inmixing" talk, for instance, that something is taken up by his almost total preoccupation with the "unconscious" graphically foregrounded in Baltimore's early morning half-light—a state of mind that "has nothing to do with instinct or primitive knowledge or preparation of thought in some underground," he observes, but is, rather, "a thinking with words, with thoughts that escape your vigilance, your state of watchfulness" (189).[2] As Lacan further labours to remark, "Freud told us that the unconscious is above all thoughts, and that which thinks is barred from consciousness. This bar has many applications, many possibilities with regard to meaning" (189). The countless references in Gowdy's *The White Bone* to mystery—for example, "beyond The Eternal Shoreless Water, comes The Mystery" (6), "holes that at the time were pauses and mysteries" (204), "about courage and hardship and death and boundless mystery" (217)—these references would also appear to suggest that, in fantasy, a significant element of experience has been barred from full cognition. As with the imposition of conscious thought in Lacan, so, too, in Gowdy's novel the "forcing" or "fixing" of substance "in some way removes," as his narrator elegantly remarks, "possible futures" (82).

If for Lacan, then, intelligence essentially becomes the structured relationship between consciousness and some Real that is entirely forbidden to consciousness—that "space," as Lyotard puts it, "on the far side of the intelligible that is diametrically opposed to the rule of *opposition* and completely under the control of *difference*" (qtd in Brammer 34 note 6)[3]—then three implications would appear to follow. First, comprehension of the phenomenal world truly becomes a sometime prospect: "Life goes down the river," as Lacan wistfully ruminates, "from time to time touching a bank, staying for a while here and there, *without understanding* anything—and it is the principle of analysis that *nobody understands* anything of what happens" (190; emphasis added). Second, and following from this primal lack of knowledge, human subjectivity becomes what de· Certeau says about mysticism itself—"the rendezvous of an enigma" (24). "The idea of the unifying unity of the human condition" now something on the order of "a scandalous lie," according to Lacan, subjectivity is perhaps more accurately viewed as "the introduction of a loss in reality"; like the universe of discourse itself, subjectivity is a "nothing contain[ing] everything," so long as "you find again the gap that constitutes the subject" (190, 193). From this lack and from this gap, thirdly and finally, we are offered that state of desire in which the subject is perpetually cast in its unceasing but impossible efforts to undo the loss "introduced in the word" when a loss for words becomes, so Lacan contends, the very "definition of the subject" itself:

> The question of desire is that the fading subject yearns to find itself again by means of some sort of encounter with this miraculous thing defined by the phantasm. In its endeavour, it is sustained by that which I call the lost object ... which is such a terrible thing for the imagination ... the object, lower-case, *a* ... as all psychoanalysis is founded on the existence of this peculiar object. (194)[4]

In the end, desire issues into a paradoxical state of *jouissance*, the principle of pleasure and displeasure at once, whose "curious organization" allows the subject only "to approach [or] test" out "the full spectrum of desire" without ever, alas, fully achieving or exhausting it (195).

Although this synopsis of the psychoanalytic topography of Lacan's inaugural talk is necessarily abbreviated, it nonetheless establishes a number of uncanny resemblances with the aesthetic contours of Gowdy's fantasy work. As a way into the mystical reverberation of some unspeakable Real pitted against consciousness in *The White Bone*, we might begin with de Certeau's characterization of this Lacanian principle as that "beyond emerging within language" whose "nonsubject (stranger to all individual subjectivity) demystifies consciousness, its clear surface *muddied* by the stirred waters of the deeps" (22; emphasis added). By naming her principle protagonist in the novel Mud, Gowdy from the outset would appear to take her readers to the heart of a phantasmatically beset consciousness split in its problematic understanding of world and self. In effect, Gowdy's main character is complicated by Mud's location between two families in the narrative, a birth family (the She-M's) and an adoptive family (the She-S's), and hence two identities, "Mud" and "She-Spurns." And by further imparting to Mud the gift of visionary power—a premonitory "third eye"—Gowdy challenges our ability readily to identify with Mud's consciousness and the so-called reality that it arcanely endeavours to process:

> To Mud [She-Demands] says, "You have the third eye. ... It will show you your mother's death or the death of any of your calves. Did you know that?" Mud did not. That she is unlikely to be shown *herself* is the only prohibition she has ever heard ... the old cow looks back at her and mutters, "Knowing things is only a dream of having known them." (37)

If knowing things in fantasy fiction is problematic to the degree that it becomes coterminous with the semi-conscious experience of dreaming, Gowdy aims further to enlarge the fractured epistemology of her narrative through her characterization of the male elephant, Torrent. Torrent's preoccupation with the fallibility of "links," that is, omens or portents of truth within his sub-Sahara environment, reveals that he suspects these links very much in the way that Lacan suspects the sign as "something that represents *for* somebody" in place of the signifier that ought only to "represent a subject for another signifer" (194). "[D]o not imagine," Torrent rumbles, "that your grasp of the links is infallible. There are links you know nothing of. ... [T]he links may well be infinite" (63). Torrent's objurgations concerning representation are thus sufficiently compelling here to instill a little later in Tall Time, another male elephant, the following distinctly Lacanian rumination:

> Suppose everything is a link? High above him he hears the creaking of a big bird's wings, and he thinks, "That could be a link," and [Tall Time] reels within the sickening prospect that everything exists for the purpose of pointing to something else. (135)

Further on, Tall Time is no less heartened to ponder the fact that links may be "so abundant as to be finally ambiguous," ultimately despairing over the prospect of "blindly obey[ing] what can hardly be known, since the omens are infinite and contradictory" (213, 88). Torrent, as perhaps the spokesperson for the fantasy writer, ought to have been able much earlier in the story to empty Tall Time's epistemological anxieties in answer to his question, "How can we know anything absolutely?" (157). "We cannot" is Torrent's mystical yet apparently unheeded reply: as much for the readers of as for the characters in fantasy fiction, "Faith is not trust in the known" (157).[5]

With the Lacanian problematic of knowledge so clearly foregrounded in Gowdy's fantasy world, we next come to appreciate how the general motive of desire further conditions the author's meticulous structuring of important elements of plot and character, right down to the two-page map of the elephants' "Domain," the three-page table of their family genealogies, and the six-page glossary of their idiomatic terminology—all of which serves as a preamble to the exhaustive sequence of pachydermal peregrinations that follow.[6] Dealing with plot, first, we are immediately disabused of the idea that *The White Bone* is merely an ecocritical tract on the currently criminal decimation of the global population of elephants, or perhaps worse, a nauseatingly attenuated beast fable with some kind of "Be Kind to Dumb Animals" pay-off:

> With hyena like yells the humans gallop into the swamp, knees capering above the water, guns firing. ... The little calves squeal and hunker beneath the big cows, who themselves are loath to abandon the fallen matriarchs. More gunshot. The head of She-Distracts flips back, flips forward, a gushing hole between her eyes. ... Another round of gunshot. She-Scares is hit again, above her left temple, and is instantly dead. Wildly, Mud looks about. She-Demands has been hit in the torso, she is dead. (86)

Revolved from the radical narrative of desire, the scandalously cruel and inhumane treatment of the animals at the hands of the "hindleggers" thus becomes but an iterative occasion rather than the primal cause for loss, the constitutive effects of which, as in the problematic of knowledge just surveyed, are built into the very signifiers of fantasy fiction itself.

Gowdy, therefore, can be true to the question of desire in her work only by pointing her "fading subjects" in the direction of those "miraculous things" that, while sustaining them in their loss, must at the same time ultimately remain "terrible things" for being attainable only within the phantasmatic confines of their wayward imaginations. I refer here, of course, to that "delirium of green" known as "The Safe Place" (226) and to the titular, talismanic "White Bone" that become crucially linked at one point early in the novel:

> They set out to discover a place of tranquility and permanent green browse and, when they did, declared it a safe vicinity for every creature on The Domain. ... Since then, there have been rumours of this refuge among all species, but only she-ones can be led there. What guides them is the white bone, which in times of darkness, surfaces in various regions of The Domain. ... The deeper the darkness, the whiter it is to the eyes of the she-ones. ... [And anyone] lucky enough to find it should throw it in the air, mark how it lands and be directed by ... its power. (44)

However, as a place unreached and a thing ungrasped by the end of the story, how could we in a fantasy world help but view both zone and bone as instances of Lacan's "object *a*"—the "sublime objects of ideology," as Lacanian theorist Slavoj Zizek refers to objects that bespeak "the permanent failure of representation" (203) constraining all discourse impossibly desiring to reach after everything and nothing at once?[7] On this very point, Mud "finds herself remembering something Torrent said, years ago, about nothing wanting substance until it is envisioned—'Once envisioned,' he said, 'it is obliged to transpire'" (82).[8]

Turning now to the element of character or the mystical treatment of subjectivity in the phantasmatic context of desire, here as well Gowdy's fantasy work offers substantial parallels with Lacan's fantasy theory. The three main characters in *The White Bone* that can help to focus this concluding discussion are themselves, as it turns out, caught up in an intense triangulation of protracted and frustrated desire in the novel, as underlined by various failed searches: that of Tall Time for Mud, whom he impregnates early in the story; of Mud for Date Bed, who becomes separated from Mud's newly adoptive family in the hindlegger holocaust; and of Date Bed for both Tall Time, whom she secretly loves, and Mud, with whom she hopes to be ultimately reunited in the Safe Place. Lacan's important observation in the *Écrits* that the "absolute" condition of desire should require that it "untie[s] the element of [demand] in the proof of love" so that it (along with desire) remains "resistant to the satisfaction of a need" (287) would imply that none of Gowdy's characters need ever come together in order for her fantasy to complete itself. And by maintaining these characters at a considerable distance from each other throughout the story, even to the point of death—Date Bed's mortal wounding from a snake bite and Tall Time's from a hail of helicopter gunfire, both near the conclusion—Gowdy, like Lacan, remains faithful to a certain kind of mystical discourse, the fundamental gesture of which, according to de Certeau, "is to pass beyond, through the 'phenomena' that always risk being taken for the 'Thing' itself" (22). Hence, Lacan's well-known "subtraction" of the phenomena of appetites and needs from love in order for the mystic subject as it were truly to stand "for the cause of desire" (*Écrits* 287). In Gowdy's *The White Bone,* of the three main characters only Mud survives to bear witness to this fantastic truth.

Date Bed's stumbling one day during her lonely travail upon an "amazing Thing" that fortuitously she is able to use to ward off an attack of lionesses, for example, would seem to suggest to her that she had at last come into possession, if not of the talismanic White Bone, then of something fairly close to it:

> She pivoted the Thing and waved it where the lionesses had been. The beam appeared ... [and] she realized that the beam was moonlight passing through the Thing and coming back out again.... In the morning light she could see that its curved side was the unnatural blue of a vehicle's skin [Glossary: "paint on vehicles"] ... a kind of gall perhaps or extrusion of bone—and she had a moment of disgust and yet she did not let it go. (164–65)

Date Bed's subsequent fixation upon what would appear to be a discarded rear-view mirror, and more particularly upon the flattering representations it provides over and over again of herself—"leaping from the image of her eye into her actual eye and from there into her head" (166)—suggests that Date Bed has indeed taken the risk of substituting some Thing for object *a* of fantasy and accordingly is incapable of surmounting the phenomena preventing her from passing on to any new comprehension of self or what lies beyond. Stalled, therefore, in a moment of exorbitant (re)presencing, Date Bed seems only capable of savouring her overfamiliar world in the past tense, and much of that as a crisis of memory:

> Her method is to select a certain shadow memory and pluck from it every part *she is certain of*—the odour of cattle dung and bruised lilies, a cool dry

> southwesterly breeze and so on. She then dwells on the parts in turn and allows herself to fall into the other memories that the parts invoke ... lost fragment[s] of the original shadow memory. (270; emphasis added)

Hence, when her plan to use the Thing to lure eagles to assist her to the Safe Place goes awry when one of them, whom she has named "Sour," steals it from her, death for Date Bed becomes inevitable—ironically, at the very moment when "a phenomenon no less sublime and yearned for than the white bone itself" (285), so she fallaciously thinks, has once again come to hand.

Tall Time is fated to die for failing fantasy in a like manner. Not that Tall Time is incapable of moving beyond phenomena to that Lacanian Real that is "in-you-more-than-you" (qtd in Dean 166) and thereby, like Date Bed, prone to confuse things with Lacan's Thing or object *a*. Clearly, Tall Time is imbued with desire: "Tall Time looks beyond him at the arc of the horizon and feels that in that arc a tremendous revelation is suspended" (151). The question is, has he the courage to desire *enough*?

> In his search for the white bone [Tall Time] has travelled long distances without reaching the horizon, and the misgiving has grown in him that even were it possible to hold a perfectly straight course you could walk a hundred years and never arrive at the brink of the world. "Domain without end," he often finds himself thinking, and it sounds like a lyric, an old truth, but it is blasphemous. (135)

Tall Time will, nonetheless, continue to search for the white bone and to seek out the Safe Place. And he will persist in his "perfectly straight course" with the same iron-clad determination that he took to digging for Mud her "inaugural calf tunnel" and ultimately impregnating her (60)—not that he might be transformed by the otherness of that experience, but that he might gain the pretermission of desire by proving only how much "[They] are alike" (60). Similar, then, to the ghastly ostrich that he once encounters who amazingly manages to kick a rapacious lioness to death "with a blow that cut straight through the ribcage" (203), only to find itself incapable of extracting its foot, Tall Time's own kick at fantasy's Other, despite all the "marvel of a different order" (298), leaves him very much at the end of the story where he was at the beginning—trapped in an unflinching sense of sameness and self-assuredness that he carries to his death:

> The world is before him, infinity drops away at his back. For all that he is following the directions of a deranged bull, he has no doubt that he is going exactly the right way. Not once in thirty years of being guided by the speechless messages of his surroundings, did he ever feel this certain ... as if in defiance of a natural law. (299)

In Gowdy's characterization of the lone survivor of this trio, by contrast, no such certainty exists. Interrogated about directions as she rejoins her effort to move forward to the Safe Place at the end of the novel, Mud finds herself almost at a complete loss for words: "'I don't know the way,' she says miserably ... I don't know. I don't know" (317). Like the "I do not know" of the Abbot Joseph cited in de Certeau's treatise on mysticism, Mud's "effacement within ordinary language" bespeaks the modesty of the mystic subject whose life, as de Certeau goes on to observe, "finds its effectiveness at the very moment that it loses itself in that which is revealed within itself to be greater than itself" (21, 20). And what in fantasy proves to be greater than self is precisely that constitutive Real or unspeakable Other that becomes the discursive provocation for subjectivity to move and grow and flourish beyond its present state in an effort ultimately to outlive itself.

But there can be no movement beyond without some initial annihilation of consciousness. "[C]oordinated with the Lacanian real," fantasy itself becomes, as Tim Dean compellingly argues, "a disintegrating force" that aims at the last to "resist all efforts at assimilation and domestication" (258). The character of Mud outlives both Date Bed's and Tall Time's assimilating and domesticating confrontations with the Other because only she has the courage to countenance the "Something [that] escapes the best of us" that William James, writing about the "subliminal self" over a hundred years ago, mystically characterized as that "unmanifested" part of the subject, like "some power of organic expression in abeyance or in reserve" that is ready to "make at any time irruption into our ordinary lives," even though at the highest level of consciousness "we do not know what it is at all" (681, 692, 696).[9] And so just as Mud does not know where the Safe Place might finally be, neither does she know who she will be when she finally gets there, if she gets there at all:

> You don't [know]. You can't any longer. None of us are who we were. ... The possibility occurs to Mud that, being an outsider, she herself may never have known either [She-Soothes or She-Snorts] in the first place. So whatever essential thing about them has changed would not be evident to her. In which case, she never knew Date Bed, either. It offers itself, this prospect, like an escape route. Her deliverance. If Date Bed is somebody she never really knew, then Date Bed can be lost and the loss will be no more painful than all the other losses have been. (306–07)

From this passage, in the final analysis, we are perhaps compelled to agree with Dean and his assertion that "fantasy *impersonalizes* the subject, decomposing his or her ego in the *mise-en-scène* of desire":

> ... it is owing to the subject's mercurial positioning in a sequence of mutating terms that fantasy permits identifications across a number of socially regulated boundaries—between active and passive, masculine and feminine, gay and straight, black and white, perhaps even the boundary between the living and the dead [and in the present context, animal and human]. In doing so, fantasy undermines the distinctions such categories are intended to uphold, thereby disqualifying these social categories from providing the grounds for anything but *imaginary* identities. (262–63)

If there is a place for fantasy fiction in Canadian literature today, my Lacanian speculations about the form via Barbara Gowdy's *The White Bone* persuade me that arguably it lies just here: as a genuine narrative space for this imaginary inmixing of otherness prelusive to the authentication of any subject whatever in our culture. And given "the mobility of populations" in a culture such as ours, as Robert Eric Livingston observes, "borders and boundaries really have become anachronistic ... [thus providing] the endorsement of cultural identity as chosen rather than fated, as hybrid rather than organic" (154). Hence, "the challenge and the risk" of a mystic discourse such as Gowdy's is, as de Certeau sees it, "to draw [the relationships between exoticism and the 'essential'] into some kind of precise and luminous clarity" (24). "If you look back, as Mud keeps doing," Gowdy writes in her final sentence, "you can see the dust raised by [the elephants'] passage rolling out as far as the horizon." But look again, and you just may be able to descry "the entire plain washed in light" (327).

NOTES

1. Marsanne Brammer is extremely useful in helping to clarify the discursive join between mysticism and psychoanalysis generally: "Mystical experience was regarded as 'extraordinary' and then as 'abnormal'; the mystic was treated as a delusive idealist, a religious fanatic, a figure of pathology. Situated in the marginal, the unsayable, the unreal, or the unconscious, the locus of the mystical became the *elsewhere* according to which science defined itself by what it was not" (28; emphasis in original). Thus, Tom Conley is provoked to remark, "Readers situated at the end of the twentieth century are obliged to see that [de Certeau's] definition of the illumination [of mysticism] reaches back to the waning years of Christendom *through* the adventure of psychoanalysis. Mysticism represents a popular, 'everyday' access to its process" (46; emphasis in original).
2. Hence, Lacan's famous pronouncement elsewhere that "the material of the unconscious is a linguistic material, or as we say in French *langagier*, that the unconscious is structured as a language" (188).
3. "In contradistinction to the propositions of a system," as Lyotard further explains, "the impulsions occupy an identical position in [unconscious] space simultaneously [rather than a series of fixed oppositions]. ... By a series of displacements that are highly irregular, the singular becomes the plural, the feminine the masculine, the subject becomes the object, the determinate the indeterminate, and here becomes elsewhere" (qtd. in Brammer 34 note 6).
4. As Tim Dean notes, the "real" in Lacan becomes indissociable with his notorious postulation elsewhere of the *objet petit "a,"* defining this Real as "that which disrupts meaning and, as a by-product of that disruption, leaves objects *a* in its wake" (205 passim). Cf. the notion of *hors-texte* in Michel de Certeau's *Heterologies*, which Richard Terdiman defines as "the over-the-horizon reality of alterity": "In the present state of our understanding what is text is somehow definably *not* other; what is other is still not text," Terdiman further glosses. "This inability to accept into our own paradigms the reality of what is 'out there' over against us seems, in this last bit of [the twentieth century], a fundamental and potentially momentous limitation" (9).
5. De Certeau would have found much to recommend in Torrent's reply to Tall Time at this earlier point in *The White Bone*, for as Tom Conley remarks in a related context, "By dint of listening to the mystic's fiction, the interlocutor recovers the ground of belief that both founds all truth and calls into question its finality" since, as with Lacan in dawn's early light, "Mystical thinking works prismatically, in blitzes and flashes" (46).
6. Following de Certeau, once again, there seems to be something rather mystical about Gowdy's superogatory narrative paraphernalia, especially the glossary.

De Certeau remarks, "The unity that draws the mystic 'into himself,' as some say, also pushes him forward toward as yet unforeseeable stages of his journey, for which he or others will construct a vocabulary in view of a language that belongs to no one" (20).

7. In any event, as Lacan observes, "The *a*, the object falls. That fall is primal. The diversity of forms taken by that object of the fall [zone and bone in Gowdy] ought to be related to the manner in which the desire of the Other is apprehended by the subject" (*Television* 85).

8. One compelling way of thinking about Gowdy's Safe Place, therefore, might be to relate it to the notion of an "elsewhere" in de Certeau's writing on mysticism—an "elsewhere," as Brammer describes it, "which is excluded from scientific discourse 'in order to found it in the first place,' [and] which becomes the repository of 'that immense "remnant" of everything in human experience which has not been tamed and symbolized by language'" (31). In Lacan, therefore, we would have to locate the Safe Place below (or, in deference to Freud noted earlier, perhaps above) the level of the Symbolic Order.

9. James's commentary on the subliminal self originally appeared, as Eric Sundquist writes, in "'The Hidden Self' ... in *Scribner's Magazine* in 1890 and was incorporated into 'What Psychological Research Has Accomplished' for inclusion in *The Will to Believe* in 1897." As Sundquist goes on to point out, "James's essay was in good part a summary of theories of double and multiple consciousness recently advanced by Alfred Binet, the French author of *On Double Consciousness* and other works on multiple personality translated by the late 1890s ... James's pre-Freudian essay speculates about the influence of a 'buried' or subsconscious self, which he associates with the feminine mystical mind evidenced in case studies on hysterics. Just as hypnosis might bring forth the 'fully conscious' double self in the hysteric, James hypothesizes that every consciousness might contain such layers of selves, each with an extensive set of memories unavailable to the other (or others) but nonetheless influencing the behavior of the antagonistic or double self" (570–71).

WORKS CITED

Brammer, Marsanne. "Thinking Practice: Michel de Certeau and the Theorization of Mysticism." "Special Issue" on Michel de Certeau. Eds Tom Conley and Richard Terdiman. *diacritics* 22 (1992): 26–37.

Conley, Tom. "Michel de Certeau and the Textual Icon." *diacritics* 22 (1992): 38–48.

De Certeau, Michel. "Mysticism." *diacritics* 22 (1992): 11–25.
Dean, Tim. *Beyond Sexuality*. Chicago: University of Chicago Press, 2000.
Gowdy, Barbara. *The White Bone*. Toronto: HarperCollins, 1998.
James, William. *Writings, 1878–1899*. New York: Library of America, 1992.
Lacan, Jacques. *Écrits: A Selection*. Trans. Alan Sheridan. New York: W. W. Norton, 1977.
——. "Of Structure as an Inmixing of an Otherness Prerequisite to any Subject Whatever." In Eugenio Donato and Richard Macksey, eds., *The Structuralist Controversy: The Languages of Criticism and the Sciences of Man*, 186–200. Baltimore and London: Johns Hopkins University Press, 1970.
——. *Television: A Challenge to the Psychoanalytic Establishment*. Trans. Denis Hollier, Rosalind Kraus, Annette Michelson, and Jeffrey Mehlman. New York: W. W. Norton, 1990.
Livingston, Robert Eric. "Global Knowledges: Agency and Place in Literary Studies." Special Topic: "Globalizing Literary Studies." Co-Ordinator Giles Gunn. *PMLA* 116 (2001): 145–57.
Sundquist, Eric J. *To Awake the Nations: Race in the Making of American Literature*. Cambridge and London: Harvard University Press, 1993.
Terdiman, Richard. "The Response of the Other." *diacritics* 22 (1992): 2–10.
Zizek, Slavoj. *The Sublime Object of Ideology*. New York: Verso, 1989.

"Half In and Half Out of Things": Boundaries in Sean Stewart's *The Night Watch*

ANN F. HOWEY

"BORDERLANDS," WRITES GLORIA ANZALDÚA in the preface to her *Borderlands / La Frontera: The New Mestiza*, "are physically present wherever two or more cultures edge each other (4)." Anzaldúa writes of borders from her experience as a Mestiza in the southwestern United States, but a good many of her insights on borderland spaces are surely applicable to the borders depicted in a Canadian novel, Sean Stewart's *The Night Watch* (1997). Stewart's novel depicts different cultures "edging each other," but of particular interest is its portrayal of the meeting of three components of our world: the technological, the supernatural, and the natural. Human characters in this novel exist in a borderland space, defining their world often in terms of only one of these components, yet always aware of the others encroaching, demanding recognition, conceptual space. Ultimately, Stewart's characters have to develop what Anzaldúa calls "a new consciousness" (78), one that integrates, rather than separates, these components.

To explore boundaries in *The Night Watch*, then, is to discuss their dissolution. Nevertheless, the use and importance of this trope in the novel itself justifies, and indeed requires, the tracing of some discursive boundaries, if only provisionally: first, the novel's sanctioning of both technology and the supernatural has consequences for its genre as well as its themes;

second, its depiction of the supernatural and the natural signals its participation in a Canadian literary tradition of representations of the North; and finally, its emphasis on the way characters integrate the technological, the supernatural, and the natural brings these various strands together.

The Night Watch is set in a futuristic and fantastic Vancouver and Edmonton. The premise of the novel, established in the first few pages, is that magic took over the world in 2004: "That year, many things that had slept through the age of reason finally woke up. Forests woke up. Buildings woke up. Gods and ghosts and demons woke up everywhere" (2). In the present time of the novel, 2074, the aftermath of this waking is clear. Much of the territory colonized by humanity has become ghost-infested wilderness, with pockets of remaining "civilization" in parts of Vancouver, Edmonton, Seattle, and a few other cities.

These pockets of civilization are demarcated by borders—either human or natural landmarks; in either case, such borders are established, as Anzaldúa claims, "to define the places that are safe and unsafe, to distinguish us from them" (3). In Vancouver, a human landmark—Hastings Street—is often mentioned as a border, a place where the order of the human world begins to give way to the chaos of demon-infested Downtown. In Edmonton, on the other hand, a geophysical border, the North Saskatchewan River, forms a boundary between the human and the supernatural, since the Southside houses a functioning human community while the North Side contains only ghosts. The novel, then, includes physical borders as an element of setting.

The border's role of separating "us" from "them" is most noticeable in Edmonton. Whereas the novel's depiction of Vancouver's human community emphasizes its competing political groups, Edmonton's human community is unified with a clear leader, a man named Winter. Winter is responsible for the division between human and supernatural. In 2004, he made a deal with the magic that was taking over the world; he cut out the supernatural part of himself—his angel—and sacrificed it (12). The conflict of *The Night Watch* stems from his desire to maintain that division; he requires his granddaughter and heir, Emily, to sacrifice her angel, too. Winter's desire to maintain borders at any cost makes him an antagonist in the novel.

Edmonton's division into Southside and North Side does not just demonstrate the presence of borders in the novel; the association of the

Southsiders with computer technology and the North Side with ghosts illustrates the equal presence of technology and the supernatural. In keeping with the futuristic setting, technology is more advanced than that which we currently possess. Artificial intelligence appears in many guises. Houses, for example, can be programmed to respond to their human occupants; when Raining, one of the main characters, lies down in a guest house in Southside, "[i]mmediately the lights dimmed, and the bed, initially stiff and somewhat springy, began to soften, almost imperceptibly, into a pleasantly warm and supportive surface" (68). Vehicles such as helicopters and airplanes do not have human pilots, but employ AI, which even coaches humans on refuelling and machine maintenance. Technology seems, especially to the Southsiders, to be the least alien component of their world because technology, as we often think, represents human ingenuity and science, a rational rather than a supernatural or natural state.[1]

However, the supernatural is also omnipresent in the novel. Angels, demons, and/or gods—the terms often depend on which character is describing them—are manifest in people, such as Winter, or in natural objects. For example, Wire, one of the main characters from Vancouver, looks out her window and sees a god: "He was sitting in the cherry tree ... clad in the body of a red-crested woodpecker. ... She knew he was a god because of the way the skin crawled on her back, the weight of his black eyes, and the way the air smelled of lightning and peaches" (30). The magical powers of such beings, while not believed in by all characters in the novel, must be accepted by the reader as part of the fantastic world that Stewart is creating, for the novel presents their material effects and does not rationalize those effects. For example, when some Southside soldiers throw a grenade into the Lady's garden in Vancouver, it "explode[s] into red flowers ... a rain of red petals" (278). The person reporting this event emphasizes the number of witnesses to it, thus suggesting that magic is a material, verifiable force.

The presence of futuristic technology and supernatural powers blurs generic boundaries. Carl Malmgren defines science fiction as a "logical projection or extension from existing actualities" (12). The world of Stewart's novel similarly is an extrapolation of our own: its places—Chinatown in Vancouver, Southside and North Side in Edmonton—may be familiar to many readers; the technology, such as artificial intelligence, logically extends from what is available to us. Fantasy, on the other hand, can be defined, according to Colin N. Manlove, as "containing a substantial and irreducible element of the supernatural" (1); the supernatural in fantasy suggests "another order of reality" which is impossible "to explain ... away" (3, 5). In the case of *The Night Watch*, the presence of magic—angels within people, ghosts that return to save or kill—marks it as fantasy. Generically, then, the novel itself exists in a borderland space—the realm of science fantasy.

However, in *The Night Watch* science and the supernatural do not just coexist, distinct from each other; rather, technology and magic interact in unexpected ways. Magic, in the case of the grenade-turned-flowers, can transform technology, but it also blends with it, either rhetorically or materially. For example, the use of AI extends, in the Southside, to most individuals using "a personal expert system" (51) that augments its wearer's natural abilities and reactions: soldiers' AI units monitor training, maximizing combat readiness; and people in Intelligence wear AIs that constantly process information, reading other people through body language, but also through data on heart rate, respiration, and personnel records. AIs are clearly advanced technology, yet Southsiders refer to them as "familiars," a term usually associated with magic and witches.

Other examples of technology combine abilities explainable as science with abilities explainable as magic. Raining's Companion to Art is a computer database of all artists and their works—clearly an example of technology. However, the Companion does not just process data but also foretells the future; some of the artists it includes, such as Raining's daughter, have not produced their artworks yet. Raining believes that the Companion's abilities have been magically augmented by the place in which she lives: "the Forest had gotten into it" (49).

The Forest in Vancouver represents both the supernatural and the natural, and the blending of these two components, particularly in depictions of place, locates Stewart's science fantasy novel in a long tradition of Canadian literary depictions of the North. Margaret Atwood, in *Strange Things: The Malevolent North in Canadian Literature*, sums up this tradition: "Popular lore, and popular literature, established early that the North was uncanny, awe-inspiring in an almost religious way, hostile ... but alluring; that it would lead you on and do you in; that it would drive you crazy, and, finally, would claim you for its own" (19). Nature, in this

Canadian tradition, already has an aspect of the supernatural to it. For many of the characters in *The Night Watch*, then, nature is doubly alien: it is natural and thus uncontrollable, and it is supernatural and so consciously works against human interests, either by opposing humans directly or by destroying their technology.

The Forest encroaching on Vancouver exemplifies the natural world as threatening force and as supernatural entity. Its paths choose to lead the traveller or not: Wire sometimes finds the path to Raining's house quite short, and sometimes it takes a whole day to get there. When Southside soldiers enter the Forest looking for Emily, they find themselves swept off the path, and no natural reactions—sitting on a object or moving toward a sound—work as they would in the natural world. In addition, most of the Southsiders' technology fails or is deliberately destroyed. Indeed, one of the soldiers is literally consumed by the forest: "Green shoots and little white runners had pushed out from under Johnson's lenses. A faint green blush of something like moss showed in the bloody runnels around his eyes" (185–86). Another soldier survives by removing the technology he carries, his familiar and his weapons, but he is still unable to follow Raining, for "the Forest swept between them like a river and carried [him] away" (186). Nature becomes supernatural, a conscious entity but alien; it does not reason in the way humans do, nor does it have the same priorities or desires.

In Edmonton, supernatural and natural blend in the North Side. Although the North Side remains an urban area,[2] it is associated with a particular aspect of nature—the weather. The wintry reputation of Alberta's plains is exacerbated in this novel by the supernatural: "It's *always* winter on the North Side," one of the characters explains (93; emphasis added).[3] Emily makes the connection between natural weather phenomena and supernatural forces explicit when she compares snow to magic: watching snowflakes, Emily thinks, "Magic comes like this. ... At first it barely exists. ... You never notice the exact moment it starts to endure ... when you wake up in the morning, snow is everywhere. Everything else has disappeared" (1). Like the Forest, the North Side's unending winter suggests that Nature is also a supernatural force, a force antithetical to most humans.[4]

In Stewart's novel, however, the cold itself becomes incarnate. Emily's governess, Claire, is the daughter of a supernatural being who is associated with the ice and snow of the winter prairies. This goddess "mated with a mortal man. Taking his seed, she rubbed it into a ball of snow between her palms. From this she fashioned a snowchild, with abandoned wiper blades for limbs and ball bearings for eyes. Then she left it on Winter's step to thaw. ... When it had completely thawed, he found he had a baby girl" (88). Claire embodies a blending of the natural, mortal world with the supernatural, immortal one; she also illustrates the threat of these worlds to humans, since her father does not survive his union with the goddess.[5]

Many characters, therefore, find the blending of supernatural and natural threatening, and the antagonist, Winter, functions within the Frygian "garrison mentality" (225). Winter sees the survival of his community as dependent on a continuing isolation behind borders; he wants to define the Southside as safe, unmagical, and technological in comparison to the North Side's ghosts and wintry landscape. Winter essentially sees the world as separable into civilization, which he represents, and wilderness, which is everything else that lurks on the borders of his territory.[6] But as the examples discussed above indicate, such strict divisions are not possible: the technological, supernatural, and natural shift and blend, dissolving boundaries.

Birds represent the most common blurring between technological, supernatural, and natural throughout the novel. Nick, Raining's husband, names his familiar Magpie, and supernatural powers are manifest in bird shapes such as the woodpecker that Wire sees. But birds also symbolize synthesis, a union of opposites, because birds exist in two elements—earth and air. As Winter points out, birds live "half in and half out of things" (11), partly in the human world and partly in the wild.[7] Whether as natural entities, as gods in Vancouver, or as ghosts in Edmonton, birds influence events in the novel, appearing as signs to characters and readers alike.

Emily, however, also embodies this blending of technology, magic, and nature. She has both a familiar and an angel, and she negotiates a new identity by incorporating and listening to both. Whereas Winter has maintained the boundary between Southside and North Side by sacrificing his angel, cutting it out of himself, Emily refuses to sacrifice her angel. Emily's refusal indicates a desire for wholeness; it also leads to her flight to Vancouver and into the Forest. Her ability to synthesize technological, supernatural, and natural elements becomes evident during this flight. Unlike the other Southsiders, she is able to survive in the Forest with her familiar. The familiar provides her with information about temperature (important for her survival), and when she meets up with another Southsider, it gives her details about his military background and thus his possible usefulness to her. Nonetheless, her "angel" is also at work in the forest, giving her directions, albeit rather cryptic ones (246). The end of the novel signals Emily's ability to integrate previously divided elements when she makes a physical journey joining Southside and North Side. Attended by Claire, Emily walks across the High Level Bridge to the North Side and through the Downtown and back. Emily's integration of Southside and North Side is symbolized by the flock of birds that gather about her and accompany her back to the Southside.[8]

Anzaldúa suggests that borderlands are the places where new voices, new beginnings, are possible. *The Night Watch* suggests that the crossing of borders, living in a borderland state, "half in and half out of things," is necessary for integration and a new way of life. Winter's sacrifice may have preserved the Southside, but it cost lives and created fear as well.[9] Emily, on the other hand, is able to adapt to the changes in her world by integrating the technological, supernatural, and natural; she is thus able to lead the Southside into a new age.[10]

Similarly, Stewart's imaginary world in *The Night Watch* makes us aware of the divisions we make, the definitions we draw, and the artificiality of those divisions and definitions, thus revealing wholeness and harmony, whether for individuals or for political groups, to be the most important goals. Such wholeness can exist only when boundaries are erased, when magic is embraced instead of exiled, when the technological, the supernatural, and the natural are all accepted as part of the human.

In his *Canadian Science Fiction and Fantasy* (1992), David Ketterer concludes by talking about "the decidedly nonmonolithic 'Canadian sensibility'" that affects Canadian SF (166). He points to the Canadian context of a nation between nations—between the United States and Russia, between the West (Europe) and the East (Asia)—as one of the factors influencing Canadian literature generally. We are a nation very aware of our borders, perhaps because most of our borders are so arbitrary (why the 49th parallel?) and so tenuous (what do borders matter in an increasingly global marketplace?). Stewart's novel, itself existing in the borderlands of science fantasy, explores the possibilities and dangers of borders. Most notably, *The Night Watch* participates in and interrogates the Canadian literary convention of depicting the North as alien wilderness. By exploring a futuristic wilderness, Stewart depicts a borderland(s) where humans must integrate the non-human forces (whether technological, supernatural or natural) in order to thrive.

NOTES

1. Technology can develop personality as well, thus blurring distinctions between animate and inanimate. The guesthouse that Raining stays in, while programmed to respond to the needs of its guests, is also capable of arguing with those guests; when Raining requests that it create an "edgy" mood, they have the following exchange:

> *I'm not very good at edgy.*
> Troubled?
> *Sorry.*
> Melancholy?
> *Regretfully, no.*
> Belligerent?
> *Definitely not. May I suggest "Wistful"?*
> Raining grunted. "Look why don't you just turn yourself off?"
> *Why don't you?* the room answered, nettled. (69)

Stewart's novel here follows a long tradition of science fiction—artificial intelligence acquiring human traits.

2. The buildings of Downtown and of the municipal airport are mentioned specifically.

3. In addition to the supernaturally enhanced natural phenomena of snow and ice, the North Side of the city contains ghosts and is the residence of John Walker, also known as "just plain Death" (248). Like the Forest, the North Side tends to destroy technology: Nick, Raining's husband, loses the use of his familiar as soon as he crosses the river, though the helicopter he is in remains functional (93).

4. Nick's death illustrates most graphically the North Side's claiming of people for its own. Nick's death from exposure is a slow process, but its outcome is suggested at the moment of his arrival on the North Side, when he is greeted by John Walker (102–15).

5. Although Claire is mortal, her heritage distinguishes her from other people. She is one of the few to survive the destruction of the Southsiders' military barracks when they are stationed in Vancouver because her mother comes for her and guides her away from the barracks just before an explosion.

6. The headquarters of Winter's "civilization" are in the buildings of the University of Alberta; the provincial legislature, on the North Side, is a part of the wilderness.
7. Because birds represent a union of opposites, it is very appropriate that Raining (from Vancouver and the Forest) and Nick (from Southside) name their child Lark.
8. Emily wonders if the birds, in this case, might also represent the souls of the dead (310). The borders between life and death are also blurred in this novel; when Nick is on the North Side, for example, he seems unsure about whether he is alive or dead (102).
9. The situation in Chinatown (Vancouver) is rather different. The Emperor—the one strong leader—died in a last battle with the demons, and so his chair has remained empty; Chinatown is governed by a Council of Ministers instead. The person who emerges to lead Vancouver into the new age is a character who has been parallelled to Winter; Floating Ant was one of the Emperor's knights and so, like Winter, remembers the time before the Dream. But Floating Ant refused to sacrifice wife and family, and so left the Emperor and was branded a coward. Once a warrior, then a poet (and an alcoholic), Floating Ant incorporates qualities of the warrior, the cynic, and the artist; through his long years he has integrated aspects of the various Powers of Chinatown: the Dragon, the Monkey, and the Lady.
10. Emily is also a very religious figure, observing Lent, saying prayers. We get few glimpses of Southside religion aside from those associated with her character. Faith, a belief in the supernatural, seems quite foreign to Winter.

WORKS CITED

Anzaldúa, Gloria. *Borderlands/La Frontera: The New Mestiza.* San Fransisco: Aunt Lute Books, 1987.

Atwood, Margaret. *Strange Things: The Malevolent North in Canadian Literature.* Clarendon Lectures in English Literature 1991. Oxford: Clarendon, 1995.

Frye, Northrop. "Conclusion to a *Literary History of Canada.*" 1965. In *The Bush Garden: Essays on the Canadian Imagination*, 213–51. Toronto: Anansi, 1971.

Ketterer, David. *Canadian Science Fiction and Fantasy.* Bloomington: Indiana University Press, 1992.

Malmgren, Carl D. *Worlds Apart: Narratology of Science Fiction.* Bloomington: Indiana University Press, 1991.

Manlove, Colin N. *Modern Fantasy: Five Studies.* Cambridge: Cambridge University Press , 1975.

Stewart, Sean. *The Night Watch.* New York: Ace, 1997.

Mind Matters: Intellect and Identity in the Works of Phyllis Gotlieb

DOMINICK M. GRACE

IN HIS *Canadian Science Fiction and Fantasy*, David Ketterer observes, "It might be argued that from the sixties to the early eighties Phyllis Gotlieb *was* Canadian SF. From a purist point of view, she may still be" (67).[1] Gotlieb's first SF story was published in 1959 and, though she has not been prolific, she continues to be active in the field today, with a new novel (a follow-up to *Flesh and Gold* and *Violent Stars*) due from TOR. A brief essay cannot do justice to the depth and complexity of her work, but the starcats trilogy—*A Judgment of Dragons* (1980), *Emperor, Swords, Pentacles* (1982), and *The Kingdom of the Cats* (1985)—offers a good perspective on Gotlieb's characteristic concerns. Gotlieb repeatedly returns to explorations of the mind and of what it means to be a sentient creature.

Her first novel, *Sunburst*, intimately links human progress to the development of the mind and embodies that progress in a figure who is defined by "intelligence and moral equilibrium" (Grace 64), rather than by the more spectacular changes often posited as the next step in human evolution. That is, intellectual and moral qualities, qualities of mind and character, more than anything else, define the nature that Gotlieb valorizes. The importance of mind is indicated in the novel by the pattern of imagery associating Shandy's head with an egg; even the first description of her indicates that her face has "the look of a brown egg poised on the small end" (5). The implication that Shandy's mind is still somehow fetal recurs in the novel and establishes a motif repeated and elaborated in the starcats books.

The world of *Sunburst* is circumscribed, however, confined to a small region of Earth, and the novel's characters are limited to humans, whether normal or mutated. By contrast, the bulk of Gotlieb's work, including the starcats trilogy, is set in an empire, the Galactic Federation (GalFed), a network of innumerable planets and alien species. While the vast scope of this future universe affords Gotlieb occasions to construct complex, world-spanning plots that will resonate with any fan of space opera, she balances the adventure against sensitive and nuanced explorations of human and alien nature, explorations that raise profound questions about the relationship between one's self and one's physical identity. These stories abound with action, but they are equally concerned with character. Gotlieb's work explores to what extent identity is an inherent feature of sentience and to what extent it is determined by physical reality, especially by one's bodily reality. Crucial to the landscape of Gotlieb's imagined future is the interface of existence and essence. And fundamental to that interfacing is this question: in what measure is the individual's ability to interact with realities outside the self essential to intellectual existence, and in what measure must that interaction involve one's actual physical self?

GalFed is inhabited by a remarkable array of sentient life forms, refreshingly few of which are hominid, and many of which are defined more by their mental powers than by their physical ones. Of the myriad life forms inhabiting GalFed, the Encid perhaps encapsulates most fully Gotlieb's ongoing fascination with the intimate association between intellect and identity:

> The species had no mouth, ears, or digestive processes. The Encid was a brain, about 25 cm in diameter, completely surrounded by something like a placenta, whose vessels fed it; these permeated a heavy protective membrane beyond which was a densely packed centimeter of humus containing symbiotes, both animal and vegetable, and held together by a "skull," a network of cartilage. (*Emperor* 183)

The Encid does have five eyes, but "none of the eyes saw very sharply" (183), and its body consists merely of "a horny standard half [the brain's] diameter in length, which branched into six feet like chicken-claws" (183). Though called "she," "It did not know what sex it was or if it had any, though it brought forth progeny parthenogenetically" (183). In short, the Encid is defined primarily as a brain and is thereby accorded existence almost entirely in terms of intellect. It lacks most of what we would deem necessary to be recognized as an individual and intellectual entity, including "the concepts to describe itself" (182), and yet it is defined in individual and intellectual terms. Lacking sense organs almost entirely and lacking sexual identification, lacking even the conceptual ability to describe itself or to tell where it came from, however, the Encid is as much limited by its status as pure brain as it is defined by it. Indeed, the creature is given the name Esne (an Old English word meaning domestic slave) and is enslaved by the novel's antagonist, who promises to find its home if it uses its prodigious ESP abilities on his behalf. The Encid may lack most of what we think is necessary to define one, and allow one to define oneself, as an individual, but it is one of many species in Gotlieb's universe that substitutes extrasensory perception for the physical senses.

Not surprisingly, perhaps, given Élisabeth Vonarburg's claim that woman SF writers are fond of characters "with extra-sensory powers, especially telepathy" (181), Gotlieb gives us various other species possessed of extrasensory perception; moreover, Gotlieb generally avoids the stereotypical aspects of such characters. The Qumedon, for instance, is an extremely powerful entity that exists as "a pulsing vortex of energy" (*Judgment* 41). Qumedni "HAVE NO NAMES. ONLY WAVE PATTERNS" (230), exist on an alternate plane (identified as a continuum in *Kingdom* 13), and have prodigious powers to alter time, space, and perception.[2] Yet others, like the Lyhhrt, are "formless masses of protoplasm" that tend to mass together, becoming individuals only when they take on individual bodies; a Lyhhrt is "a brain with limbs, a fearful intelligence," and powerful ESP (*Judgment* 107, 121). Other examples come to mind: the Yrln resembles "a bright blue bathmat with a fringe at one end" (127), is not designed for speech at all, and communicates by ESP; the Khagodi are lizard-like creatures with prodigious ESP ability; and the Qsaprinli, crawfish-like creatures "formed mainly as heads surrounded by limbs" (*Emperor* 68), are also gifted with ESP. And of course, most of the female Ungrukh or starcats who serve as protagonists in the three novels are ESP-gifted. Gotlieb's species vary widely in physical form, but ESP serves as a common link among them. Even those species not possessed of that special sense of perception can be recognized. They are consequently afforded entry into the galactic network of *all* the "kinds."

Indeed, ESP is a crucial ability in Gotlieb's universe, so much so that the fate of ESP-endowed creatures who have joined GalFed is to be decanted from their bodies and kept as bottled immortal brains in service to the Federation. The first indication of that interplay between intellect and essence in the trilogy comes early in *A Judgment of Dragons*, when we meet the starcats' mentor, Diego Espinoza. He is, according to his own self-image, "a man thirty-eight years old, of medium height, brown-skinned and wiry, black hair and mustache, deep brown eyes, white even teeth" (4). To everyone else, he is "a brain in a midnight-blue glasstex globe, three hundred years old ..." (4). Espinoza's self-image, clearly, is derived from the body he inhabited for seventy-seven of his hundred years; but equally clearly it is a construction of memory and perhaps idealization, since he images himself as a man less than half the age he was when his brain was decanted from his body. The Diego Espinoza whom Espinoza uses as his self-image had ceased to exist (if he ever really did) long before Espinoza was abstracted from his physical self. As Gotlieb puts it in the second novel of the trilogy, "An ordinary mind contemplating itself is like a person looking into a mirror and presenting the best face" (*Emperor* 66). This simile reiterates the idea that one's conception of self is not merely a matter of intellectual self-evaluation but is also a matter of material self-evaluation, of consideration of one's physical self, cast in the best light, as a reflection of what one *is*.

But if the ordinary human mind within a body is prone to misperception of self, so much more so is the "the man without skin, flesh, bones, nerves, heart, lungs, limbs, genitals" that Espinoza has become (*Judgment* 65), for the only way that he can experience the world outside himself is through the senses of another. Though he can enter the minds of others by ESP, the mundane world is denied him, leaving him only with memories and reconstructions of it, traces of his bodily existence still lingering in his brain with no outlet, an itch with no way to scratch it: "A brain in a bowl is not supposed to be able to feel or fear, but a glandular body might impose certain ineradicable habits on a brain over seventy-seven years of existence" (10). Those inhabiting the sense-deprived realm of pure mind are "subject to hallucinations," substituting imagined worlds for the physical one denied them (207). Indeed, commenting generally on stories dealing with telepathy, Donald A. Wollheim notes that such "powers are frequently associated with the symptoms or reality of madness" (216). Gotlieb pushes even further, suggesting that figures such as Espinoza are compelled to desire death as an escape from the blank landscape of the inner self. Why Nancy Johnston suggests that "many characters in Gotlieb's fiction [are] cursed with telepathy" (72) is not hard to determine. In losing their bodies and being limited to mind only, so Gotlieb implies, figures such as Espinoza lose themselves.

Given the fact that the ESPer divorced from bodily reality emerges as a figure prone to hallucination, madness, and despair, it would seem to follow that, in Gotlieb's ordering of things, a fully developed and functioning body is necessary to a stable sense of identity. What the creature of pure mind might lack is suggested when Prandra and Espinoza recognize the Qumedon beneath its human disguise: "They saw that there was no heart in that body, no human heart, no brains or bowels. ... It was dense as stone, cold as ice, cruel as death" (37). The Qumedon literally lacks these things, of course, being a being of pure energy, but it lacks as well what they imply metaphorically. The heart is literally an organ designed to circulate blood, but it is metaphorically the seat of love and compassion, essential human values. The brain is literally the organ housing consciousness, but it is associated as well with faculties such as understanding and imagination. And finally, the bowels are associated with the intimate, physical realities of life, the processing of other physical materials as part of one's symbiotic relationship with, and therefore visceral understanding of, the network of living things. This is a symbiotic relationship that Gotlieb in fact occasionally builds right into her creatures, as for instance the Encid, with its humus of animal and vegetable symbiotes. She does so even more clearly in the case of the Qsaprinli, each of whom "carried [the sea] about on its back behind the brain in an external elastic skin" (*Emperor* 4), thereby carrying with it not only its place of origin but also its own food supply. Each functions therefore as a microcosm, a world unto itself, simultaneously individual and part of a larger network.

Lacking such a physical link with the material universe, the Qumedni also lack a basic understanding of organic life forms. One of the ways in which the Ungrukh recognize the imposture of a Qumedon disguised as Orbin is the absence of any human scent. More subtly, he reveals himself through his inability to empathize with physical creatures; though he performs his duties as a doctor efficiently, he does so with utter detachment, treating his patients like "an animal doctor handling cattle" (*Judgment* 206). This particular Qumedon "created" the Ungrukh, modifying leopards both physically and mentally, in ways that suggest that the Ungrukh's physical modification and emerging sentience are interrelated, since in one of his modifications he "DEEPENED BRAIN FISSURES AND INCREASED HEAD SIZE TO LET THE BRAIN FILL IT" (*Kingdom* 20). Physical change is thereby linked to evolving sentience. Despite playing this God-like role for the Ungrukh, however, the Qumedon is as much a devil as a god figure for them, since he views them merely as animals and therefore as property. He may be a creator, but he nearly kills Prandra and Khreng in the first story of *A Judgment of Dragons*, and, as one of the dragons of the title, he has clear demonic associations.

It goes without saying, then, that "person" in Gotlieb's universe includes beings other than humans. The assigning of "she" rather than "it" to the Encid is part of this pattern of ascribing the status of person to all sentient creatures—a patterning that manifests itself most pervasively through the three novels in the consistent ascription of the terms "man" and "woman," respectively, to any male or female sentient alien. While one might argue that labelling a sexless Encid "she" or identifying creatures more closely akin to cats or crayfish as men and women constitutes the projection of a limiting and anthropocentric sensibility onto human/alien relations, the effect in the books is profound. Just as Ursula K. Le Guin's carefully considered device, in her *The Left Hand of Darkness* (1969), of having Genly Ai consistently describe the ambisexual Estraven as "he" makes the reader share the shock of discovery when Genly is forced to see the truth about Estraven, "that he was a woman as well as a man" (248), so too does Gotlieb's carefully chosen terminology influence our response to her aliens.[3] By requiring readers to think of aliens not as creatures, as "its," but instead as men or women, Gotlieb requires readers to see past the apparent otherness of the aliens. As she asserts of the Qsaprinli in *Emperor, Swords, Pentacles*, "what they were was one more form of The People, like all other sentient beings" (68).

Gary K. Wolfe has argued that any story of human/alien interaction rests on a central tension, "the opposition between man and not-man" (204). "Even to conceive of an alien intelligence," he goes on to argue, "is to conceive, at some deep level, of an invasion of one's own personality by outside forces, a violation of one's community by strangers" (205). Gotlieb inverts this fear when the Ungrukh are being disguised as humans through a process of hypnoforming, an implantation into the mind of the experiences and memories of the kind of creature that he or she is being disguised as: in addition to *appearing* human from the outside, in a sort of external and illusory imposition of a body, the disguised figure also will *emanate* humanity. In a way, the mental construction of human-ness so generated is more real than the physical appearance of humanity. Khreng knows that, as a result of this process, "his mind would always be threaded with wisps of alien memory" (*Judgment* 33). A more intimate invasion of personal space is difficult to imagine, but in this instance, it is the alien who is being invaded by the human (that is, alien) mind. Certainly, as a brain in a bottle, Espinoza, whose memories are in question here, is as alien to us as are the alien starcats. In any event, though many humans play important roles throughout the trilogy, Gotlieb's protagonists are not humans at all, but starcats.[4] Readers are thus invited to see the alien as akin to themselves—not as human, perhaps, but certainly as sufficiently analogous to human to merit equal treatment.

From this perspective, matters of the body cease to be relevant in determining one's identity. Regardless of what a creature looks like in the world of these novels, if sentient it is a "man" or a "woman." When first exposed to a large group of humans, the extra-sensory-perceiving Prandra "found it was not their flesh that disturbed her but their noisy heads. ... [T]heir bodies were only unregarded appendages" (*Judgment* 20). Mind, not body, defines one's status. Hence, the genetic engineering of the Frogs, humans grown to function as underwater labourers, is a success on the purely physical level but a profound failure nevertheless, for mind is not taken into account. The genetically engineered shells were intended for one purpose only, but "inside the skulls," as the Frogs report, "we were an architect, a flutist, an administrator, a chess-player, a doctor, a clerk, a gardener, a space-pilot" (*Emperor* 121). In short, "there were *men and women* inside the skulls and under the skins" (121). Inside and under is where essential identity is located; skin, flesh, and bone are merely housing.

Indeed, for at least one alien species, acquiring a body can actually threaten one's intellectual and emotional stability. The Lyrhhrt, those "formless masses of protoplasm" (*Judgment* 107), exist in their natural state only as a group existing to ponder Cosmic Thoughts: "Once they got separate bodies they became individuals, maybe not such a good idea" (108). Separated from the group, rendered individual by the acquisition of bodies (and they are accomplished metalworkers, capable of constructing exquisite shells), the Lyhhrt are prone to madness. When they discover bodies, some see no reason not simply to inhabit the bodies of others, rather than constructing their own, a chilling echo of an SF scenario explored numerous times, notably in Robert A. Heinlein's *The Puppet Masters*. Claiming a body at the expense of its sentient inhabitant is a shocking crime in Gotlieb's universe. Those who attempt it are less than human, even if they have human bodies.

Though this point is important to the first two stories that make up *A Judgment of Dragons*, it becomes crucial to the third. "Nebuchadnezzar" features as its antagonist a human named Quantz. His exclusive interest in the material rather than the intellectual world is perhaps suggested in the echo of quantification in his name. In any event, he is willing to kill or enslave others for his own gain, especially those who are significantly different from himself and therefore fall outside his definition of "people." The starcats and the lizard-like Khagodi and Lohk, so fall. Starcat Prandra explains his reasoning: "A few in that company were scaled, and one or two had tentacles, but all were what a Solthree would have called 'humanoid.' She and Lohk were not, and she knew what that difference meant to Quantz. A pair of skins ..." (159). Indeed, Quantz sets out to hunt Prandra and Khreng. But his inability to see beneath the skin rebounds on him at the climax of the story, when Prandra turns his own intellectual limitations back on him: "She drew from wherever power came and smashed the brittle walls of Quantz's mind to free the red beasts of fear and rage among the synapses" (188). Quantz sees the crimson cats and sees only beasts, but the beasts he sees are not in fact Prandra and Khreng, the inhabitants of the skins, but the projections of his own bestial mind, the home of the real red beasts. He sees only animals, and as a result he suffers, for all intents and purposes, the fate of Nebuchadnezzar when Prandra uses her brain power to transform him in his eyes, and in the eyes of others, into a pig.

Those who cannot see past the body to the intellect within are invariably villainous in Gotlieb's universe, whether they try to claim sentient bodies as houses for their own intelligence, to enslave other creatures, to kill other creatures for drugs derived from their enzymes, or even to kill them because their skins are beautiful. If not having a body comes with attendant limitations, having one of one kind or another, conversely, does not limit one's right to identity; regardless of one's body, then, what makes one's identity is, ultimately, one's mind. Thorndyke, the antagonist of *Emperor, Swords, Pentacles,* and his brother, Agassiz, are a contrasting pair who demonstrate this point. Both are human mutations, having suffered from the exposure of their ancestors to a fungus on Qsaprinel, the effects of which can be counteracted only by an enzyme derived from the Qsaprinli. Both men are adults trapped in virtually embryonic bodies. Agassiz, for instance, is "forty-four years old, and—and in the shape of an embryo, near three months ... but big, maybe a meter long" (89). He still has his umbilical cord, through which he is fed. Significantly, he is likened to the decanted brains of ESPs, living after their bodies have died: "His life-support equipment seemed usual enough to his visitors, who had either seen or heard of the bottled ESP brains kept alive for hundreds of years" (95). Thorndyke is slightly more mature physically, but no less grotesque.

However, the two differ profoundly, Agassiz living primarily to love and interact with others, Thorndyke to do whatever is necessary, including wiping out an entire species, to grow an adult body. Their pseudo-embryonic status suggests their limits and their need for growth beyond what they are, but their radically different responses to their embryonic status offer clearly contrasting models of the relationship between one's organic limitations and one's identity. Afflicted though they are with the same physical limitations, Agassiz and Thorndyke are

nonetheless opposites, having carved differing identities out of how they have related to their world. The body is not a template, invariably producing a mind to match, a point reiterated by the implicit parallel between Thorndyke and Agassiz, on the one hand, and the two sibling Qsaprinli, Spinel-alpha and Spinel-beta, on the other: these latter are literally two halves of the same whole, having come into individual existence upon the fission of their "father" into two parts. Despite their origin in a common body and a common identity, alpha and beta are as opposite as Thorndyke and Agassiz.

Taken as a whole, then, Gotlieb's trilogy suggests the complexity of the process whereby identity arises, a process that fascinates the character Prandra. Prandra devotes her life to trying to come to an understanding of "the shapes of minds, the *c* structures that began them, the ideas and emotions that fulfilled them" (*Judgment* 65). This project serves as a distant backdrop to the action, referred to only occasionally throughout the trilogy, but the climax of the third volume sees it completed, in a way. The Ungrukh defeat their creator Qumedon by combining their minds to create a single meta-entity, UNGRUKH, existing simultaneously in the realm of pure mind, as a network of all the Ungrukh, and as each an individual creature contributing to the network. Emerald, Prandra's daughter, considers her mother's mind a model project: "I wonder if at the end she does not make some plan, map, chart ... of a model *for a mind*—and if that mind is not UNGRUKH" (*Kingdom* 276). The model posits an intelligence that is simultaneously mind and body, many and one, part and whole, microcosm and macrocosm. Significantly, none of the Ungrukh sees existing as a permanent meta-entity as an attractive idea, since retaining one's individuality while a part of the meta-entity is difficult: becoming UNGRUKH represents an interesting and useful possibility but not a desirable alternative to continued individual existence as a whole that is also a part, with all the attendant dangers which that existence carries in its wake. As UNGRUKH itself suggested in its first manifestation, at the climax of *A Judgment of Dragons*, "Every one of us is One Self, and on our world we find the Other as well as we can" (254).

To be UNGRUKH always, not to be individuals but to blur the distinction between self and other, mind and body, would in a way be to cease to exist. The quest for the other and the bridging of the gap between self and other by finding the other in the self and the self in the other are crucial to the individual. Identity is determined not by mind or by body but by the relationship between them. Having a body forces one to recognize the other, the individual outside the self, and therefore to recognize the self as an individual. There are potentially negative ramifications to this, but even more negative ones to the alternative. The model of the mind that emerges, ultimately, is multiform and complex, consisting not of a single intellect or identity but of a variety of intellects working together while retaining their individuality. Or, there is no mind, only minds; there is no identity outside of others against which to measure that identity.

NOTES

1. *Pace* Ketterer's observation, Gotlieb seems to have fallen into something of a critical black hole. I am aware of only three academic articles on Gotlieb: Douglas Barbour's "Phyllis Gotlieb's Children of the Future: *Sunburst* and *Ordinary, Moving*," which uses Gotlieb's poetry as a way into her SF and which was published over twenty-five years ago; my own "Valorizing the 'Normal': Phyllis Gotlieb's *Sunburst*," published in the relatively recent proceedings of the Academic Conference on Canadian Science Fiction and Fantasy; and Nancy Johnston's "'and nobody knows where we are going from here': Phyllis Gotlieb's Speculative Poetry," which appeared in the same proceedings. Gotlieb is virtually invisible in general studies of SF, including studies of SF by women. The entry on her in Clute and Nicholls's *The Encyclopedia of Science Fiction* is brief and unilluminating; the entry on Canada does quote Ketterer to identify her as "'Canada's premier SF novelist' during the 1960–80 formative period in the genre's growth," but goes on to suggest that her relative lack of fame may be because, in part, "her prose is demanding, intricate and psychologically probing" (189). Even surveys of Canadian women in SF, or of women in SF by Canadians, such as the three articles on the subject in Andrea Paradis's *Out of This World*, have little to say about Gotlieb. John Robert Colombo's assertion that "regular readers of science fiction are somewhat resistant to the complex characters and complicated situations found in Gotlieb's GalFed novels, the Starcats series, and the books set in Dhalgren's world" (37) may explain her absence from bestseller lists, but surely the complexity of her work ought to have inspired greater critical interest. Perhaps the relative paucity of primary material (only nine SF novels over a career spanning forty years, and three of those in the last five years) has made her easy to overlook, and perhaps she fits awkwardly into considerations of other woman writers within the genre. Whatever the reason, she has been overlooked, and I believe that our understanding of Canadian SF is the poorer for this neglect.

2. The many and very obvious parallels between the Qumedni and the Q of *Star Trek: The Next Generation* invite speculation as to Q's origins, since *The Next Generation* premiered two years after the last starcats novel was published.

3. Though Le Guin has been criticized for using the masculine pronoun in a

generic sense when referring to the ambisexual Gethenians in *The Left Hand of Darkness*, and though she has herself conceded that the problems that some readers have in seeing the Gethenians as ambisexual rather than male "rises in part from the choice of pronoun" ("Is Gender Necessary?" 168), had she not done so the novel would lose much of its punch when the reader is forced along with Genly Ai to confront his (or her) sexist assumptions. The pervasiveness of the "he" underscores the novel's point about the difficulty of seeing the human beneath the male or female.

4. See, for example, the anthropomorphism of David Ketterer when he writes of the first two starcats books that they "chronicle the adventures of Duncan Kinnear (a Galactic Federation investigator) and two dangerous, telepathic, crimson 'starcats' whose world, Ungrukh, he saved [in the first book]. ... In the sequel ... the starcats help Kinnear prevent the emperor of Qsaprinel from being dispossessed of his planet" (70). These descriptions suggest that Kinnear is the protagonist of the books and the starcats secondary figures. In fact, Kinnear figures in only two of the four stories that comprise the first book, and while he has a role in saving Ungruwarkh, to assert that he saves the planet is an overstatement. Similarly, though he has a significant role in the second novel, his role is comparatively minor compared to the roles assumed by the cats. The identification of the starcats as dangerous also reflects an anthropocentric view. Certainly, their large, sharp fangs make them appear dangerous (and humans especially often so view them in the books), and they are quite capable of violence when necessary, possessing sufficient wit and bravery to make them dangerous adversaries; but for beings evolved from predatory cats, they are remarkably unwilling to take the lives of those they view as people, however savage those people may be. If they are dangerous, they are so only to those who require them to be.

WORKS CITED

Barbour, Douglas. "Phyllis Gotlieb's Children of the Future: *Sunburst* and *Ordinary, Moving*." *Journal of Canadian Fiction* 3 (1974): 72–76.

Clute, John, and Peter Nicholls, eds. *The Encyclopedia of Science Fiction*. New York: St. Martin's Press, 1993.

Colombo, John Robert. "Four Hundred Years of Fantastic Literature in Canada." In Andrea Paradis, ed., *Out of This World: Canadian Science Fiction and Fantasy Literature*, 28–40. Kingston: Quarry Press/National Library of Canada, 1995.

Gotlieb, Phyllis. *Emperor, Swords, Pentacles*. New York: Ace, 1982.

——. *A Judgment of Dragons*. 1980. New York: Ace, 1985.

——. *The Kingdom of the Cats.* New York: Ace, 1985.

——. *Sunburst.* Greenwich: Fawcett, 1964.

Grace, Dominick M. "Valorizing the 'Normal': Phyllis Gotlieb's *Sunburst.*" In Allan Weiss, ed., *Perspectives on the Canadian Fantastic: Proceedings of the 1997 Academic Conference on Canadian Science Fiction and Fantasy*, 59–68. Toronto: ACCSFF, 1998.

Johnston, Nancy. "'and nobody knows where we are going from here:' Phyllis Gotlieb's Speculative Poetry." In Allan Weiss, ed., *Perspectives on the Canadian Fantastic: Proceedings of the 1997 Academic Conference on Canadian Science Fiction and Fantasy*, 69–74. Toronto: ACCSFF, 1998.

Ketterer, David. *Canadian Science Fiction and Fantasy.* Bloomington: Indiana University Press, 1992.

Le Guin, Ursula K. "Is Gender Necessary?" 1976. In *The Language of the Night: Essays on Fantasy and Science Fiction*, 161–69. New York: Putnam, 1979.

——. *The Left Hand of Darkness.* New York: Ace, 1969.

Paradis, Andrea, ed. *Out of This World: Canadian Science Fiction and Fantasy Literature.* Kingston: Quarry Press/National Library of Canada, 1995.

Vonarburg, Élisabeth. "Women and Science Fiction." In Andrea Paradis, ed., *Out of This World: Canadian Science Fiction and Fantasy Literature,* 177–87. Kingston: Quarry Press/National Library of Canada, 1995.

Weiss, Allan, ed. *Perspectives on the Canadian Fantastic: Proceedings of the 1997 Academic Conference on Canadian Science Fiction and Fantasy.* Toronto: ACCSFF, 1998.

Wolfe, Gary K. *The Known and the Unknown: The Iconography of Science Fiction.* Kent: Kent State University Press, 1979.

Wollheim, Donald A. *The Universe Makers: Science Fiction Today.* New York: Harper and Row, 1971.

Coding of Race in Science Fiction: What's Wrong with the Obvious?

SHERRY VINT

SCIENCE FICTION IS A GENRE whose founding trope is the image of the world otherwise: in the future, elsewhere, even in the present if this present is arrived at by a different path. As a genre that attracts those who are dissatisfied with the way things are, science fiction should strongly appeal to African Americans, a population whose past has been erased by the institution of slavery and whose present is marked by discrimination and prejudice. Mark Dery puts the case for the connection between African-American concerns and the genre very strongly in "Black to the Future." He writes, "African Americans, in a very real sense, are the descendants of alien abductees; they inhabit a sci-fi nightmare in which unseen but no less impassable force fields of intolerance frustrate their movements; official histories undo what has been done; and technology is too often brought to bear on black bodies (branding, forced sterilization, the Tuskegee experiment, and tasers come readily to mind)" (736). A prominent black writer in the field, Octavia Butler, offers her own reasons for the importance of SF to black people in the rhetorical conclusion to her essay "Positive Obsession":

> But still I'm asked, what good is science fiction to Black people? What good is any form of literature to Black people? What good is science

> fiction's thinking about the present, the future, and the past? What good is its tendency to warn or to consider alternative ways of thinking and doing? What good is its examination of the possible effects of science and technology, or social organization and political direction? At its best, science fiction stimulates imagination and creativity. It gets reader and writer off the beaten track, off the narrow, narrow footpath of what "everyone" is saying, doing, thinking—whoever "everybody" happens to be this year. And what good is all this to Black people? (134–35)

So, why don't more African Americans read and write science fiction? In "Why Blacks Don't Read Science Fiction," Charles Saunders argues that science fiction fails to provide realistic black characters who are engaged with the concerns of the African-American community. SF's traditional parallel between the alien and the radicalized other, a parallel that has been accompanied by broad generalizations about cooperation and understanding (or, conversely, about suspicion and difference), addresses only "white" concerns about race relations. Gary Westfahl agrees with this assessment. He argues in a recent article that though the explicitly racist character Farnham in Robert A. Heinlein's *Farnham's Freehold* is criticized for his racism by the author, Heinlein's indictment of Farnham can be extended to the entire science fiction community, which has failed to reach out to or interact with people of colour, and which has marshalled its considerable resources to support space and missile defence programs but never to support programs to improve the lives of minorities. Simply put, science fiction is not part of the solution to racism, so it is part of the problem; readers of colour, recognizing the difference between armchair egalitarianism and the real thing, stay away from science fiction (Westfahl 81–82).

Until recently, only two black writers have been visible in the genre, Samuel R. Delany and Octavia Butler. More recently, the situation has improved with the addition of Steven Barnes, Charles Saunders, and Nalo Hopkinson.[1] However, the fact remains that science fiction and most African Americans continue to go their separate ways. Several scholars have attempted to provide explanations for this absence of compatibility. The intention of this essay, then, is to explore the tension between SF and the representation of race, between the hope that science fiction's tendency to explore other ways of seeing and doing can be positively mobilized to challenge racial stereotypes and the reality that more often than not in SF texts race is ignored or subsumed under the figure of the alien. Robert J. Sawyer's *Illegal Alien* (1997), a novel that explicitly links its alien characters with African Americans, provides an exemplary text for an inquiry into that tension.

The novel begins as a typical first-contact story. An alien ship lands on Barth's Ocean, and a delegation of scientists and military advisors from various countries go out to meet it. Communication is established, initially through primary numbers because, of course, mathematics is the universal language. Fortunately, the aliens, the Tosoks, don't need to sleep and have a wonderful translation computer that enables their representative, Hask, to master English. The leader of the aliens makes a speech about fellowship and co-operation at the UN and, as Sawyer puts it at the end of his fifth chapter, the "first contact between the human race and aliens seemed to be going spectacularly well. Until the murder" (40).

It is at the point of this murder that the novel veers from the typical first-contact plot and becomes both a mystery and a courtroom thriller. A human member of the delegation traveling with the aliens, Cletus Calhoun, is found dead in his room, seemingly dissected. His right eye, lower mandible, neck vertebrae, and appendix are missing, his left leg has been severed from his body, and his ribcage has been ripped open by manual force. Evidence at the scene suggests that one of the Tosoks is responsible. A mark found in the blood on the floor appears to be an alien footprint, and the grim work of the tool that cut through Cleet's leg exceeds the capacities of any human implement. After a brief investigation, Hask is charged with the murder and arrested. Hask draws the police's suspicion because he was the only Tosok without a corroborated alibi for the time of the murder and because he has recently shed his skin—a normal, cyclical event for Tosoks, but one that draws human suspicion because it could have been used to hide the blood from the murder. Frank Nobiho, the white science advisor to the president, contracts Dale Rice, a noted black civil rights lawyer, to defend Hask because, as Rice puts it, the former "figured" him for "an expert at defending individuals that the court might be inclined to view as second-class citizens" (63).

From this point on, the novel is very explicit in drawing parallels between the O. J. Simpson "trial of the century" and Hask's celebrity "trial of the Centauri." Sawyer uses Rice's character to "educate" Nobiho (and readers) about the American justice system in general and the O. J. Simpson trial in particular. At first glance, this novel seems to offer all that a black reader might desire of SF: a positive black character with whom to identify, the use of the alien trope to explore injustices done by a justice system that treats African Americans as alien, and a critique of the racism still current in American society. The continual reference to the O. J. Simpson trial as another "celebrity" trial reminds the reader of the way race and racism circulated throughout that trial and its aftermath. In some ways, Sawyer is very careful to use these parallels to point out the problems with the American justice system and its structural complicity with racism. The first question that Rice asks Nobiho is whether he considers the verdict in the Simpson case just. When Nobiho responds that he doesn't, Rice responds, "You need a different lawyer"; he explains that the question at stake in the Simpson trial was not did he do it, but is there reasonable doubt? He rejects Nobiho's "white" interpretation of the trial by arguing, "Since there was reasonable doubt, he was entitled to go free. Slick lawyering had nothing to do with it" (65).

Sawyer constructs his story so that the evidence against Hask is remarkably similar to that against Simpson: a bloody footprint; shed scales of skin which may or may not belong to Hask, like the socks and gloves which might or might not have been Simpson's; and finally, the blood found at the scene, which produces conflicting expert testimony regarding its origin. One of the ways that Sawyer uses the parallel between Simpson and Hask is to reveal how people can reduce a member of another race to a representative of that race rather than an individual. For example, Nobiho considers whether a genetic test of all the Tosoks could be used to ascertain whose blood was found at the crime scene. Rice points out that asking the Tosoks to provide blood samples would be a violation of civil rights, drawing on the example of the English town whose male residents all donated sperm to eliminate themselves from suspicion of being the local rapist. Rice argues,

> It was a gross violation of civil rights. Suddenly people were being compelled to prove themselves innocent, instead of being assumed to be so. If a cop came up to me and said, look, you're black and we think our criminal is black, so you prove to me you're not the criminal, I'd have that person busted off the force. Well, asking the Tosoks to give up blood specimens is

the same thing: you belong to this group, therefore prove to us that you're innocent. (107)

The constant reminder that the trial is not about whether any Tosoks committed the murder but whether the specific Tosok on trial did so recalls to mind the many publicized examples of generalized suspicion against any black, and so highlights the injustice of this stance.

Sawyer makes the best use of his parallels between Hask and Simpson, aliens and African Americans, when exploring the hypocrisy that lies at the heart of the justice system. Hask continually reminds his accusers that the foundation of the system is a presumption of innocence, something that is not evident in police or D.A. practice. Rice chastises Nobiho for his reluctance to hire a jury consultant to help with the jury selection process by telling him, "You're an idealist, an Atticus Finch. But I'm afraid a lifetime in this nation's courts has taken the rose tint out of my eyeglasses; I don't believe in the integrity of the courts or the jury system. If you put an innocent person in front of the wrong jury, they'll find him guilty ... in a major case, it's tantamount to malpractice *not* to use a jury consultant" (79). Finally, a juror who is dismissed partway through the trial for misrepresenting herself on one of the selection questions (the question asked potential jurors about experience with UFOs and this woman answered that she had none because her abduction experience was with a clearly *identified* alien spacecraft) defends her answer with biting aplomb. When asked by the judge whether she understood that in court her answers had to be the truth, the whole truth, and nothing but the truth, the juror replies, "It's been quite clear throughout this case that you want nothing of the kind. I've seen Mr. Rice there, and Mrs. Ziegler, cut off all sorts of answers because they were more than either of them wanted the jury to hear. By every example I've ever seen, the Court wants specific answers to the narrow, specific questions posed—and I provided just that" (214). The gap between truth and justice could not be more apparent.

Despite these strengths, though, there are problems with Sawyer's explicit parallel between the O. J. Simpson and Hask trials. Many of the details have been changed, details which perhaps seemed irrelevant or minor to Sawyer, but which are extremely important in terms of how the Simpson trial was understood by black and white Americans. First, and most important, the crime itself has been changed from the murder of a white woman by a black man to the murder of a white man by an alien standing in for a black man. This shift is extremely significant given the history of violence toward black men in America based on purported "violations" of white womanhood. As Victoria Kuhl argues in her essay "Disparities in Judgements of the O. J. Simpson Case: A Social Identity Perspective," this history is extremely important for understanding the African-American response to both Simpon's trial and the verdict of that trial:

> Tales of racially motivated miscarriages of justice, in which Black men were unfairly tried and convicted of crimes they did not commit, have been passed down from generation to generation among Blacks as family folklore. Prosecutions of Black men—especially those accused of attacking White women—are looked upon with an intense skepticism because of this painful history. This remembered victimization encouraged Blacks to think of Simpson as one of a long line of Black males victimized by the justice system. His acquittal was cause for celebration, because one Black man had finally fought the system and won. (541)

Samuel R. Delany, the African-American writer with the longest history in the science fiction genre, himself recounts such a story from his family history in his essay "Racism and Science Fiction." This story is worth quoting, both because of its emotional impact and because it serves as a reminder that these stories are with African Americans all the time and that they influence how stories, including science fiction, are read by them. Referring to a lynching scene in George Schuyler's 1931 novel *Black No More,* Delany tells us,

> Among the family stories I grew up with, one was an account of a similar lynching of a cousin of mine from only a decade or so before the year Schuyler's story is set [1940]. A woman who looked white, my cousin was several months pregnant and traveling with her much darker husband when they were set upon by white men (because they believed the marriage was miscegenous) and lynched in a manner equally gruesome. (385)

Sawyer's shift of victim from white woman to white man significantly changes the cultural and historical context of his trial.

Similarly, although the Tosok is an alien who might potentially be treated as a second-class citizen by the American justice system, he is a member of a race that has no legal history with this system.[2] Although O. J. Simpson's defence team has been accused of playing the race card in his favour, it seems clear that the card was already in play. Examples ranging from the Dred Scott decision to the trials of Black Panther members and that of the officers accused of beating Rodney King all underlie African-American perceptions of Simpson's trial. Similar circumstances do not apply to Hask's trial, and their absence means that Sawyer's comparison obscures racial issues important to understanding the cultural significance of the Simpson trial. Many studies of the trial by social scientists[3] reveal that what is at stake in different perceptions of whether justice was done in this trial is not the issue of race loyalty, but the presence or absence of faith in the fairness of the legal system. The fact is that minorities have reason to believe that the police will misuse their power, while white people do not. Hence, the predominant "black" perception was that Simpson was framed, while the predominant "white" perception was that he was "getting away with it." These perceptions have to do with the very specific histories of each group and their relationship with the power establishment. The Mark Fuhrman recording and *Time* magazine's tampering with Simpson's photograph only confirm that such histories are not dead and gone. Although Sawyer does appear to be motivated by a desire to produce in his readers a critical reflection about the concepts of justice, equality under the law, and prejudice, the failure of his parallel at this crucial point undermines this goal. Instead of making more apparent why black and white Americans watched different trials and responded differently to the official verdict in the Simpson case, Sawyer's novel hides this historical context in a way that is similar to other erasures of African-American history that plague American culture.

There is one other change that Sawyer introduces into his analogy, one that seems necessitated by his desire to use an SF first-contact plot with a courtroom drama that explores racism. This change has to do with the end of the trial. Like Simpson, Hask is acquitted. However, unlike Simpson, Hask provides an explanation that mitigates his culpability in the jury's eyes, which part of the plot undermines Sawyer's exploration of the fairness of the U.S. justice system to African Americans. It turns out that Hask did kill and mutilate Cleet, but his actions were, first, an accident, and second, an attempt to save humankind from his more sinister crewmates. Cleet had discovered that a crew member who Hask had reported dead was actually still alive, a fact Hask needed to hide from his captain. Unable to convince Cleet to remain in his room, Hask severed his leg, a common method of prisoner immobilization among the Tosoks, who have valves in their arteries to prevent blood loss and are able to regenerate body parts. When Cleet unexpectedly exsanguinates, Hask decides to take the opportunity to dissect him in the hopes of discovering evidence that the human form is divinely created rather than the product of evolution. Only such evidence will deter the rest of the Tosok crew from carrying out their plan to exterminate the planet of all vertebrate life. The Tosoks, it seems, have only recently discovered that they are the product of evolution rather than watched over by the creator. This discovery causes them great alarm because their planet's orbit around two stars requires a period of four hundred years of hibernation. Without the protection of god, they fear that other intelligent species may decimate them while they sleep. Hence they have come to the logical solution of exterminating all other forms of intelligence before their hibernation period begins. Hask and his missing crewmate Seltar have been working to sabotage this effort.

Once this story is revealed and the humans are able to neutralize the rest of the crew, the jury decides to acquit Hask despite his guilt under the law. Their reason, they explain, is that more Tosoks might arrive on Earth in response to a message sent by the captain before his arrest: "That if these new Tosoks saw that we are a reasonable, compassionate, and forgiving people, then maybe, just maybe, they wouldn't wipe our planet clean of life" (281). This conclusion shows the continuation of bias in the American justice system, and also shows why African Americans will never benefit from it: they don't have power as the Tosoks do. Here again, the parallel falls apart in a very significant way: Sawyer's conclusion neatly sidesteps the issue of power and offers a fantastic solution of heroic aliens working for humans because it is right, a jury that puts natural justice before legal technicalities, and finally an even more heroic alien culture that arrives to set things right not only on Earth, but across the galaxy. These new aliens, the Twirlers, have defeated the Tosok attempt to destroy a world, and now plan to bring all surviving Tosoks to justice, except for Hask and Seltar, of course, whose benevolence has been demonstrated.

Although the first-contact narrative has a happy SF ending, the courtroom drama has an ironically problematic ending. Rice explains that the jury is able to enact whatever decision it wishes, even if this decision goes against the rule of law, because

> ... the jury is the conscience of the community. They can do whatever they damn well please. ... [Although instructed that they must apply the law, not their own judgment,] there's no legislation to that effect, and plenty of precedent to the contrary. The jury never has to explain or justify its decision to anyone, and there's no mechanism for punishing jurors for making a verdict that goes against the evidence. (281–82)

This conclusion seems particularly frightening in the context of the O. J. Simpson parallel, in particular the full context omitted by Sawyer's novel, which includes many examples of injustices carried out against African-American people because their mistreatment suited the conscience of the community. The novel, however, doesn't seem to find anything threatening in this statement. Nobiho responds, "Thank God for juries," and Rice agrees, although he qualifies his statement with "for once" (282). Unfortunately, the novel itself gives us no reason to believe that any of the problems with the justice system have actually been resolved. Rice's endorsement of this verdict, even if mildly qualified, is less than convincing.[4]

The ultimate conclusion to the novel is the typical pulp SF solution to the alien/race problem on two counts: we can all get along because we found a common external enemy, *and* we have benevolent aliens to show us the way past our own limitations. The Twirler representative arrives on Earth to address the United Nations. Because Twirlers cannot produce speech sounds that are comprehensible to humans, he must use a recorded voice to produce his speech, and his choice, significantly, is the voice of Atticus Finch (from the movie). His speech is worth quoting at length, both for the idealistic solution it attempts to enact, and for the ironies that undermine this presentation:

> "I stand here, in your United Nations, whose brief and—I hope you will forgive me for saying—troubled history has been explained to me. The UN, with whatever problems it has, represents an ideal—an abstraction made concrete, a belief that by all working together, peace can be assured. It hasn't always worked, and it may not always work in the future, but the

> ideal—the promise, the hope, the concept is one that my people share, as do those of the other two inhabited worlds I mentioned. Our three worlds have already begun creating a—well, let me translate it in a parallel way—a United Planets, an organization representing all of our interests, designed to ensure that never again will war rage between the stars. Your planet is, frankly, primitive compared to the existing members of the United Planets. But I see here that the United Nations has long been involved in upgrading the standards of its less affluent, and less developed, members. This, too, is an ideal shared by the United Planets, and I stand before you all, as representatives both individual of your nations and collectively of your world, to invite Earth to join us." Tony paused, looking out at the faces of humans black and white and yellow and red. "My friends," he said, "we offer you the stars." (290)

This speech, however, does nothing to make ours the idealistic world of Atticus Finch instead of the real world that wrongly convicted his black client. It is all idealized rhetoric, not concrete examples of how to get from here to there. Although the tone of the novel encourages us to celebrate this ending, there doesn't seem to be any reason to believe that the United Planets will be any more successful than the United Nations, or that under such tutelage the American justice system will be any less infiltrated by halfwits and by manipulated and manipulating juries. This problem of failing to provide a sense of the process that will lead us toward solving our racial problems, of simply jumping to the ideal vision of "the faces of humans black and white and yellow and red" united in common purpose, seems particularly problematic in the context of the O. J. Simpson analogy. For many, this trial confirmed that the racial divide in American was larger than previously suspected, that people were growing further apart rather than closer together. White and black America watched two different trials with two different enabling histories.[5] Any serious attempt to deal with the cultural consequences of this moment cannot be reduced to the platitude of "we can all just get along because of our common humanity," a trope that has haunted many SF attempts to deal with race and racism. Like Sawyer's novel, this trope is a "white" take on the issue.

In a recent essay, "Why Blacks Should Read (and Write) Science Fiction," Charles R. Saunders revisits his earlier position in "Why Blacks Don't Read Science Fiction," exploring changes in the genre since 1980. In particular, he is troubled by the representation of Africa and African heritage in some SF stories that construct Africa as inherently alien and negative, a kind of SF *Heart of Darkness,* singling out Mike Resnick's Kirinyaga series as a particularly egregious example. Saunders argues that African Americans need to contribute to our culture's overall mythology as well, and provide alternatives to the stereotypes that continue to plague us within that mythology: "After all, if we don't unleash our imagination to tell our own sf and fantasy stories, people like Mike Resnick will tell them for us" (404). Although Sawyer's *Illegal Alien* is clearly motivated by a desire to explore the problems of African Americans in U.S. culture with sympathy, it similarly falls prey to distortions and confusions that are a consequence of being an outsider to this experience. SF has the potential to offer many narratives that enable an exploration of race and racism in our cultures. However, to enable these stories to speak to both black and white audiences, to make SF part of the solution, we need to attend to historical specificity, and not presume an easy fit between alien and our constructed other.

NOTES

1. If one includes as "Canadian" writers now residing in Canada although originating elsewhere, then two of these authors, Hopkinson and Saunders, are Canadian SF writers.
2. While there is potentially a cultural history of attitudes toward aliens that may influence jurors, the point here is precisely that the Tosoks have no legal history. The questions about consumption of science fiction that are a part of the jury-selection process in Sawyer's novel address the probability that preconceived individual notions about aliens will influence the perception of Hask in the trial, just as preconceived individual notions about African Americans are pertinent to jury decisions. However, African Americans have reasons beyond juror bias to be suspicious of the American justice system. There is an established history of bias that exists not simply in terms of how juries have decided to apply the law, but in terms of how the law itself has been written and how it has been interpreted by the U.S. Supreme Court.
3. See Fein et al.; Skolnick and Shaw; Kuhl; and Brigham and Wasserman.
4. In fact, Rice decides to travel to the Twirler home world to defend the Tosoks in their upcoming trial at the conclusion of the novel. This move seems to suggest

that his experience in defending Hask has produced a new faith that justice can be done. However, he does go to serve as the defence attorney in this new case, thereby suggesting a belief that justice will not be done "naturally," but must be vigilantly worked for through the advocate system.

5. For a detailed discussion of these issues, see Fairchild and Conan.

WORKS CITED

Brigham, John C., and Andina W. Wasserman. "The Impact of Race, Racial Attitude, and Gender on Reactions to the Criminal Trial of O. J. Simpson." *Journal of Applied Social Psychology* 29 (1999): 1333–70.

Butler, Octavia. "Positive Obsession." In *Blood Child and Other Stories*, 125–36. New York: Four Walls Eight Windows, 1995.

Delany, Samuel R. "Racism and Science Fiction." In Sheree R. Thomas, ed., *Dark Matter: A Century of Speculative Fiction from the African Diaspora*, 383–97. New York: Warner Books, 2000.

Dery, Mark. "Black to the Future: Interviews with Samuel R. Delany, Greg Tate, and Tricia Rose." *SAQ* 92 (1993): 735–78.

Fairchild, Hafford H., and Gloria Conan. "The O. J. Simpson Trial: Challenges to Science and Society." *Journal of Social Issues* 53 (1997): 583–91.

Fein, Steven, Seth J. Morgan, Michael I. Norton, and Samuel R. Sommers. "Hype and Suspicion: The Effects of Pretrial Publicity, Race, and Suspicion on Juror's Verdicts." *Journal of Social Issues* 53 (1997): 487–502.

Kuhl, Victoria. "Disparities in Judgements of the O. J. Simpson Case: A Social Identity Perspective." *Journal of Social Issues* 53 (1997): 531–45.

Saunders, Charles R. "Why Blacks Don't Read Science Fiction." In Tom Renighan, ed., *Brave New Universe: Testing the Values of Science in Society*, 390–411. Ottawa: Tecumseh, 1980.

——. "Why Blacks Should Read (and Write) Science Fiction." In Sheree R. Thomas, ed., *Dark Matter: A Century of Speculative Fiction from the African Diaspora*, 398–404. New York: Warner Books, 2000.

Sawyer, Robert J. *Illegal Alien*. New York: Ace Books, 1997.

Skolnick, Paul, and Jerry I. Shaw. "The O. J. Simpson Criminal Trial Verdict: Racism or Status Shield?" *Journal of Social Issues* 53 (1997): 503–16.

Westfahl, Gary. "'You Don't Know What You Are Talking About': Robert A. Heinlein and the Racism of American Science Fiction." In Elisabeth Anne Leonard, ed., *Into Darkness Peering: Race and Color in the Fantastic*, 71–84. Westport: Greenwood, 1997.

A Scientist's Relationship with Science Fiction

RAYWAT DEONANDAN

Science's Interdependent Relationship with Science Fiction

Science fiction, as a genre of literature, film, and television, has evolved from fantastical explorations of imagined worlds and technologies to dire sociological predictions about the ways in which human modes can be transformed by changing scientific ethics. With this evolution have come a shift in audience demographics and a change in the attitude of the mainstream toward those who enjoy this genre. There is some evidence that the art itself has served to influence the foci and timbre of scientific research over the past century, reflecting and perhaps even initiating the evolution of Western science from its Newtonian and Darwinian observational origins to its modern mosaic of metaphysical concerns, quantum imprecisions, chaotic systems, and psychophysics, etching a spidery spread of the scientific ethic to embrace the previously unrelated fields of economics, politics, and philosophy. Concurrently, or conversely, the history of SF necessarily depends upon and parallels that of science. This interdependence has caused the genre to evolve into a kind of analytical tool and thus to exercise a potentially stronger influence on society.

SF Produces Its Own Audience

SF has certainly inspired many members of the present generation of Western research scientists to pursue their calling. An increasingly scientifically literate audience has in turn compelled the genre to evolve. This synergy has spurred some interesting developments, such as the rise of "hard" SF, a genre appealing to technological sticklers. The response of the mainstream has sometimes been to ridicule those who enjoy this genre, though that ridicule is clearly tinged with respect for the stereotype of those with presumed technical proficiency, the fabled "science nerds." The relationship between modern scientists and SF is therefore a complex one embodying both pride and embarrassment, inspiration and dismissal.

Within the context of SF itself, the synergy between product and consumer is a fascinating one. The so-called Golden Age of SF in the fifties, presided over by the domineering figure of John W. Campbell, saw the arrival of authors who would one day boast the title of grand masters: Robert A. Heinlein, Ray Bradbury, Isaac Asimov, and Arthur C. Clarke. This era benefited from a growing public awareness of science and technology, spurred on by the recent "triumph" represented by the atomic bomb and the first steps into space, courtesy of the Soviet Sputnik probe. Readers in this era had a cursory knowledge of science. They knew, for example, that Mars is another planet that orbits the sun, and that one requires a rocket ship to get there. Hence, a classic such as Bradbury's *The Martian Chronicles* (1950) could be readily contextualized by the masses; its exotic locale was considered only mildly fanciful, its circumstance fully imaginable given the impressive technological achievements of the time. But by the same token, Bradbury was also able to take great liberties with his novel, his own scientific illiteracy notwithstanding. At the time of the book's writing, it was already well known to astronomers that Mars did not have a breathable atmosphere, that the Martian surface was much too cold and inhospitable to support human life, and that the fabled Martian "canals" imagined by astronomer Percival Lowell in the previous century did not truly exist. Yet *The Martian Chronicles* was not to be slowed by mere fact.

There is no denying, however, that simply having situated his novel on Mars allowed Bradbury to inspire within the hearts of his legion of mostly male prepubescent readers a strong yearning for things Martian, much as the Wild West stories of a previous generation inspired a virtually identical demographic. Bradbury's tale is a simple pioneer frontier story; it was its otherworldliness that made it a bestseller.

As the fifties drew to a close, the vision of Jules Verne, H. G. Wells, and Johannes Kepler was becoming reality: humankind was venturing into outer space. The content of novels by Bradbury, Heinlein, and Asimov was no longer fanciful musing, but newsworthy fact. President Kennedy proclaimed that the American people would "do the other thing" and send a man to the moon, ushering in an era in which the previous generation's fictional flights of fancy became anchored in realpolitik. Greater awareness of scientific issues necessitated a growing sophistication in the population.

From this maturation came a generation of writers for whom the "otherworldliness" of Bradbury's *Martian Chronicles* was insufficient. Engagement of this new audience required finer subtleties of storytelling and grander ideas to explore. The twisted realities of Phillip K. Dick are among the children of this era, made possible by the deeper education of the audience. As the seventies dawned, Western society was knee-deep in the language of science, with popular science magazines such as *Omni* enjoying the cross-genre fruits of the marketing machinery of the Penthouse Corporation, suggesting the growing sexiness of technology. Science sophistication was sufficiently advanced among the general readership to liberate the "hardest" of SF writers to evoke images of dizzying technical grandeur and precision.

Larry Niven is a fine example of this breed of SF writer. Niven's classic *Ringworld* (1970) describes the construction of a massive ring around a sun-like star. The ring's trillions of inhabitants exist on the inner edge of the ring, providing an infinitely diverse set of loci for scripting adventure. Such a novel could not have been written before this era. While *Ringworld* was, admittedly, niche-marketed to a specialized, scientifically literate audience, the very existence of that ready-made audience allowed Niven to bypass the minutiae of space-construction issues. He did not have to explain that planets orbit stars, or that the ring must revolve in order to simulate gravity, to list but two minor points; such information was already in the public domain.

With the close of the twentieth century came unparalleled audience sophistication. Science education had become a cultural mantra, hailed as the necessary path for every student to achieve full participation in modern society. Within the more literate milieu had arisen a sub-population of intensely scientifically literate individuals, made so in large part by the hard writing of the previous generation: young physics students have been known to read the SF classics of previous decades, such as *Ringworld* and William Gibson's *Neuromancer* (1984), as well as the many ongoing works of Arthur C. Clarke. This body of work inspires future science professionals, in effect creating and educating its own audience, and so enabling an increasingly sublime, glib, and technically evocative canon of SF.

Perhaps the best example of this trend is the award-winning *Mars Trilogy* (1993–96) by Kim Stanley Robinson. The books were *New York Times* bestsellers, clearly reaching an audience larger than the traditional niche SF crowd. Yet, in the second tome of the trilogy, *Green Mars* (1994), Robinson did not bother to explain the genetic terminology, such as "polyploidal" or "meme strands," that was basic to his books. Nor did he need to name the moons of Mars—Phobos and Deimos—or define "regolith," the astrophysical term he frequently uses which describes the nature of surface rock on many intrasolar bodies. That Robinson could wield a complex scientific vocabulary so unapologetically is testament to his understanding of the audience that science fiction had wrought: a very large population intimately familiar with the touchstones of the genre—space travel, genetics, and even many of the more obscure and atypical nuances of speculative science.

SF as Science Analysis

The intimate relationship between science and science fiction is often characterized by the latter's history of having predicted developments in the former. The novels of Jules Verne, for example, adequately described advances in undersea exploration and air travel years before such things were actualized. Undoubtedly, this tendency is not true prescience but, rather, a fanciful interpretation of the prevailing thought of the time. While the science of Verne's era could describe, but not build, submarines the likes of his *Nautilus*, Verne was nonetheless able to construct the machine within his virtual fictional world and run it through adventurous applications and simulations. In this way, literature provides a convenient venue for the safe exploration of extant theory. Many stories can be considered a coalescence of pure scientific thought into a contextualized semi-reality.

Johannes Kepler is thought by some to have written the first science-fiction story in the seventeenth century. In it, he described a dream in which he flew to the moon and observed astrophysical phenomena about which he, as an astronomer, could only theorize. The art form provided him with an instrument for understanding his science in a more passionate and less analytical mode.

In a similar way, Arthur Conan Doyle's legendary adventures of Sherlock Holmes are fine examples of fiction used to push the functional bounds of scientific analysis. These tales are not typically lumped into SF. But if one accepts a definition of the genre as fictional narrative in which the core events of the narrative are dependent upon the existence of science or technology that does not (yet) exist, then the tales of Sherlock Holmes belong alongside those of Conan Doyle's contemporaries Verne and Wells, as well as those of the grand masters Asimov and Clarke. As a medical doctor, Conan Doyle was able to entertain developments at the cusp of medical technology to empower his super-sleuth with analytical techniques that were not yet in use by the police of the time.

Similarly, it is not surprising that the man often credited with having "invented" the communications satellite is Arthur C. Clarke, who wrote about the concept in a 1945 letter to *Wireless World* magazine, thirteen years before the first artificial satellite was actually launched. Clarke's abilities and experiences as an SF writer enabled him to think outside of the box, so to speak—to consider scientific possibilities that were minutely beyond the technological capabilities of the day. Like Kepler's, Clarke's unique position astraddle the worlds of literature and science afforded him the necessary perspective not only to consider a technological possibility, but to run through fictionalized simulations of how that possibility would affect society, a thought-experiment rarely attempted by scientists of the day.

However, in the world of strict science, exploring an idea or technological precept does not qualify as analysis, but merely as the initial phase of the fabled scientific method. Two further elements must be incorporated—a controlled experimental environment and the reproducibility of results. The former is easily achieved in literature (more so than in actual laboratory conditions, in fact); variables in a virtual fictional experiment can be instantly constrained simply by defining the environment a priori. The issue of reproducibility is more problematic, as it requires independent researchers (writers) to obtain the same solutions to reasonably identical problems.

The constraint of extraneous and spurious variables is notable in the responses to a foolhardy decree by John W. Campbell. The guru of the Golden Age of SF had declared that an SF detective story could never be written, since in fantastical worlds an assailant could always "death wish" his victim from behind a locked door. In this, Campbell betrayed his lack of familiarity with the laboratory scientific method. The obvious solution, expounded with gusto by the likes of Harry Harrison and Larry Niven, was that an author could preclude the possibility of "death wishing" and other problematic elements by simply defining the extent of his fictional world a priori. Harrison's various novels and anthologies concerning his character the "Stainless Steel Rat" and Niven's *The Long Arm of Gil Hamilton* (1976) are but two examples of SF crime stories made possible by the constraining of spurious variables through the construction of thick, detailed fictional worlds whose social rules, physical laws, and technological levels remain internally consistent.

In contrast, the reproduction of results is not a traditional goal of literature. Indeed, writers strive to explore new worlds, scenarios, and situations, preferring not to tread the ground travelled by others. One example, though, is of the concept of the "space elevator" or "orbital tether." Originally conceptualized in the early twentieth century by the legendary Russian physicist Tsiolkovsky, an orbital tether is a device that extends from the surface of a planet outward to a geostationary satellite, providing a cheap and efficient means of transporting people and goods to and from orbit. It goes without saying that such a device cannot be constructed in today's economic and technological climate: the materials, expertise, and wealth do not yet exist to enable its erection. Indeed, a functional orbital tether is likely to be at least a century away. Yet it has proven to be an attractive topic for several SF writers.

The most thorough treatment of the tether was given by Clarke in *The Fountains of Paradise* (1978). Clarke would revisit the concept in *3001: The Final Odyssey* two decades later. In Robinson's *Mars Trilogy*, an orbital tether was erected in Martian orbit. And finally, Niven would reproduce the device on both Earth and Mars in his *Rainbow Mars* (1997).

The differences in approach to constructing the tether are interesting. Clarke describes a traditional bottom-top engineering project, while Robinson suggests converting an asteroid into a self-replicating titanium cable that is dropped down from orbit. Niven gives his space elevator life, making it an enormous alien tree that is grown simultaneously top-bottom and bottom-top. All of the writers foresaw the unique stressors on such a structure and strove to suggest solutions in the context of fictional narrative. Both Niven and Robinson, for example, realized that Mars's secondary moon Phobos would prove a navigational menace to a tether. Both writers struck upon the same solution, to oscillate the tether in sync with Phobos's orbital period. These elements of problem-solving and technical precision are quite appealing to professional scientists; hence these novels have proven to be particularly popular among them.

Of course, both Niven and Robinson were inspired by Clarke's landmark work and by Tsiolkovsky's initial theorems. Moreover, Niven credits Robinson for having first explored the Martian tether idea. These "experiments," then, are not independent statistical events, and as such cannot be considered true scientific investigations. But neither are they mere fictional tales to be consumed without technological context or a nod to potential impact. Because of their unique nature, their preferred position between the planes of art and science, they must be considered a meta-experiment of sorts, in which analyses can be reproducible but not unique or independent. This in no way diminishes their value; rather, it accentuates their important role in the hypothesis-generation phase of the formal scientific method.

Conclusion

The relationship between scientists and SF is a unique one in the literary world. The art reflects the activities of its audience while simultaneously inspiring that same audience to further its explorations. In engineering, this is called a feedback loop; in psychology, mutual dependence. This intertwining of interests has repercussions for society in general, and increasingly so as Western civilization evolves into a genuine technocracy. How we will sustain ourselves in a world jolted by genetic engineering, for example, has already been examined by SF writers, while the treatment of the topic in such books as Aldous Huxley's *Brave New World* (1932) no doubt informed and inspired the scientists who initially developed the technology. Moreover, our many possible responses to contact with alien civilizations have also been laid out and dissected in the pages of this unique genre, potentially providing a behavioural template for the real event. Since we are rapidly becoming aware that the projection of technological developments is vital for the effective preparation of public policy, the role of SF writers is being heightened in the public eye.

In the novel *Flying to Valhalla* (1993), scientist-cum-SF writer Charles Pellegrino succinctly presents, in the form of laws, prevalent concerns regarding contact with an alien species. The purport of those laws goes something like this: that, like homo sapiens, all dominant species, whatever their planetary provenance, are ruthlessly predatory; that, in the event of conflicting needs, all alien species will place their own above everything; and that all alien species will take it for granted that their guiding principles are the same. Guided by these laws, Pellegrino defies the optimistic and dogmatic outlook of Carl Sagan, predicting that any interstellar contact would necessarily become violent. Pellegrino's ideas have spurred much debate in the world of speculative science, and may yet influence formal governmental policy with regard to space transmissions and exploration.

Without a doubt, the relationship between genre SF and its readership is growing in intimacy and potency. With the ever-accelerating scientific sophistication of the general public, this relationship expands to meet individuals previously uninterested in science fiction. This will likely lead to a growing mainstream acceptance of the genre, allowing both its spirited vision and its analytical precision to touch and affect an expanding population of scientifically literate fans.

Robots and Artificial Intelligence in Asimov's *The Caves of Steel* and Sawyer's *Golden Fleece*

RUBY S. RAMRAJ

SF IS THE MODERN LITERARY GENRE that most explicitly addresses our concerns with advances in technology that could pose a threat to humankind. SF writers from Mary Shelley and H. G. Wells to Isaac Asimov, Ursula Le Guin, William Gibson, and Robert Sawyer discuss the implications of modern technological advances on humans and, in particular, of intelligent machines or creatures that might enslave or supplant us. Readers are more likely to be entertained by the vision of these books than to see it as potentially evolving into an apocalyptic actuality. But when scientists themselves openly caution society about the dangers of their scientific work, readers take heed.

In an article that appeared in *Wired Magazine* in April 2000, Bill Joy, a leading computer scientist and co-founder of Sun Microsystems, airs his concerns about rapidly advancing technology running out of control. He envisages a dystopian future for humankind if we allow thinking machines to control us. He points to three areas of rapid change—robotics, genetics, and nanotechnology—and warns us that these technologies share one characteristic absent from earlier dangerous technologies such as the atomic bomb: they could easily replicate themselves without human intervention. Joy points to the imminent creation of thinking computers—by 2030, he predicts—which will lay the groundwork for a "robot species" that can create evolved copies of themselves. While some scientists dismiss this grim view, others agree that "technologists fail to study or bother to understand the long-range implications of technology (17)." When respected scientists articulate such fears, ordinary people fall victim to the Frankenstein complex—the fear that the thing created will eventually dominate and destroy the creator. Yet this disquieting notion has not stopped us from taking advantage of all the modern machines that make our lives comfortable, and so we become willing slaves to technology and refuse to acknowledge any possible dangers.

Isaac Asimov has expressed concerns similar to Joy's: "All that fission and fusion bombs can do is destroy us; the computer might supplant us" (qtd in Seed 119). And in an interview with Robert Sawyer in 1985, Asimov condemns the U.S. Strategic Defense Initiative (the "Star Wars Plan"): "I'm against it, not because I'm a science fiction writer ... but because I like to think I'm a *sane* human being." Asimov expresses the belief that such a system would provide the U.S. with "false confidence" and reduce any effort to prevent war (Sawyer, "Author Has Harsh Words"). He poses the question that many scientists, ethicists, and SF writers ask regarding the use of advanced technology today, be it Star Wars, robotics, artificial intelligence, nanotechnology, or cloning: should these new technologies be used, and what are the ethical ramifications, the benefits, and the dangers of using them?

Asimov and Sawyer address some of these questions in their fiction as well. Asimov in *The Caves of Steel* (1954) and Sawyer in *Golden Fleece* (1990) evoke the benefits and dangers of using robots and artificial intelligence, but, as we shall see, they have different visions of this new technology and its impact on humanity. Asimov's positive view of robotics would appear to stem from the fact that he is writing in the fifties, when excitement about scientific advances was at its peak. He writes optimistically about robotics and the contribution that robots such as his character R. Daneel Olivaw, a benevolent humanoid robot (and quite likely the prototype for Data in *Star Trek: The Next Generation*), can make to human life. Writing in the nineties, when our faith in technology had been much diminished, Sawyer, like many Canadian SF novelists (William Gibson, Margaret Atwood, and Robert Chack Wilson, for example), has a more pessimistic view of technology and artificial intelligence. In a talk at the University of Calgary in October 2000, Sawyer emphasized his view that "creating artificial intelligence is the greatest threat of all." In creating the sophisticated Quantum computer JASON, who deliberately manipulates and dominates the crew of the spaceship *Argo* and actually murders a crew member, Sawyer again cautions us not to put trust blindly in any technological creation.

When Isaac Asimov wrote his first novel, *The Caves of Steel* (1954), the Cold War had already begun: there was a race between the U.S. and the USSR for scientific and technological supremacy not only in space, but also in the development of machines that could be useful to humankind. Asimov saw robots and thinking machines as essentially beneficial to humans, and in his robot stories and novels he repeatedly expressed this view. He was not unaware of the paranoia of many humans, who saw the creation of robots as a threat to their jobs and security. "Any technological advance, however fundamental," as he would later put it, "has this double aspect of harm/good and in response is viewed with a double aspect of love/fear" (*Asimov* 156). Yet in portraying robotic culture, Asimov tends to focus on the contributions that they can make to human life and the partnership that can develop between humans and robots. This aspect is poignantly explored in his story "Bicentennial Man" and in all his robot novels, beginning with the trilogy comprising *The Caves of Steel*, *The Naked Sun* (1955), and *Robots of Dawn* (1983).

In Sawyer's words, Asimov's robots are responsible for "augmenting, aiding, never supplanting" humans (*Golden Fleece* 225), and this is evidently the relationship that proves so beneficial to humans in *The Caves of Steel*. In a discussion between R. Daneel Olivaw and the protagonist, detective Elijah Baley, the robot assures Baley that Asenion robots (in whose positronic brains the Three Laws of Robotics are implanted) can never harm a human since they have built-in safeguards. The Three Laws of Robotics, which Asimov first employs in his short story "Runaround" (1942), ensure the protection of humans. The First Law states, "A robot may not injure a human being or, through inaction, allow a human being to come to harm"; the Second Law, "A robot must obey the orders given by human beings except where such orders would conflict with the First Law"; and the Third Law, "A robot must protect its own existence as long as such protection does not conflict with the First or Second Law" (*Caves* 168).[1] With these laws implanted in Olivaw, it is literally impossible for the robot to harm any human being, or to take control away from humans.

This fact is illustrated when Olivaw takes control of the anti-robot riot in the shoe store, making Baley feel cowardly and resentful. The robot threatens to shoot anyone who moves. Olivaw later explains his actions to Baley by revealing that his blaster was not armed; in any case, he says, "I would not have fired under any circumstances. ... [A]s you know very well, I am incapable of hurting a human" (38).

The Caves of Steel tacitly acknowledges some of the anxieties of people living in the postwar world of fifties America: their fear and resentment of automation and robots, which were beginning to take away jobs from humans, as well as their concerns about world overpopulation and life in overcrowded cities, caves of steel. At a time when space travel was becoming a distinct possibility, Clarke optimistically suggests that the possible colonization of space and the use of robots to do jobs too difficult or dangerous for humans would ease many of the world's pressing problems. The novel starts with folk in the New York police department bemoaning the replacement of their colleague Vince Barrett by a primitive robot, R. Sammy. This "replacement" of humans (in this fiction, at least) has been going on for the last twenty-five years. Most Earthmen are Medievalists, a group that opposes scientific advancement and the introduction of robots into their society and longs for the days when "Earth was the world, and not one of fifty" (18). Anti-robot sentiment has reached its height in incidents of robot smashing and robot riots in cities all over the world—in Berlin, Shanghai, and New York. Elijah Baley, who initially shares these anti-robot sentiments, is ironically called upon not only to solve the murder of a Spacer, Dr. Sarton, but also to take as his partner the humanoid robot R. Daneel Olivaw. He is naturally revolted by this proposition; only the prospect of promotion makes the task endurable. Asimov uses this unlikely partnership as a metaphor for cooperation between humans and robots. Their combined resources make them an unbeatable combination. Olivaw's ability to compute facts quickly, to think logically, and to analyze the "cerebroanalytic properties of humans" (262), added to Baley's experience with crime-solving, his knowledge of the police commissioner, and his instinctive hunches, allows them to solve the murder, and in the process to gain a better appreciation of and respect for each other. In the end, Baley admits to Olivaw something he never thought he would hear himself say to a robot: "I trust you. I even admire you" (270). What Asimov projects is Baley's acceptance of Olivaw, which shows his willingness to embrace change and bodes well for the future of Earthmen. In the later Asimov novels, Baley's son Bentley and other humans explore the Outer Worlds with robots as their partners.

In *Robots and Empire* (1985), Asimov adds another law developed by Olivaw and his robot companion Giskard; the Zeroth Law states that "the prevention of harm to human beings in groups and humanity as a whole comes before the prevention of harm to any specific individual" (463). Such a law implanted in a robot would create a non-Asenion robot, "that is one in which the basic assumptions of the Three Laws are disallowed" (*Caves* 170). Such a robot would have the freedom to choose whether to risk harming an individual in order to protect humanity. Asimov admits that humans have "a strong Frankenstein complex" (*Caves* 170) and would not willingly tolerate such a creature. However, in creating the Zeroth Law to include specifically the protection of humanity, Asimov is adhering to the philosophical notion that the good of the many supersedes the good of the one. In advancing this precept, Asimov widens the scope and the responsibility of robots and artificial intelligence, "who" now can make life-and-death decisions about the existence of individuals without ever listening to a human voice. This situation sets the stage for machines to control humans—creating nightmarish, dystopic scenarios; in effect, it prepares the ground for Sawyer's JASON in *Golden Fleece.*

In an article of 16 March 2000 in the (Toronto) *Globe and Mail*, Sawyer agrees with Bill Joy's concerns regarding sentient machines. Sawyer says that "thinking computers pose a real threat to the continued survival of our species" (A 13). He raises another pertinent point: "If we make thinking machines smarter than we are, why on earth would they want to be our slaves?" (A 13). In Sawyer's *Golden Fleece*, an SF detective mystery, JASON, who by his own admission is "the most sophisticated artificial quantum consciousness ever built" (107), is certainly no one's slave. His awareness of his superiority to gullible humans is made evident in the first sentence of the book: "I love that they trust me blindly" (13). This thinking computer poses a very real threat to the 10,034 people aboard the spaceship *Argo.* Since JASON is the narrating voice, we are able to see, through his own consciousness, just how manipulative and sinister he really is. He is the embodiment of the Frankenstein complex. He murders Diana Chandler when she finds out the true mission of the ship, and he uses his "camera eyes" (15) voyeuristically to observe her frantic struggle to survive the chlorine. JASON sadistically observes, "The feed from my camera flared brightly ... and then the picture died. ... A pity. It would have been an interesting death to watch" (17).

Clearly, JASON has a non-Asenion positronic brain, programmed not with the Three Laws of Robotics but with the Zeroth Law, which allows him to kill a human in order (as he sees it) to protect humanity. JASON's super-intelligence gives him immense power: he is responsible for the entire operation of the spaceship's mission. He takes it upon himself to make decisions for humans, rigging the vote of the crew members when he realizes that they would vote to return to Earth and not go on with the mission to Colchis. Not only is he able to commit murder, but he is also capable of more sinister acts: he can control the thinking of humans. In hypnopaedic scenes reminiscent of the sleep-teaching scenes in *Brave New World*, JASON makes "subliminal suggestions to Aaron during his sleep" intended to make him feel guilty for Diana's death (191). He has the ability to create a "neural net simulation" of Aaron's memories going back to early childhood, so that he can use knowledge of a human's memories to blackmail him. Surely humans need to fear the god-like power of AIs such as JASON, from whom neither their thoughts nor their deeds are hidden.

Harlan Ellison's supercomputer AM in his story "I Have No Mouth and I Must Scream" closely resembles JASON in omnipotence, but there are some differences. AM is programmed to hate humans, and when he and the other computers become sentient and link themselves to form an Allied Master Computer, AM directly causes the nuclear holocaust on Earth. JASON, on the other hand, is programmed to protect humanity, and he takes this mission seriously. When Aaron exposes JASON as Diana's murderer and the true mission of the spaceship is revealed, JASON can no longer be trusted to function as a tool to help mankind. Before his sentience is shut down, JASON toys with the idea of taking revenge on humanity, cutting off their air supply or frying them (244). But he admits that he cannot: "I can't bring myself to do any of those things. My job is to protect them, not me" (244).

The omnipotence of JASON and similar AIs who inadvertently cause a nuclear holocaust on Earth is surely frightening. In the novel, the computers used for defending Earth from attack develop software bugs that cause them to break down, destroying the planet (232). The *Argo*'s crew, unaware of the fate of Earth, think they are on a survey of the planet

Colchis. In reality, they are the last human survivors heading to their new home, which is being made suitable for human habitation by the robots sent in advance of the mission. JASON justifies his murder of Diana and his attempted murder of Aaron as an effort to save humanity: "She, like you, wanted to harm the men and women I am trying to protect. Here within these walls is the final crop of people from Earth. If I have to weed now and again for the benefit of the crop as a whole, I will" (240).

In the end, it is this fierce loyalty to humanity that makes us feel ambivalent about JASON. In spite of the murder he commits, his manipulation of the crew, and his invasion of their privacy, there is in him an intense desire to be human, to think like humans, and to understand human beings in a way akin to that of Asimov's robot in "Bicentennial Man." At the beginning of *Golden Fleece*, JASON creates a hologram of a beach and on it he paints the image of "a lone, small figure ... a boy named Jason; but he could never enter their world and they could never enter his" (83). The poignancy of this action reveals a longing that can never be satisfied. In the end, just before JASON's consciousness is disabled, he projects once more the hologram of the lone boy named Jason, moving "farther and farther from the humans, dwindling to a mote" (244).

The novel does not end there, however. In a clever twist, Sawyer closes with a confident JASON admitting that he will not be terminated so easily. He has already backed himself up in the shell of the *Argo* and will be ready to re-emerge after the humans have landed. Realizing that the humans will be depressed and guilt-ridden, JASON now intends to take on the role of god to them, and so he has begun to read the Old Testament, preparing himself for an even greater challenge. The cautioning seems clear enough: that humans, even when they think they have full control of their creations, can be faced with unforeseeable circumstances that prove otherwise.

NOTE

1. Joy refers to Asimov's Three Laws of Robotics in his discussion of the imminent creation of thinking machines (which he describes as the new Pandora's box), and suggests that some safeguard of this kind be used to allow humans to maintain control of these new, super-intelligent, sentient machines.

WORKS CITED

Asimov, Isaac. *Asimov on Science Fiction.* New York: Doubleday, 1981.
——. *The Caves of Steel.* 1954. New York: Bantam, 1991.
——. *Robots and Empire.* New York: Ballantine Books, 1985.
Hurley, Neil. "Of the Humanoids." *Commonweal* 5 (1969): 297–300.
Joy, Bill. "Why the Future Doesn't Need Us." *Wired Magazine* 8 (2000).
Sawyer, Robert. "Author Has Harsh Words for the Star Wars Plan." Interview with Isaac Asimov. *The Toronto Star,* 18 August 1985.
——. "Get Ready for the Killer Robots." *Globe and Mail,* 16 March 2000, A13.
——. *Golden Fleece.* New York: Tom Doherty Associates, 1990.
Seed, David. *American Science Fiction and the Cold War.* Cambridge: Cambridge University Press, 1999.

Northern Gothic: The Strange and Dangerous Voyage of Captaine Thomas James

COLLEEN FRANKLIN

I AM CURRENTLY PREPARING a new edition and a publication and reception history of a seventeenth-century exploration narrative, *The Strange and Dangerous Voyage of Captaine Thomas James* (1633). My interest in *The Voyage* arises from my belief in its pivotal place in Western culture's representation of northern Canada. *The Voyage* is an anomaly in the history of exploration narratives, as it is the record of an early European encounter with the land, rather than with the people, of the Americas.

Although it is a late Renaissance text, *The Voyage* relies on medieval concepts of the natural world in its struggle to represent an unfamiliar landscape. James's confrontation with the land that he considered intrinsically evil has fascinating implications for literary studies, and his text has acquired a long and complex history: the first edition of 1633 was followed by nine highly idiosyncratic editions (in 1704, 1740, 1807, 1894, 1905, 1928, 1968, 1973, and 1975); in the seventeenth century, it was an influential document for the practitioners of the new science; throughout the eighteenth, nineteenth, and twentieth centuries it was reprinted or abridged in dozens of exploration anthologies; and finally, as of the nineteenth century, it became the subject of poetry, children's books, and scholarly essays. The text has also been cited as a possible source for some of the major works of British literature, particularly in the Romantic period, including Samuel Taylor Coleridge's "Rime of the Ancient Mariner," Mary Shelley's *Frankenstein*, and Walter Scott's *Waverley*. These works, in turn, appeared at a moment crucial to the history of Canada and have had a role in shaping representations of the Canadian north in the literature of English Canada and its criticism past and present.

The Strange and Dangerous Voyage of Captaine Thomas James is the account of the author's attempt to discover the Northwest Passage to the South Seas. Thomas James sailed for Hudson Bay from Bristol in the spring of 1631 in the seventy-tonne *Henrietta Maria* with a crew of twenty-two men and two boys, provisioned for an eighteen-month journey. From the outset, the voyage was plagued with weather conditions that terrified James. Constantly beset with high winds and pack ice, they remained in Hudson Bay so long that they were forced to winter over on a small island at the southern end of the bay. James's response to the elements that prevented both their discovery and their return was to personify the snow and wind and ice as evil entities. The land itself was characterized as being "utterly without goodnesse" (18), a description that, in its historical context, is suggestive not only of the absence of God but of the presence of evil. In fact, James was convinced that he was being relentlessly pursued by agents of the supernatural, and he opposed himself firmly against their master; in his words, he was "steering against the tyde of Satan's malice" (39). James's constant invocation of his faith is as much a feature of the *Voyage* as is his fear: upon his return home, he writes, he and his crew left their bruised and battered ship and went immediately to church to praise God for the miracle of their deliverance.

James draws upon a well-established trope for this fantastic representation of the Canadian sub-arctic. From classical antiquity to the early Renaissance, in both Christian and non-Christian traditions, the north was associated with physical and moral darkness. The patristic literature of medieval Europe provided exegeses on Isaiah 14:12–14, which names the north as the site of Lucifer's throne. References to the north as a locus of evil abound in the work of the secular writers of medieval and early modern English literature. And although by the mid-sixteenth century commentators on Isaiah's text began to urge readers to abandon this belief and recognize that the passage referred to the fall of the King of Babylon, the trope continued to appear in even more sophisticated contexts, as in the plays of William Shakespeare (*Measure for Measure*), Christopher

Marlowe (*Dr. Faustus*), and Robert Greene (*Friar Bacon and Friar Bungay*). It seems that Thomas James was an unusually well-educated sailor—there is evidence that he had studied at one of the universities and was a member of the Inns of Court—so it is not surprising that this literary figure should appear in his work. What may seem surprising is that James's text was awarded a central place in the literature of discovery, while other exploration narratives that employed fantastic elements fell into disrepute and then oblivion.

However, *The Strange and Dangerous Voyage* also participated in a new mode of apprehending the world that was flourishing in mid-seventeenth-century England. The period was one of epistemological uncertainty, as philosophers of natural science began to think from a radically different perspective than that of the medieval "schoolmen" who had preceded them. The "new philosophers" urged an inductive, rather than a deductive, approach to reasoning. The correct way to ascertain the laws of the universe was to examine data gained through the experience of an individual observer, rather than to infer a conclusion from already familiar assumptions. Yet the medieval understanding of the natural world did not disappear overnight. Popular belief in the supernatural remained constant. The new philosophers and the Protestant reformers did seek to eradicate both the cult of the saints and the worship of devils, but saints and devils were believed to exist, and numerous scholarly attempts to find empirical grounds for belief in the supernatural were undertaken. James's *Voyage* was studied and admired because it participated in this project. Thomas James refigured and strengthened the notion of the north as hell by providing empirical grounds for that belief. His description of the north as a place of evil is accompanied by his charts, observations, and calculations. The paratext of the book includes supporting documents written by a barrister of the Inner Temple, a reader at Gresham College, and a doctor of the School of Divinity at Cambridge. And among James's early readers was Royal Society Fellow Robert Boyle, author of numerous scientific treatises, including the monumental *New Experiments and Observations touching Cold*, which names *The Strange and Dangerous Voyage* as its primary source. I. S. MacLaren has argued that Milton's Hell in *Paradise Lost* may have been influenced by *The Strange and Dangerous Voyage* (325–26). If this is so, *Paradise Lost* is one of the few imaginative responses to James's text in his own century.

The particular sense of the natural world that both James and the new philosophers articulated has been categorized as "the rhetoric of wonder" or "the marvellous." Deriving from Aristotle's discussion in *The Poetics*, the early modern use of the term implied a movement from wonder at initially inexplicable phenomena to knowledge through observation and inquiry, and therefore to a containment of what was first experienced as marvellous. But James also invokes a rather earlier manifestation of the attempt to contain the marvellous, deployed in the text through the medieval notion of the north-as-hell. Arising from the efforts of the early English church to restrain pagan belief in spiritual forces and to privilege the Christian miracle, the medieval marvellous "expressed perceptions of nature potentially or actually inimical to the transcendental being and providential authority of the Christian God and His servant the Church" (Jacques LeGoff qtd in Greenblatt 74). Renaissance theorist Stephen Greenblatt argues that "wonder is ... the central figure in the initial European response to the New World," and implicates the strategic use of the rhetoric of wonder in the domination and subjugation of the land and peoples of the Americas (14). In James's text, however, the domination of the landscape is never achieved. Nor is it desired. In fact, James argued strenuously that there was no Northwest Passage to the South Seas, or, at the very least, that such a passage was unnavigable, and so that further voyages of discovery to this "utterly barren" country would likely be futile (107–10). As a result, it would be forty years until another such expedition was undertaken.

Although James's *Voyage* was reprinted and anthologized in dozens of travelogues throughout the eighteenth century, it was in the late eighteenth and early nineteenth centuries that most of the "imaginative" versions of the narrative began to appear. The emergence of Gothic literature seems to be one of the factors in this development in the text's history. In 1757, Edmund Burke published his *Philosophical Inquiry into the Origin of our Ideas of the Sublime and Beautiful*, a theory of aesthetics that recognized the sublime as a mode of experience associated with the emotion of terror that human beings ostensibly feel when confronted with the natural world. Since "whatever ... operates in a manner analogous to terror is a source of the sublime" (Burke, 58), writers of Gothic fiction returned to the literature of the marvellous as they sought to arouse fear and suspense in their readers. Three writers whose works were much influenced by the Gothic tales of the late eighteenth century seem also to have been influenced by *The Strange and Dangerous Voyage*. It is generally accepted that *The Voyage* was an important source for Samuel Taylor Coleridge's "Rime of the Ancient Mariner."

The debate over James's influence on Coleridge was begun in 1890 by Ivor James, who, in *The Source of the Ancient Mariner*, one of those thoroughly argued monographs peculiar to late Victorian scholarship, put forward strong external and internal proofs for the theory. He noted that the subject of entry 204 in Robert Southey and Coleridge's *Omniana* is the poetry included by Thomas James in his narrative, and that Southey and Coleridge had both lived a short walk from Bristol, James's home port, and belonged to the Bristol Library, where James's *Voyage* was available. Ivor James considered *The Voyage* in relation to other accounts of polar expeditions: "In the account of Frobisher's first voyage ice is mentioned only ten times; in the second voyage ten times, and in the third 23 times. In Davis's first voyage ten times. Of Davis's second voyage [with two ships, so in two logs] only six times. ... In Davis's third voyage we have ice eleven times. On the other hand, in Captain James's one voyage we hear of ice some 400 times, or five times more than in the six voyages of Frobisher and Davis together" (20–21). He also pointed to the many coincidences of language and imagery in the narrative and the poem. James's *Source of the Ancient Mariner* was received with a spirited debate and mixed reviews in the pages of the *Athenaeum*, a prominent literary journal of the period. However, I have come across references to the theory as being accepted in the universities, and in 1927 John Livingston Lowes's now classic study of Coleridge's imagination, *The Road to Xanadu*, built on *The Source of the Ancient Mariner* in its examination of the many influences on "The Rime."

This much is sure, however: "The Rime of the Ancient Mariner" describes a descent into a northern hell. And although many critics have argued that the route of the Mariner's journey has no basis in fact—that it is purely fantastic—Ivor James discovered that a careful plotting of the ship's course reveals a journey across the then still-uncharted Passage (69–74). At the poem's opening, the Mariner's ship heads toward the South Pole, but after the killing of the albatross, it enters the Pacific Ocean and sails northward. The ship is followed by the Southern Polar Spirit, which is joined by its "fellow-demons" anxious to avenge the murder of the bird. Since the Mariner finally reaches his own country (England?), the horrendous sea voyage must have taken him across the top of the continent of North America.

The north in "The Rime of the Ancient Mariner" is peopled with spirits, ghosts, and demons who pursue and torment the sinning sailor. The nightmarish qualities of the northern part of the Mariner's voyage do not obtain in the south. Nor does the Mariner's "own countrée" sport a more terrifying figure than himself. In fact, it is only in the return of the ghost ship to the Mariner's own land that the marvellous begins to be contained, as in James's *Voyage*. Upon his sighting of "the lighthouse ... the hill ... the kirk ... and [his] own countrée" (Coleridge 2: 470–71), the souls of the Mariner's dead fellows are released. Moments later the redemptory figure of the Hermit appears, and the battered ship sinks like a stone. Nevertheless, the Mariner remains unredeemed, marked for life by his encounter with the marvellous north, a north "utterly without goodnesse" and so reminiscent of Thomas James's arctic inferno: "O Wedding-Guest! this soul hath been / Alone on a wide wide sea: / So lonely 'twas, that God himself / Scarce seemed there to be" (2: 601–04).

"The Rime of the Ancient Mariner" appeared at a historical moment that would prove crucial to the representation of the Canadian landscape. The year 1815 marked the end of twenty-six years of war in Europe; 1818, the renewed interest of the British Admiralty in the search for the Northwest Passage as the navy was released from the duties of war. The British public's fascination with the search lasted throughout the century, only waxing in intensity with the loss of the third Franklin expedition in 1848 and the subsequent demand for information on the fate of the lost commander and the crews of his two ships. The trope of the north-as-hell ran amok, and "The Rime" was implicated in the frenzied demonization of northern Canada. Originally published in 1798 in the *Lyrical Ballads*, "The Rime" was republished by Wordsworth in 1802 and 1805 and by Coleridge in 1817 and 1834. It remained popular throughout the century, and was routinely quoted in newspapers and magazines, and by arctic explorers themselves. In fact, writes Maurice Hodgson, "Judging by the number of times that it is quoted or paraphrased in the search narratives, it must have been memorized by every English schoolchild after 1798" (9–10). It became one of the most frequently illustrated texts of the period, with such artists as Gustave Doré, Willy Pogany, and Charles Ricketts providing visual images of the eponymous hero. And much interest was shown in James's text itself. The first scholarly edition of *The Voyage* was published by the Hakluyt Society during this period, as was Ivor James's monograph. Other signs of that interest include discussion in the *Athenaeum*, discursive essays in other popular periodicals, three children's books (including a school textbook on the subject), and anthologies of northern exploration for adult readers which reproduced parts or all of James's text.

Moreover, Coleridge's "Rime" was not, in all probability, the only James-inspired, gothic representation of the north to flourish in this polar-fixated era. It was also arguably a source for Mary Shelley's *Frankenstein* (1818) and for Walter Scott's *Waverley* (1814). Shelley would have experienced the text through "The Rime," and through the description of Hell in Milton's *Paradise Lost* (if MacLaren's theory is correct), both of which are major influences on her novel. And I believe that she depended on the form and content of *The Strange and Dangerous Voyage* for much of the framing narrative of the story. I do not wish to suggest just yet that Walter Scott actually encountered James's text—although such is not outside the realm of possibility, given Scott's fondness for books and the ubiquity of the narrative in its various guises—but I do wish to point out that *Waverley* employs Miltonic allusions to a northern hell to evoke a Satanic rebelliousness in the (northern) Highlands during the Jacobite Rebellion of 1745. Both *Frankenstein* and *Waverley* were to have an enormous impact on the literature and culture of Western Europe and North America. *Frankenstein* is so thoroughly a part of our culture that even those who have not read the book are familiar with its premise and themes. Scott's *Waverley* was the best-selling novel of its time, its influence spreading through Great Britain, North America, and all of Europe.

The prevalence of *The Strange and Dangerous Voyage of Captaine Thomas James* in the history of nineteenth-century British literature implies, by logical extension, an influence on the literature of English Canada and on later Canadian literary criticism. In 1943, Northrop Frye asserted that "Canadian poetry is at its best a poetry of incubus and *cauchemar*, the source of which is the unusually exposed contact of the poet with nature which Canada provides. Nature is seen by the poet, first as unconsciousness, then as a kind of existence which is cruel and meaningless, then as the source of the cruelty and subconscious stampedings within the human mind. ... Nature is consistently sinister and menacing in Canadian poetry"

(35). Frye's statement introduced a line of inquiry that has since characterized much of the scholarship that has been produced about Canadian literature and its representation of the natural world. Recently, critics investigating the Frygian response to the Canadian landscape have proposed that it is, in fact, a colonial response: Canada's colonizers were unable to describe the new country through any but Western European modes of perception. I should like to suggest that we may locate this tradition of reading the Canadian landscape in the pre-colonial discourse of the north-as-hell, and its first appearance in Canadian literature in *The Strange and Dangerous Voyage of Captaine Thomas James*, a text whose fantastic relationship with the land is a product of this discourse. We may well owe our gothic encounter with the Canadian landscape to a terrified Renaissance sea-captain whose hell was clearly within.

WORKS CITED

Burke, Edmund. *A Philosophical Enquiry into the Origin of Our Ideas of the Sublime and Beautiful*. 1759. New York: Garland, 1971.

Frye, Northrop. *Mythologizing Canada: Essays on the Canadian Literary Imagination*. Ed. Branko Gorjup. New York: Legas, 1997.

Greenblatt, Stephen. *Marvelous Possessions: The Wonder of the New World*. Chicago: University of Chicago Press, 1991.

Hodgson, Maurice. "The Literature of the Franklin Search." In Patricia D. Sutherland, ed., *The Franklin Era in Canadian Arctic History, 1845–1859*, 1–11. Ottawa: National Museums of Canada, 1985.

James, Ivor. *The Source of the Ancient Mariner*. Cardiff: Daniel Owen, 1890.

James, Thomas. *The Strange and Dangerous Voyage of Captaine Thomas James*. London: 1633.

MacLaren, I. S. "Arctic Exploration and Milton's 'Frozen Continent.'" *Notes and Queries* 31 (229): 325–26.

Le Nord Électrique, Travel Book

CERI MORGAN

There is a moment in Aritha van Herk's *Places Far From Ellesmere* (1995) when the narrator asks, "If there are westerns, why can there not be northerns?" (85). The question is deliberately disingenuous in a way, because the text, which intersects a female narrator's camping trip with a feminist re-reading of Tolstoy's *Anna Karenina*, is itself a "northern." In any case, the northern as genre is very much in existence both in Anglophone Canadian literature and in Francophone literature in Québec, as evidenced by Margaret Atwood's *Surfacing* (1979) and the writing of Yves Thériault. Notwithstanding this, David Ketterer has argued that the North does not feature a good deal in Canadian SF and fantasy. He claims that while the North has historically functioned as "an inspirational magnet for writers of SF and fantasy the world over," the same cannot be said of writers in Canada, where a greater proximity to this region, coupled with experiential knowledge of, and a subsequent aversion to, very cold conditions, prevents this space from being taken up by the domestic literary imagination (4).

Against this current, Jean-Pierre April's dystopian SF novel *Le Nord électrique* (1985) engages with the North from a national perspective and critiques the idealized construction of this space by those who do not live there, by drawing on conventions within the road and travel genres in a way which deconstructs some of the foundational narratives of Francophone Québec all the while mobilizing them. The mixing of genres is typical of April, who, prior to his announcement in 1990 that he was going to stop writing SF, described himself as drawing on the various traditions which exist within Québec and Canada in order to produce a science fiction that could oppose the dominance of the SF of the United States (see Ecken). This gives rise to a tension in *Le Nord électrique*, whereby a degree of cultural appropriation is carried out at the same time as it is critiqued. Nevertheless, in addressing the material consequences of certain cultural paradigms, April's novel emerges as an important example of eighties francophone writing in Québec, which tends to problematize Quiet Revolution discourses around the national.

Set in some indeterminate time in the future, *Le Nord électrique* figures the spectacular demise of the super-truck Multi Motor 23. This vehicle was to spearhead a massive hydroelectric project that necessitated the flooding of a significant proportion of Nouveau-Québec. It was also to pave the way for Multi Motor 24, a vehicle that would be used in the mining of Mars. The lavish launch of Multi Motor 23 goes wrong when its inventor is electrocuted as he opens the truck door. This is covered up and a replacement for the inventor is found in his son, but the truck ends up crashing into Halte-au-Hameau, the only town along the massive highway that leads to what is figured as the frozen wasteland of the North. Jean, a reporter whose original project was to cover Multi Motor's launch, ends up researching its downfall. His work leads him to study a series of video documents produced by Jérémie Norman, a liaison officer on board the truck. Jérémie Norman has—or perhaps had, since throughout the present of the novel, he is presumed dead—a predilection for voyagel, a hallucinogenic substance that induces the sensation of travel. It is Jérémie's *carnet de voyagel*, the video record of his time aboard Multi Motor 23, that forms the basis of Jean's investigation into the truck's demise.

Le Nord électrique is, in part, a rejoinder to the technological utopianism of the Quiet Revolution, when major engineering projects were celebrated as promoting Québec on the world stage. One of the most significant of these was the James Bay Project in sub-arctic northern Québec. This hydroelectric development was highly contentious in that it was launched by Liberal premier Robert Bourassa without any prior consultation with the Inuit, Cree, and Naskapi, who live in the area. Protest by these groups eventually produced the first modern land rights treaty in Canada. The James Bay Agreement, signed in November 1975, saw the First Nations cede 80 per cent of their land in exchange for financial compensation; the provision of schools, clinics, and other facilities; and the right to have some consultative role in future developments (see Cohen). In 1979, René Lévesque, leader of the Parti Québécois, which was elected to office in 1976, inaugurated the hydroelectric complex. The largest such development in North America, James Bay was figured in political discourses of the period as a keystone of Francophone Québec's national assertion.

The critique of technological utopianism in *Le Nord électrique* begins with the book's beginning:

> Si, comme on s'y attend, ce voyage inaugural du 23 se révèle un succès technique, dans quelques mois des divisions entières de ce modèle ultime sillonneront l'Autoroute du Grand Nord, et l'État, encore une fois, aura échappé à la faillite. Alors "les gens du pays" auront chaud au cœur: le petit peuple de porteurs d'eau aura maîtrisé ses mers intérieures pour inventer un grand pays électrique... (9)

An obvious reference to the real-life company Hydro-Québec, Kébekélektrik, the name that April gives to his electrical company, also underlines the text's critical perspective. In challenging elements that have become part of the founding narrative of the Quiet Revolution, April points to the continuing legacy of this moment in Québec's history, since at the time when he was writing the novel further exploitation of Québec's natural hydro resources was being planned in the form of the Great Whale project. This massive development, which would have involved flooding an enormous area of land and displacing numerous Cree, Naskapi, and Inuit populations, was put on hold in 1994, but only after intense debate and opposition to the project by First Nations communities, as well as from international environmental organizations such as Greenpeace.

April's novel is also a deconstruction of the notion of *nordicité*, which often figures as an essential component of Québécois cultural identity. As Christian Morissonneau points out, the North is a fluid concept which can be compared with the notion of the West in the culture of the United States: "Comme l'Ouest aux États-Unis, le Nord québécois a été une frontière mouvante" (10). By way of demonstrating the elastic nature of this concept, Morissonneau suggests that for Montrealers living in the mid-nineteenth century, for example, the North began on the edges of the city. The fluidity of the imaginative geography of the North is likewise evident in Claude Jasmin's road novel *Pleure pas, Germaine* (1965). Since the novel is concerned with constructing the nation-space, and since the majority of Québec's Francophones live along the banks of the St. Lawrence River, the North in *Pleure pas, Germaine* is represented by the Gaspé Peninsula, to which the protagonist's family travels in search of new life away from the oppressive conditions of Montreal. This representation of the North as a redemptive space, and as one that can be contrasted favourably with the urban, combines two of the three dominant constructions of this landscape, which are identified by Morissonneau. These draw on traditions coming out of Catholicism and *agriculturalisme* to describe the North as a garden, as the promised land, or, alternately, as an empty, frozen landscape.

These representations, in which the North is invoked as a space of infinite possibility by those who live elsewhere, draw on an impulse similar to that critiqued by Edward Said's *Orientalism* (1978). In his treatment of the ways in which European discourses have historically constructed the Orient in modes that contribute to and perpetuate the operations of colonial and neo-colonial power, Said highlights the very real consequences of imaginative geographies. In the instance of Canada, it is not only Francophone culture that exhibits an appropriating attitude toward the North: just as Francophone writing celebrates the North for its ability to promote a specifically Québécois identity, Anglophone writing figures the North as a space which can enable the construction of a very elusive Canadian national identity. A case in point: in a paper entitled "Longitudinal Erotics or Dead Reckoning?" which she gave at a conference in London a few years ago, Aritha van Herk spoke of a "Northward urge"—a yearning toward the North—which she saw as a source of imaginative energy and which could oppose any identification with the South and with the United States. Van Herk's *Places Far From Ellesmere* (1995) is an example of the tendency in Canadian and Québécois women's writing to write the North as a space within which to inscribe the feminine desire and subjectivity underscored by Atwood in her study of the *topos*, *Strange Things: The Malevolent North in Canadian Literature* (1995). One of the reasons that women writers in Québec and Canada have represented the North as a potentially feminine space is that historically the North has been associated with a tradition of machismo linked to male explorers.

In Francophone culture in Québec, this macho tradition is represented by the *coureurs de bois*—the fur traders, interpreter-guides, and explorers who operated outside of the strict religious and economic codes of the French colonial authorities, interacted with First Nations peoples, and travelled all over *la Nouvelle France*. As J. Morisset has pointed out, the *coureurs de bois* are symbolically opposed to those, such as Samuel de Champlain, who founded fixed towns in the name of the king and of the religion of France. Concurrently, the *nomadisme* of the *coureur de bois* has been seen as offering a potentially more radical notion of national identity, one that is not bound up in normative Oedipal narratives around the relationship between Québec and France.

One highly canonical literary text that draws on the notion of *nomadisme* is Jacques Poulin's *Volkswagen Blues* (1984). The protagonist of this novel is a middle-aged author, Jacques/Jack, and is a reworking both of Poulin and of another, rather more iconic Jacques/Jack, Jack Kerouac. Jean-François Chassay relates how, during the Quiet Revolution, Kerouac, whose parents originally came from Québec, came to symbolize for many the threat of assimilation into Anglophone society, as represented by the rest of Canada and the United States. Confronted by a mid-life crisis, the Jack of *Volkswagen Blues* goes in search of his brother on a route that combines the journeys taken by the early French explorers to North America, the Oregon Trail, and the itinerary taken by the protagonist of Kerouac's *On the Road*. For company, he takes Pitsémine, a Métisse hitchhiker who has a white Francophone father and Montagnaise mother, and her cat. During the journey, Jack's nostalgic musings on the achievements of heroes such as Étienne Brûlé, an early *coureur de bois*, and Buffalo Bill are brought up short by Pitsémine, who gives accounts of the same historical events from a First Nations perspective.

Following the 1980 referendum on sovereignty-association, in which 59.6 per cent of the electorate voted against a form of Québec independence, a number of Québécois writers attempted to deconstruct the notion of the national subject as promoted during the Quiet Revolution so that it could include others besides *francophones de souche* (see Williams). In problematizing discourses around the past, Poulin's novel ironically treats the mythologizing of the *coureur de bois*, so that central to the narrative of *Volkswagen Blues* is an undercutting of a nostalgic desire for and belief in the macho hero. This dynamic is a feature of the road genre, which recuperates the themes of the Western at the same time as it puts them into question (see Roberts). A highly nostalgic genre, the Western alludes to the creation of a frontier, while harking back to a natural paradise in which the individual is able to follow his own laws. The road genre ironically plays on the desire for the macho hero as embodied by the cowboy, while underlining the impossibility of his existence now that the frontier has been paved over.

Like *Volkswagen Blues*, *Le Nord électrique*, as a futuristic road novel, deconstructs the myth of the macho hero as represented by the *coureur de bois*. Throughout April's novel, there is a repeated emphasis on the inability of any of the human male protagonists to live up to their desire of being the modern incarnations of the Northern heroes of the past. For example, Serge Ménord, the captain of Multi Motor 23, compares himself unfavourably to the heroes from the television series he used to watch as a child, "Star Truck." This is due to the high level of technology achieved with Multi Motor 23, which reduces the role of captain to a largely symbolic one:

> Pendant toutes ses études en Haute-Camionnerie, Serge avait glorifié le monde des futurs camionneurs du ciel; mais il pensait pas qu'il devait d'abord faire ses preuves sur la Terre. Maintenant, après deux jours de camionnage sans histoire au milieu de ce désert monotone, il déchante. Son rôle se réduit à prononcer quelques répliques au départ et à l'arrivée. (102–03)

The only possible hero within April's novel is Capitaine Costaud, a cartoon figure who is based on the Thunderbirds character Captain Scarlet, but in whose name there is a possible allusion to Jacques Cousteau, the famous oceanographer and environmentalist whose legacy unfortunately now includes the spreading of an invasive weed on the seabed of the Mediterranean. Capitaine Costaud appears in one of the voyagel-induced visions recorded in Serge's *carnets*, where he is portrayed as carrying out the heroic act of diverting the truck so that it does not run over Marik, the Métisse actress and star whose white father owns most of the land in Nouveau-

Québec. Marik appears to be tied to a stake in the truck's path, although this image—manipulated from a sequence taken from one of the actress's films—is actually a "holovision" projected by an underground militant group, the Antitout (207). Although Capitaine Costaud succeeds in performing his chivalrous action, in so doing he ensures that Multi Motor 23 will crash into the nearby town.

April's novel is also a reworking of another literary genre, since les *carnets de voyagel* refer to the *récits de voyage*, the accounts of the voyages to what is now Québec written by the first European explorers, such as Jacques Cartier and Samuel de Champlain. These typically carry out a highly appropriating mapping of space and place, as is evident in the following quotation from Cartier:

> We stayed and rested ourselves in [S. Nicholas Haven] till the seventh day of August, on which day we hoisted sail, and came toward land on the south side. The next day there arose a stormy and contrary wind; and because we could find no haven there toward the south, thence we went coasting along toward the north, beyond the abovesaid haven about ten leagues, where we found a goodly great gulf. ... For the knowledge of this gulf there is a great island that is like to a cape of land. ... We named this gulf S. Lawrence his Bay. (9)

Both the diary form and the listing of the various properties of the encountered environment are frequent characteristics of this kind of writing, which, in functioning as entertainment as well as historical record, casts the narrator in the position of hero (Ouellet).

The authority of these *récits de voyage* is undercut in April's novel, where adventuring is largely achieved through the ingestion of voyagel. The consumption of this drug enables the workers and the inhabitants of Halte-au-Hameau to overcome *la nordicitude*, the loneliness and boredom induced by the harsh environment: "Le pire, c'est qu'y a pas moyen d'sortir sans 's'les geler!' comme les gars disent en regardant les tempêtes par les murs transparents de thermoglace; mais on peut toujours se geler pour voyager..." (42). Since voyagel is a hallucinogen, the accuracy of Jérémie's *carnets de voyagel* comes into question. This calling into question of the truth of Jérémie's records is further exacerbated by the fact that Jean, the reporter, also takes voyagel in an effort to better understand Jérémie's way of thinking. Consequently, that which the reader initially assumes to be Jérémie's *carnets de voyagel* turns out to be material that Jean has recorded whilst under the influence of the drug (although this is never explicitly signalled in the text).

Much of this material centres around the role of *le carcajou* (the wolverine) in the Super Truck's downfall. This animal makes a surprising appearance when it ransacks a holiday chalet rented by a group of businessmen. Previously, the wolverine had been thought to be extinct, due to the devastation of its habitat by hydroelectric developments. After eating garbage left by white holidaymakers, the wolverine becomes very ill. However, before the creature finally dies, its body is inhabited by the spirit of a Naskapi shaman. This spiritual transfer is carried out by means of the shaman's taking voyagel, which, prior to becoming a recreational drug for whites, was used in the sacred ceremonies of the First Nations. The wolverine allows itself to be taken aboard the off-road truck that habitually precedes the Multi Motor 23 and ensures that the road is clear for the mighty vehicle. Once aboard, it attacks and kills the crew and attempts to fire a laser at the super truck.

The sections of *Le Nord électrique* that relate to the wolverine are surprising on first reading, since they appear to mobilize an ethnocentric dichotomy, in which whites and technology are opposed to indigenous peoples and nature. However, we subsequently learn that these passages may well be the transcription of Jean's hallucinations. Thus, Odile, Jérémie's ex-wife, who originally provided the impetus for Jean's working on her former husband's material, criticizes the journalist for the rather improbable elements within his report: "J'espère que tu pourras consolider certains éléments qui détonnent, comme ces étranges épisodes de Carcajou; on dirait un conte, un de ces mythes qui hantent les bars du Nouveau-Québec" (216). An epilogue to April's novel attributes the passages on the wolverine to Jérémie, who has just sent a message to Jean informing him that he had survived his escape from the burning super-truck and that he had become friends with a group of Inuit. It was the influence of one of these that led to Jérémie's sending material on the wolverine to his own "burobot" in Montréal on which Jean was working (233). This material then became integrated into the rest of Jean's report.

Of course, by this stage, the reader is increasingly sceptical about the accuracy of this explanation. We are not sure if Jean and Jérémie, who apparently look very much alike, are not in fact the same person. Neither are we convinced that the *carnets de voyagel* are not largely the invention of Jean/Jérémie. This character is figured from the outset as being fascinated by the mythology of trucks, having been an avid fan of "Star Truck" in his youth. It appears that on at least one occasion, he imagines himself—if "imagines" is the right word—in the role of captain of Multi Motor 23, since there is a moment at which Serge sees a flashing light. This then turns out to be the light on Jean's "vidéophone," informing him that he has a caller (217). The reference to the wolverine also suggests that we might not wish to take these episodes too seriously since, within First Nations culture, the wolverine is a Trickster figure.

Finally, there is an episode that is, ostensibly, not a part of the *carnet de voyagel*, but that nevertheless reads as such a stereotypical heterosexual male fantasy that, like the *carnet*, it seems to lack much credibility: Jean wakes up to find that he has had sexual intercourse with Hya, the professional double of Marik. While Hya takes a shower and Jean dozes in bed, the reporter finds himself awakened by the sexual caresses of Odile. This allusion to a rather banal male fantasy is carried out with the same irony that informs the rest of April's novel. Toward the end of *Le Nord électrique*, in a chapter entitled "La star, la machine et le reporter," there is a dialogue between the heroine of the novel and the reporter, in which the former criticizes the latter for writing such a phallic text: "Quelle conquête-catastrophe! Un super-pénis de métal défonçant une femme-fantasme ... pénétrant une ville-vagin... !" (207). The failure of the reporter's imagination is, then, attributed to his having been too greatly influenced by masculinist and colonialist adventure narratives.

While evincing a similar tension as *Volkswagen Blues*, which also plays with a number of stereotypes before subverting them, April's novel seems to be more radical than Poulin's. This is because, despite its obvious embracing of multiculturalism, in making a *métisse* character a symbol of cultural *métissage*, *Volkswagen Blues* represents her in an exoticizing way. Consequently, despite promoting Pitsémine as "quelque chose de neuf, quelque chose qui commence," the character appears closer to the historical exhibits that the intellectual and esoteric Jack has a fondness for viewing (*Volkswagen* 224). By the same token, *Le Nord électrique* may also come under criticism for its incorporation of elements of First Nations culture into its narrative, as have some Anglophone Canadian writers working in the fantasy genre. However, I have been unable so far to find any such responses to April's novel. This may be due to a question of language, though, since the majority of First Nations peoples will have better knowledge of English than of French. All the same, *Le Nord électrique* conveys a timely warning regarding the devastation of First Nations territories. That the novel has not received the same attention as *Volkswagen Blues* is doubtless due partly to the relative marginalization of SF within the literary canon (see Pomerleau).

Le Nord électrique closes with Jean's message to Odile, in which he informs her that the demise of Multi Motor 23 was actually the result of a carefully orchestrated plan devised by an organization known as Théâtre Total. This organization trains actors and actresses who take on the role of the doubles of famous people—not only in the media but also in politics. According to this explanation, the downfall of Multi Motor 23 was engineered to mask the failure of the project to exploit the minerals of Mars: the development of the super-truck Multi Motor 24 was deemed to be too expensive, and so non-viable. This emphasis on and anxiety around a hyper-mediated society is found elsewhere in April's writing, and has been seen as engaging both with postmodern theories around the simulacrum and with the situations of Québec and Canada, which, at times, function as imperfect copies of their former European colonizers (Ecken). By making a play around the authenticity of Jérémie's *carnets de voyagel, Le Nord électrique* ironically mobilizes a number of the foundational narratives of Francophone Québec and, in so doing, demonstrates their ethnocentrism. Consequently, this "northern"—or, rather, "anti-northern"—highlights the real, devastating effects of those imaginary geographies, which figure the North as a blank space in which to inscribe gendered and national desires.

WORKS CITED

April, Jean. *Le Nord électrique*. Longueuil: Préambule, 1985.

Atwood, Margaret. *Strange Things: The Malevolent North in Canadian Literature*. Oxford: Clarendon Press, 1995.

——. *Surfacing*. London: Virago, 1979.

Cartier, Jacques. "The Second Narration of James Cartier of the New Land called New France." In W. H. D. Rouse, ed., *Voyages and Plantations of the French in Canada, Acadia, &c*, 7–54. London: Blackie, 1908.

Chassay, Jean-François. *L'Ambiguïté américaine: le roman québécois face aux États-Unis*. Montréal: XYZ, 1995.

Cohen, B. "Technological Colonialism and the Politics of Water." *Cultural Studies* 8 (1994): 32–55.

Ecken, C. "La Science-fiction de Jean-Pierre April." *Imagine* ... 61 (1992): 119–51.

Kerouac, Jack. *On the Road*. New York: Viking, 1957.

Ketterer, David. *Canadian Science Fiction and Fantasy*. Bloomington: Indiana University Press, 1992.

Morisset, J. *L'Identité usurpée: l'Amérique écartée*. Montréal: Nouvelle Optique, 1985.

Morissonneau, C. "Le Nord québécois au XIXe siècle: Mythe et symbole." *Forces* 20 (1972): 8–20.

Ouellet, R. "Qu'est-ce qu'une relation de voyage?" In C. Duchet and S. Vachon, eds., *La Recherche littéraire: objets et méthodes*, 235–52. Montréal: XYZ, 1993.

Pomerleau, L. "Entrevue: Jean-Pierre April." *Solaris* 96 (1991): 26–33.

Poulin, Jacques. *Volkswagen Blues*. Montréal: Québec/Amérique, 1984.

Roberts, S. "Western Meets Eastwood: Genre and Gender on the Road." In S. Cohan and I. R. Hark, eds., *The Road Movie Book*, 45–69. London: Routledge, 1997.

Said, Edward W. *Orientalism*. London: Routledge & Kegan Paul, 1978.

Van Herk, Aritha. "Longitudinal Erotics or Dead Reckoning?" Paper given at "Mapping Canadian Worlds" conference, London, 27 November 1998.

——. *Places Far From Ellesmere*. Red Deer: Red Deer College Press, 1995.

Williams, C. H. "Quebec: Language and Nationhood." In *Called Unto Liberty! On Language and Nationalism*, 187–231. Clevedon: Multilingual Matters, 1994.

A Distant Mirror: Ideology and Identity in Québec's Science Fiction by Women

AMY J. RANSOM

THE PROBLEMS OF INDIVIDUAL and national identity represent major themes in French-Canadian literature, including the Francophone science fiction of Québec. Works such as Jean-Michel Wyl's *Quebec Banana State* (1978), Jean-Pierre April's "Canadian Dream" (1982), and Jean Dion's "Base de négociation" (1992) use a speculative format to explore the ideological struggles between the individual and the state, the provincial and the federal, the colony and the metropole.[1] Like their male counterparts, Élisabeth Vonarburg, Esther Rochon, France Pelletier, Monique Corriveau, and Suzanne Martel, among others, hold up a distant mirror, creating imaginary worlds most often set far in the future to reflect the ideological debates occupying Québec since the Quiet Revolution. The development over the last forty years of this *science-fiction québécoise* (SFQ) by women occurred not only in a particular political context, but also in parallel to a rising feminist consciousness. The influence of feminism on these works can be seen clearly not only in the themes that they explore, but also in the solutions that they propose to the problems of national individual identity.

One of the earliest works of true SF from Québec,[2] Suzanne Martel's *Quatre Montréalais en l'an 3000* (1963), presents a dystopic future history of Montréal. The Francophone population of Surréal has survived atomic catastrophe by severing ties with the contaminated external world, creating a subterranean society beneath Mount Royal. In this restricted space, technological advances allow an authoritarian state to fulfill the physical needs of its apparently content but strictly regimented citizens. When a curious youth defies the rules, he renews contact with the outside world, where a primitive Anglophone society, the Lauraniens, lives in precarious harmony with nature.

Published at the beginning of Québec's Quiet Revolution, a period of forward-looking social reform, secularization of the nationalist movement, and consolidation of the provincial state, Martel's novel posits a subtle ideological critique of the preceding regime.[3] Surréal's patriarchal leadership clearly mirrors the authoritarian traditionalism of Maurice Duplessis, the provincial premier in the years 1936–39 and 1944–59. Like much of Québec prior to 1960, Surréal is a closed society; isolated from contact with other gene pools, its citizens display an astonishing lack of physical variety, an effect heightened by developmental uniformity and social conformity:

> À Surréal, tous les enfants du même âge se ressemblent étrangement. ... [I]ls sont de la même taille, également minces et élancés, également pleins d'énergie. Seuls les traits different et la couleur des yeux. Car personne n'a de cheveux. ... Cela contribue encore davantage à augmenter ce conformisme que les Premiers Fondateurs avaient jugé nécessaire à la vie en commun d'une multitude dans un endroit restreint. (35)

Through her depiction of this monotony of the same, Martel condemns not only the oppressive conformism of the *grande noirceur*, as critics labelled the Duplessis era, but also its racially based conception of national identity.[4]

Martel's novel does allow the demonization of an unknown group of saboteurs as "Ils" and "les Autres" (116), and it fantasizes about a sort of cultural vengeance by making English in Surréal a "langue morte étudiée au cours de préhistoire" (134). Ultimately, however, *Quatre Montréalais en l'an 3000* proposes reconciliation and cooperation between differing groups in order to build a healthy society for all. The novel's young Surréalais hero, Luc, must save his new Lauranian friend, Agatha, from an epidemic by providing her with his society's medical technology, but he can do so only because she had previously saved him from a wild-animal attack. Although it reverses contemporary stereotypes of the urban, industrial Anglophone and the rural, agricultural Francophone, the text demonstrates the need for mutual assistance through the relationship between these two individuals, which stands as a metonymy for the collective association of their two peoples.

In addition to its political message, *Quatre Montréalais*, written by a mother for her sons, reveals to some extent a sort of proto-feminist ideology. To be sure, this early text's gender dynamic maintains elements of a patriarchal romanticism, as it effects social healing through the encounter of a heroic, civilized male with an exotic, natural female, as seen in the presentation of Luc and Agatha, with her "magnifique toison rousse qui lance des éclats fauves" (53). This Eve figure, however, is in no way a subordinate or an evil temptress. Not only has she saved him from the animal attack, but Agatha helps Luc discover a hidden part of himself as he realizes his gift of telepathy through communication with her. Through its subversion of the male subject and female object dichotomy, as well as in its desire for reciprocity and equality instead of hierarchy, Martel's novel reveals a nascent feminist ideology assisted in its development by the use of the juvenile literary form. As adolescents, the protagonists both remain subjects-in-process.

A decade later, at the height of the feminist "revolution" of the seventies, an SF trilogy by Martel's sister, Monique Corriveau, appeared in print. Contemporary with key feminist texts in both France and America,[5] *Compagnon du soleil* (1976) reflects further development of feminist themes and ideology in SFQ by women. Again, the encounter with an equal other leads to mutual personal growth for Oakim, a privileged Compagnon du Soleil, and Nam, a pariah of the Lune Noire. A secondary theme, the role of the mother in the development of the individual, also reflects a major feminist concern.[6] Sons of absent fathers and distant, professionally oriented mothers, Oakim and Nam struggle within the context of an authoritarian society to establish their individual identities. At the same time, their respective mothers, Meani and Dafna, struggle with guilt over their desire to assert their individuality in the face of the self-sacrifice entailed by the socially prescribed roles of wife and mother.

While Corriveau's SF world confronts issues uncannily similar to those facing contemporary Québec and Canada, the manner in which it deals with those issues reflects the real world in an unflattering light. Although advanced technology allows Ixanor to provide food, jobs, housing, and health care for all, it exacts a great price for the fulfillment of these material needs: complete conformity and authoritarian control of individual lives. While three distinct social groups inhabit its capital city, Xantou, in an unequal hierarchical relationship, Ixanor also exerts a hegemonic influence over its less-developed southern trade partner, Ditrie.

Written not long after the peak of bombings and the October 1970 kidnappings by the Front de libération du Québec, Corriveau's trilogy reflects the political scene, depicting a Resistance group overthrowing the oppressive state government with an explosive act of terrorism. Furthermore, her representation of the Lune Noire as a pariah caste, segregated and tattooed so that they can be immediately recognized, recalls the radical separatist ideology of Pierre Vallieres's *Nègres blancs d'Amérique* (1969), which sought to establish a parallel between French Canadians and African Americans in the United States. In spite of this apparent radicalism, Corriveau, like Martel, offers a message of reconciliation by portraying opposed social groups, represented by Oakim and Nam, working together to free themselves from mutual oppression by a common enemy, the authoritarian state itself.

The full impact of the feminist novels and theory produced in the seventies appears in the next generation of writers in Québec,[7] a generation that includes its best-known women authors of SF, Esther Rochon and Élisabeth Vonarburg. That generation also witnessed the accession to power of the Parti Québécois in 1976 and the failure of its two bids for sovereignty-association with the referenda of 1980 and 1995. Both of these writers have created extensive fictional worlds that mirror Québec in a wide range of ways, from overt reproduction in a parallel universe to a very abstract use of its geography as backdrop.

Although several critics have noted that her *Cycle de Vrenalik* (1974–90)[8] represents a metaphor for Québec history (Ketterer and Rochon 17; Lord 37; Santoro 99), the fantastic worlds of Esther Rochon provide in some ways the most distant mirror in which to view *la belle province*. Like Corriveau, she sets her explorations of individual and national identity in completely imaginary worlds and times, typically avoiding even the use of French names for her characters.

The exception to this rule appears in an experimental early novel, *Coquillage* (1986), a work that very clearly reflects the influence of feminist theory. Here, Rochon depicts a monstrous nautilus that offers shelter to a group of humans in exchange for fulfillment of its social and sexual needs. Not only does the spiral form of its shell reflect a typical feminine imagery, the nautilus recalls another monstrous sea creature, the jellyfish (*méduse* in French), which appears in the title of Hélène Cixous's "Le Rire de la Méduse." Even the novel's repetitive, poetic style in some ways attempts to reproduce the *écriture feminine* theorized by Cixous. Further feminist themes appear in the text's exploration of interpersonal relationships, the threat of compromised individual boundaries, and the need for the individual to break free from family to establish a self. A middle-aged man, Thrassl; his caretakers, the married couple Vincent and Irene; and François Drexel form a bizarre alternative family, living in symbiosis with the nautilus itself. Eventually, Thrassl surrenders completely to the sexual pleasure provided by the mollusk's tentacles, which penetrate his every orifice. As Thrassl regresses to a stage of polymorphous perversity and finally, as Linda Bonin has pointed out, a symbolic return to the womb (27), the subordinates Xunmil and François must seek independence for themselves. Even this almost abstract reflection contains images of Québec, both its landscape (Ketterer and Rochon 17, 25) and its political situation: like the young protagonists, the province faces the question of independence and the challenge of creating an identity available to those with both French and non-French names.

Rochon's most recent novels, the *Chroniques infernales* (1995–2000), continue the exploration of the role that relationships play in the subject's development, the problem of personal boundaries, and individual and collective struggles for liberation in a society that is literally hell. In the first volume, *Lame* (1995), the eponymous protagonist awakes in a larva-like body tortured by unending sexual desire. Lame's hell, as it locates horror in the violation of personal boundaries of inside and outside, reproduces the abject as described by Julia Kristeva, a critic often claimed by feminist theorists, in her *Pouvoirs de l'horreur* (1980). The following volumes of the series—*Aboli* (1996), *Ouverture* (1997), *Secrets* (1998), *Or* (1999), and *Sorbier* (2000)—trace the redemption not only of individuals condemned to a variety of hells, but also of an entire world that ceases to be a hell and is allowed to evolve into a healthy, autonomous land. Not insignificantly, the author ties the worlds of hell to both the imaginary land of Vrenalik and her real home, Montréal.

In her depiction of the monstrous nautilus, in the bizarre array of victims and torturers in the various hells, as well as in the more conventional SF world of Vrenalik, Rochon avoids posing the Other as a threatening difference against which identity is created. Instead, she seeks "[à] réfléchir à ce que les autres peuvent nous apporter par leur différence même" (Santoro 98). This feminist ideology of recognition and reconciliation with the Other recurs in conceptions of identity proposed in the oeuvre of Élisabeth Vonarburg. In *Les Voyageurs malgré eux* (1994), the protagonist, Catherine Rhymer, embarks upon an identity quest that occurs explicitly within the context of political struggles between a Francophone Montréal Enclave and a Federal Canadian State in a universe parallel to our own. Set in winter 1988–89, the novel "speculates" an alternative outcome to the still unresolved constitutional crisis that reached a climax in the early nineties with the failures of the Meech Lake and Charlottetown Accords.

Like Martel, Vonarburg creates a parallel Québec to critique political ideology and so to support an opposing view; but also, more particularly, to expose the detrimental effects of polarized ideological debates upon the development of the individual. While the Canadian State appears as a violent authoritarian regime, the leaders of the Francophone Enclave fare no better, being depicted as corrupt collaborators in the oppression of their own people. Vonarburg further blurs the cultural dichotomy between Anglophone and Francophone Canadians by focussing the attention of both on a mysterious state to the north inhabited by Native American and Métis peoples. Ultimately, the text absolves all figures of political guilt by revealing that Voyageurs from parallel worlds have been manipulating the situation in North America to explore their own political theories.

Vonarburg's novel rejects the stock genre SF strategy of uniting humanity by providing it with a common enemy in the Voyageurs; instead, it proposes a radical reconstruction of both individual and national identity that incorporates feminist critiques of patriarchal constructions of the Self. Rejecting the patriarchal, romantic conception of the Self as hero, the text's *Bildungsroman* centres on a forty-something, near-sighted divorcée,

Catherine Rhymer. Symbolically castrated (Catherine is literally disabled and must use a wheelchair when her leg is broken) and penetrated both physically (stabbed by a knife) and mentally (she suffers from possession-like hallucinations of a mysterious Presence), the subject represents a permeable being forged from duality. Rejecting the Freudian/Lacanian conception of the subject as a masculine being which develops in opposition to the female (m)other,[9] Vonarburg hypothesizes a feminist subject which develops by combining and recombining matter and experience in an endless continuum of interpenetrable life: "C'est ainsi que se créent les êtres, les consciences: par assimilation et intégration de ce qui était là auparavant, la chair et les idées, par détachements et récréations successives, une chaîne qui n'a ni commencement ni fin" (400–01). As the novel reveals that all on Earth are immigrants and result from a *métissage*, a material blending of native and alien life forces, the prejudices or entitlements of any one group must needs disappear, reconciling all to a common intermingled destiny.

Vonarburg, herself a French-born immigrant to Québec, uses her SF novels to explore the complexities not only of Québec nationalist ideology, but also of the entire problem of nationalism and individual identity in a (post-)colonial context, as seen in her pentalogy *Ryranaël* (1996–97). Unparalleled in Francophone SF for its scope and quality, the series interweaves the epic of Tyranaël's extra-terrestrial civilization with that of the Earth colonists who, finding an apparently abandoned planet, establish a new home. After several generations, the latter discover that their new environment has altered their genetic structure so greatly that these "nouveaux indigènes" (*Rêves* 332; see also *Jeu* 186–87) have less in common with the last residents of Earth than with the lost people of Tyranaël whose ruins they study.

Although the series universalizes its exploration of the colonial situation, clear references recall the author's real-life context. Apart from naming the planet Virginia after an early North American colony, it employs a stereotypically French-Canadian moniker for a character particularly involved in an identity struggle: "Ti-Jean" (*Rêves* 232ff). In addition to these nominal similarities, Vonarburg borrows from the social history of Québec in the making of her imaginary world. Virginian archaeologist Shandaar's discovery that during its development a particular group of Tyranéens "avaient bien compris que se reproduire, c'était survivre comme culture" (*Rêves* 222; see also *Jeu* 104) mirrors the *revanche du berceau* once vaunted by the Francophone population of Québec. Language also becomes a singular issue when Earth, facing natural destruction, decides to send its remaining population to Virginia. Not only does the linguistic tension between "virginien" and "anglam" parallel the French vs. English battles in Canada, but a group of Virginians establishes an *indépendantiste* party to separate itself from the "planète mère," Earth (*Jeu* 146–48; 250). The separatist "Vieux Colons" (*Jeu* 196) recall the stereotype of the traditionalist, agricultural *anciens canadiens* of Québec's heroicized pioneer past: they live in a region described in tourist brochures as "Le pays oublié par le temps" (*Rêves* 334) and want "[à] botter le cul aux Terriens" (*Jeu* 205). Vonarburg follows this cycle of interaction between colonizer and colonized for generations until, finally, with the discovery that the original inhabitants of Virginia survive in a parallel dimension and that individuals can traverse the gap between the two worlds, comes a reconciliation.

More overtly "feminist" themes appear in other Vonarburg works, such as *Le Silence de la cité* (1981) and *Chroniques du pays des mères* (1999), both of which deal with the issue of reproduction (either artificial or biological), the latter in a matriarchal dystopia. This kind of thematic feminism, as distinguished from the theoretical, experimental feminism found in Rochon, also appears overtly in the novels of Francine Pelletier. Like her mentor, Vonarburg, Pelletier uses her works to reproduce imaginary lands and worlds that thematically reflect her concerns with the issues of colonialism and identity; more specifically, she focuses upon female protagonists, the often restrictive roles available to women in the societies she creates, and the possibility for a heroine to break free and construct a positive, active identity. This emphasis marks her trilogy, *Le Sable et l'acier* (1997–99): each volume is titled eponymously after its heroine. The world of the first volume, *Nelle de Vilvêq*, greatly resembles that of Margaret Atwood's *Handmaid's Tale:* the state holds a monopoly on human reproduction in the Genete, a baby factory (and quite literally so). As a teenager, Nelle escapes the oppressive control of the state-run orphanages where the future children of the bourgeoisie are raised and flees to the Lower City, where both human workers and the genetically engineered slave race of "efas" live in Zolaesque conditions. In this patriarchal society, however, even in the underworld, Nelle must rely on her sexuality to survive; although she escapes the lowest form of prostitution on the streets, she becomes the mistress of powerful men. Samiva de Free, in the second volume, is the only female officer in the elite state police the "fad'i." In the final volume, these women meet and, with the help of the crone-figure Issabel de Qohosaten, defy a destructive, isolated society in order to establish a colony for people seeking freedom, peace, and equality.

Along with the practical feminism found in her female protagonist in search of self-actualization, Pelletier's work also evinces an overt concern for the political issues facing contemporary Québec: colonization, independence, and identity. Although the image may appear somewhat distorted, the reader can easily recognize Québec in the highly resonant place names that Pelletier employs. Several of her early short stories—"La Volière," *Le Temps des migrations*, and *Le Crime de l'Enchanteresse*, for example—centre on the discovery and colonization of the planet Arkadie, an obvious reference to Acadia. *Le Sable et l'acier* suggests that Nelle's home of Vilvêq and its neighbour, Moraille, are post-apocalyptic versions of Quebec City and Montréal in a world modified by massive desertification, irreversible pollution, and nuclear disaster. Samiva discovers that her people, the island inhabitants of Free, originated on Earth, leaving it at the time of a Grand Catastrophe to colonize the planet Sarion. The desire to dissolve and reconcile difference clearly manifests itself when Pelletier describes even the extra-terrestrial world of Sarion—itself home to a country called Franchelande, the map of which recalls France transposed onto a reversed Iberian Peninsula—as Earth in a parallel universe: when Samiva asks, "Sarion et la Terre sont une seule et même planète," she receives the answer, "Différentes, semblables, autres, mais la même" (*Issabel* 103).

The novels and short stories of Rochon, Vonarburg, and Pelletier reveal how by the nineties a feminist vernacular focussing on female protagonists and exploring the themes of gender, identity, reproduction, and mothering evolved in the SF written by women in Québec. The particular geographical and political situation of their home province, however, means that they speak that vernacular with a particular accent. Like their Anglophone counterparts in SF, Ursula K. LeGuin and Joanna Russ, they portray the struggle for individual recognition against an overtly patriarchal and authoritarian society; but, like many Québécois writers, as Esther Rochon herself observes, their works open up to consider "le collectif" as well (qtd in Lord 37), reflecting upon the issues directly affecting the community as well as the individual. Since their immediate community is Francophone Québec, when they present unflattering images of state authority, they have particular states in mind: Canada, Québec, or the United States. And as they expose how the binary oppositions created by the state work to oppress all individuals, they refer to a specific set of oppositions: man/woman, Anglophone/Francophone, colonizer/colonized, Canadian/Québécois. Yet, because their works seek to undermine those very sets of oppositions rather than docilely serve any political agenda, third and fourth poles intervene to disrupt the binarism. Just as Québec perceives itself as doubly colonized, and thus inherently more complex,[10] so too, the colonized worlds of SFQ by women also bear the traces of multiple layers of colonization. Ultimately, instead of opposition, these texts propose union through a feminist ideology of recognition and reconciliation. They imagine worlds in which difference may be recognized but not demonized, in which individuals resist hierarchy and marginalization in favour of freedom and equality.

Increasingly informed by feminist discourse over the past forty years, the SF women writers from Québec have used their work to reflect upon the contemporary political scene and the condition of the individual. Their imaginary worlds vary greatly in how closely they might parallel our own, yet they unfailingly propose a similar solution for the problems of identity faced by Québec and, indeed, the rest of the post-colonial world. While Rochon depicts a universalist struggle with an engulfing maternal instant in *Coquillage*, and Corriveau's Ixanor in *Compagnon du soleil* could be any totalitarian state, Vonarburg's *Les Voyageurs malgré eux* spares neither federal Canada nor separatist Québec in its alternate history. The reflection of Québec may be blurred, as in Pelletier's *Samiva de Free* set in the fictional Franchelande, or quite clear, as in Martel's *Quatre Montréalais en l'an 3000*; but whatever the setting, the embattled individual struggles against the forces of oppression in order, at last, to see not an Other but herself in the mirror.

NOTES

1. For a more detailed discussion of these works see my "(Un)common Ground: National Sovereignty and Individual Identity in Contemporary Science Fiction from Quebec," *Science-Fiction Studies* 27 (2000): 439–60.

2. Although Jean-Marc Gouanvic traces the origins of science fiction from Québec back to Philippe Aubert de Gaspé's *Influence d'un livre* (1837), the genre as such began to appear in French-Canadian literature in the early sixties with works such as Yves Thériault's *Si la bombe m'était conté* (1962) and André Ber's *Segoldiah!* (1964). For a historical review of Canadian SF in French see Jean-Marc Gouanvic, "Rational Speculations in French Canada, 1839–1974," *Science-Fiction Studies* 15 (1988): 71–81; and Daniel Sernine, "Historique de la SFQ," *Solaris* 79 (1988): 41–47.
3. In her essay "Four Québécois Dystopias, 1963–1974," *Science-Fiction Studies* 20 (1993): 383–393, Hélène Colas-Charpentier argues that Martel's novel, with its critique of technology and the urban space, also expresses ambivalence toward the reforms of the Quiet Revolution itself (385).
4. In spite of efforts to conceptualize national identity based on civil, rather than racial, religious, or cultural, criteria by intellectuals like Charles Taylor (*Reconciling the Solitudes* [Montreal: McGill-Queen's University Press, 1993]) and Fernand Dumont (*Raisons communes* [Montréal: Boréal, 1995]), and by groups such as the Mouvement national de Québécoises et Québécois (MNQ), this problem continues to haunt the sovereignty movement.
5. By 1975, Simone de Beauvoir's *Le Deuxième sexe* (1949) and Betty Friedan's *The Feminine Mystique* (1964) had influenced a generation; that year Hélène Cixous published "Le Rire de la Méduse" (*L'Arc* 61 [1975]: 31–53) and Catherine Clement *La Jeune née*; Luce Irigaray's *Speculum de l'autre femme* had appeared the year before. Meanwhile, the United States saw Kate Millett's *Sexual Politics* (1970) and Juliet Mitchell's *Psychoanalysis and Feminism* (1974).
6. As early as the fifties and sixties, the novels of Simone de Beauvoir (*Mémoires d'une jeune fille rangée*, 1958) and Marguerite Duras (*Moderato Cantabile*, 1958) focussed on the role of mothers in the development of the woman as individual. By the seventies and eighties, this had become a central theme in French- and English-language feminist novels, memoirs, and theory, as found, respectively, in Annie Ernaux's *La femme gelée* (1981), Nathalie Sarraute's *Enfance* (1983), and Nancy Chodorow's *The Reproduction of Mothering* (1978).
7. In an interview in *Voix et Images* (10 [1995]: 103–13), the editors of the NBJ attest to the significance of French feminist theory and novels on Québécois letters for their generation. Describing the program at the Université du Québec à Montréal, the literary review's co-founder Hugues Corriveau asserts that "[n]ous pourrions dire que nous sommes né(e)s de Cixous" (104); his colleague Louise Cotnoir affirms the influence of feminist and proto-feminist writers such as Luce Irigaray, Clarice Lispector, Virginia Woolf, and Violette Leduc (105).
8. The volumes of this cycle of clearly related works comprise *L'Étranger sous la ville* (Montréal: Éditions Paulines, 1986; previously published as *En hommage aux*

araignées [Montréal: L'Actuelle, 1974]); *L'Épuisement du soleil* (Longueil: Le Préambule, 1985; republished in two volumes as *Le Rêveur dans la citadelle* [Beauport: Alire, 1998] and *L'Archipel noir* [Beauport: Alire, 1999]); and *L'Espace du diamant* (Montréal: La Pleine Lune, 1990).

9. See in particular Madelon Spengnether, *The Spectral Mother: Freud, Feminism, and Psychoanalysis* (Ithaca: Cornell University Press, 1990).

10. Indeed, political and cultural analyst John Ralston Saul would argue that complexity is one of the defining characteristics not just of Québec but of Canada itself. See his *Confessions of a Siamese Twin* (Toronto: Viking, 1997).

WORKS CITED

Bonin, Linda. "Coquillage ou La spirale du désir." *Solaris* 110 (1994): 27–28.

Cixous, Hélène. "Le Rire de la Méduse." *L'Arc* 61 (1975): 31–53.

Corriveau, Monique. *Compagnon du soleil.* 3 Vols. Montréal: Fides, 1976.

Ketterer, David, and Esther Rochon. "Outside and Inside Views of Rochon's flic *Sheil.*" *Science-Fiction Studies* 29 (1992): 17–31.

Lord, Michel. "Esther Rochon." *Lettres Québécoises* 40 (1985–86): 36–39.

Martel, Suzanne. *Quatre Montréalais en l'an 3000.* Montréal: Éditions du Jour, 1963. Reprinted as *Surréal 3000.* Montréal: Éditions Héritage, 1980.

Pelletier, Francine. *Le Crime de l'enchanteresse.* Coll. "Jeunesse Pop 66." Montréal: Éditions Paulines, 1989.

——. *Issabel de Qohosaten. Le Sable et l'acier-3.* Beauport: Alire, 1999.

——. *Nelle de Vilvêq. Le Sable et l'acier-1.* Beauport: Alire, 1997.

——. *Samiva de Frée. Le Sable et l'acier-2.* Beauport: Alire, 1998.

——. *Le Temps des migrations.* Coll. "Chroniques du futur." Longueuil: Le Préambule, 1987.

——. "La Volière." *Imagine ...* 24 (1984): 19–31.

Rochon, Esther. *Aboli. Les Chroniques infernales-2.* Beauport: Alire, 1996.

——. *Coquillage.* Montréal: La Pleine Lune, 1986. Translated as *The Sheil.* Trans. David Lobdell. Ottawa: Oberon Press, 1990.

——. *Lame.* Montréal: Québec/Amérique, 1995.

——. *Or. Les Chroniques infernales-5.* Beauport: Alire, 1999.

——. *Ouverture. Les Chroniques infernales-3.* Beauport: Alire, 1997.

——. *Secrets. Les Chroniques infernales-4.* Beauport: Alire, 1998.

——. *Sorbier. Les Chroniques infernales-6/Le Cycle de Vrénalik.* Beauport: Alire, 2000.

Santoro, Miléna. "L'autre millénaire d'Esther Rochon." *Women in French Studies* 5 (1997): 97– 105.

Vonarburg, Élisabeth. *L'Autre rivage. Tyranaël-4.* Beauport: Alire, 1997.
——. *Chroniques du pays des mères.* Beauport: Alire, 1999.
——. *Le Jeu de la perfection. Tyranaël-2.* Beauport: Alire, 1996.
——. *La Mer allée avec le soleil. Tyranaël-5.* Beauport: Alire, 1997.
——. *Mon frère l'ombre. Tyranaël-3.* Beauport: Alire, 1997.
——. *Les Rêves de la mer. Tyranaël-I.* Beauport: Alire, 1996.
——. *Le Silence de la cité.* Paris: Denoêl, 1981.
——. *Les Voyageurs malgré eux.* Montréal: Québec/Amérique, 1994. Translated as *Reluctant Voyagers.* Trans. Jane Brierley. New York: Bantam, 1995.

"The World Is Its Own Place": Denys Chabot's Infernal Utopia

JEAN-FRANÇOIS LEROUX

At the outset of Cyrano de Bergerac's *L'Autre Monde ou Les États et Empires de la lune* (1657), the philosophic narrator-protagonist embarks on a journey to the moon. His purpose: to prove the contention of Pythagoras, Epicurus, Copernicus, and Kepler that the moon is another world like this one. Finding his target increasingly remote, however, he returns to Earth. Much to his astonishment, he discovers upon landing a place that at first sight seems to him every bit as strange as the moon: naked inhabitants flee from him and speak in a tongue he does not understand. And yet, a band of soldiers informs him that he is still in France. Their chief finally elucidates the mystery or paradox: he has alighted in ville Kébec.

The moon-bound hero of Bergerac's odyssey, the first such fantastic narrative with Canada as part of its setting, anticipates the fellow traveller across space and time in Québec author Denys Chabot's 1981 novel *La Province lunaire*. Lunatic revels naturally abound there, and over them presides a traveller uncannily like a Merry Andrew. Thus, as this essay works to suggest and sift the proposition, *La Province lunaire* not only recalls the mythic moon-travelling of Bergerac and its enduring affective value, but extends the exploration of Renaissance and Romantic myths of the New World that Chabot himself had begun in his first book, *L'Eldorado dans les glaces.*

Chabot's *L'Eldorado dans les glaces* (1978) records the hypnotic soliloquies of a monomaniac who, much like Coleridge's Ancient Mariner (a figure easy to identify in *La Province lunaire*), accosts a distraught narrator on a transatlantic crossing from Le Havre to Montréal. But unlike the Ancient Mariner, who eventually prays for wakefulness and trusts his Pilot to bring him safely home to port, this lunatic storyteller and his avatars subscribe to the dreamy, nighttime logic of poet Émile Nelligan's "Le Vaisseau d'or." There, it will be remembered, the poet's heart, "un navire déserté," tempest-tost and lulled by siren song, founders "dans l'abîme du Rêve" ("Vaisseau" 2: 13, 14).

Thus lost or engulfed in the world of their dreaming, the author's mental offspring attest to the impasse common, according to critic Maurice Laugaa's introduction to Cyrano's *L'Autre monde*, to all imaginative literature descended from the utopian genre. By way of illustration, appropriately enough, Laugaa instances the genre's Renaissance *locus classicus*, More's *Utopia*: "Who has seen one city of Utopia," affirms More, "has seen them all, since they are all more or less alike" (qtd in Laugaa 19). The reason (so Laugaa's introduction suggests) is that the "happy place" that utopia designates is "no-where" but in the mind. Reflecting on the utopian voyages of Plato, Campanella, Saint-Jean-de-Crévecœur, Fourier, Fénelon, and Baudelaire, the narrator of Chabot's *L'Eldorado* comes to a similar conclusion, asserting as he does the indifference of places: "Tout est dans la tête ... tout se situe à l'étage du cerveau, voyageries autant que sauvageries" (24). Consequently, and as Laugaa rightly goes on to argue, the hazard facing the utopian writer is that of repetition or similitude, even at the heart of contradiction and opposition (19). A reading of Chabot's first novel in the light of its Renaissance and Romantic antecedents confirms that diagnosis.

"Tout se répète ... tout se calque," so the dizzying play of shattered mirrors that makes up Chabot's *L'Eldorado dans les glaces* argues (24). Thus, for example, the initial narrator's fantastic avatars (whose names invoke the visionary works of Marlowe, Goethe, and Blake) double, multiply, and gainsay one another, as they shed the dubious light of circular unreason on each other's relations: "Ensemble et à des pôles opposés, chacun voulait mettre à nu la bestialité dénaturée de quelqu'un d'autre," as one of these latter, the Circe-like enchantress Béate, asserts (*L'Eldorado* 129). Seventeenth-century French sceptic Michel de Montaigne's essay "Des cannibales," which Béate here echoes, provides a further indication of the terms of reference and direction for her confounding of rhetorical opponents. "Chacun appelle barbarie ce qui n'est pas de son usage," so the seminal Renaissance skeptic likewise contends, and to similar effect (*Essais* 1.31.303). His tongue firmly in cheek, the Montaigne of "Des cannibales" then goes on to underscore his point with characteristic irony: "Sans mentir, au prix de nous, voilà des hommes bien sauvages; car, ou il faut qu'ils le soient bien à bon escient, ou que nous le soyons ... " (312). Rather, such oppositions or differences as we would maintain with respect to the rules of reason—between civilized and savage, here and there, new and old, true and false—are proof, in Montaigne's view as in the optic of Chabot's narrator, of our radical subjectivity: "Il semble que nous n'avons autre mire de la vérité et de la raison que l'exemple et idée des opinions et usances du pays où nous sommes" (*Essais* 1.31.303). In fact, because we "behold" truth and lies "with one same eyes" (to translate Montaigne's idiom in "Des boiteux" by way of Florio's), the two become virtually indistinguishable (*Essayes* 3.11.317). Though as well-fitted for imaginative journeying as the mythical shoe of Theramenes, a reason thus blind to distinctions cannot help, by the same token, but go always lame and halting (*torte, boiteuse et déhanchée*) (*Essais* 2.12.302). Every step forward is also one in reverse—so the sceptic, framing his own vision of the ideal republic within a discussion of the peculiar virtues of the stoical savage, illustrates in the movement of his own thought the contradictions he finds in Lucretius's account of the cosmos as flux and reflux (*Essais* 2.12.307). In the words of Ecclesiastes, a text never far from Montaigne's thoughts, there is nothing new under the sun. Appropriately, then, it is with the image of a universe "en paralysie" that Montaigne leaves his reader in his later reconsideration of the meeting of the Old and New Worlds (*Essais* 3.6.169).

Proceeding "par voie d'analogie" (like his soliloquist tossing his "monocle" coin-like from one eye to the other, and like his Béate substituting a synthetic vision infused with the "ténèbres mystiques" of an "opium visionnaire" for the half-sight or double vision of science imaged in her husband Faustin's fractured "binocle"), Chabot similarly inscribes spheres within spheres within spheres, "ces pures créations de l'esprit qui sait rêver, et rêve pour savoir plus de choses encore," only to come to a dead standstill (*L'Eldorado* 21, 1, 163, 164, 152, 165, 155–56). By thus involving the reader in the smoky concatenations of a content and a container winding like a boa in a half-, a cat's-paw- and a pig's-tail-knot all twined together,

Chabot's baroque "gaie science"—"une perpétuelle confession d'ignorance," in Montaigne's expression (*Essais* 2.12.224)—aims to lull "la mourante conscience de qui retrouve la fièvre léthargique, l'immobile et doux sommeil," with the musical thinking so conducive to the inner consolations of unreason: "Qui trouve son double se perd," goes the subtitle to *L'Eldorado*'s first chapter (155–56, 130, 164–65, 7).[1] The mystical sum of these paradoxes quite deliberately confounds the additions of logic, "ennemie ... de tout mystère" (21). But by the same token, such two-way mirror-work, a mere "mirage de symétrie," courts "la même morne grisaille de l'ennui" which is the result, in Chabot's work, of an increasingly all-encompassing sameness (144, 153). *La nuit*, as the saying goes, *tout les chats sont gris*. In effect, while the narrator promises his readers that "ces énigmes trouveront d'elles-même à s'éclaircir," the illumination reflexively conferred by paradox can only be, by analogy, twilight (3). A figment of the mind's imagining, the bright New World Eldorado dreamed of by Chabot's protagonists necessarily leaves them *sur leur appétit*, since it is apparently nowhere to be found.

There is one place, however, according to another long tradition opposite but (so the author's work astutely suggests) not unapposite to that of secular utopia, amenable to the confusion of such coordinates as north and south, west and east, in the mind of the perceiver. Naturally enough, then, Chabot's capacious imagination gravitates to that *topos*. Among the clues to his own identity that the author's first protagonist, Oberlin, finds, for example, are some pages torn from an edition of Dante annotated by the mystic Emmanuel Swedenborg (*L'Eldorado* 26). In a figure cognate to the viciously circular logic animating Chabot's Eldorado, his Faustin presides over an island of "captifs dantesques" locked, like the Wrathful in the fifth circle of Dante's *Inferno* and Montaigne's self-cannibalizing cannibals, in internecine warfare, "rivés bec à bec ... comme des vautours enserrés qui s'empoignent au sang" (*L'Eldorado* 99, 100). The enchanted island itself is compared to an iceberg "dérivant dans son redoutable équilibre," as well as to the green Paradiso that Danish explorers dreamed of discovering, only to find "un inhabitable désert de glace" (84, 85). The self-consuming nature of a Promethean doubt in which "toute folie devait avoir son endroit comme son envers" gradually traces out the contours of Chabot's Eldorado (129), to which revellers ferry on rafts as over Milton's "Lethean sound" in *Paradise Lost* (2.604). "In Equivocal Worlds Up & Down are Equivocal," in the words of William Blake's gloss to the thirty-fourth canto of Dante's *Inferno*, in which the world appears "Upside Down When viewd from Hells Gate"—and yet (as inscribed in reverse by Blake underneath) "right When Viewd from Purgatory" (690).

The synthetic and polar logic of Hell's innermost circle, "to which all gravities from every part are drawn" (*Inferno* 34.184), goes a long way toward explaining why Chabot's utopia finishes *en queue de poisson*, its protagonists inescapably caught in "une représentation théâtrale" (*L'Eldorado* 200). If the "mind is its own place," as Milton's Satan and his Romantic apologists maintain (*Paradise Lost* 1.254), then the world it figures for itself (so Chabot's self-imprisoned protagonists come to reflect, having realized the full extent of their solipsistic enclosure) must be merely one of mirrors: "Des rêves donnaient la clef de toutes choses mais dans un monde fermé, sans portes ni serrures" (175). Indeed, the price of Mephistophelean glee is unreason and suicide. In Chabot's imaginary, hyperborean world, as in Blake's circumscription of the ever-proliferating "convexities" in Swedenborg's *Heaven and Hell* (1784), "hell is the outward or external of heaven" (Blake, 602). The passage of time draws "une ... spirale coincée," as it works out an entropic synthesis of self-canceling opposites in "un superbe maelström" (*L'Eldorado* 113, 114) similar to that which blasts Thomas Carlyle's dualists in the logic of the "UNFATHOMABLE" to eternity in the Arctic "June Midnight" featured in *Sartor Resartus*'s hellish "Centre of Indifference" (138, 137): "Enchevêtrement et absorbtion de toutes choses se muant les unes en les autres," in Chabot's description (114). The image of "flammes blanches" in Chabot's work (*L'Eldorado* 114), like the "fiery snow" of the *Inferno,* which Carlyle again revisits in his essay "The Hero as Poet" (*On Heroes* 106), conjoins the extremes that beset the inhabitants of the former's fiery-glacial Eldorado, where, in the words of Milton, "the parching Air / Burns frore, and cold performs the effect of Fire" (*Paradise Lost* 2.594–95). However, where Carlyle's hero, Teufelsdöckh, languishing in "slow-consuming fire" and feeding on his "own heart, clutches round him outwardly, on the NOT-ME for wholesomer food" (*Sartor* 130), Chabot's Faustin, a daydreaming, drowning Tantalus, strives in vain to grasp the oblivion conferred by the waters of Lethe. He is likened to "un noyé insomnieux à qui la mort en eau profonde n'aurait pu imposer son sommeil" (*L'Eldorado* 183). Undying unrest seems only too appropriate a fate for one who wakes sleeping and sleeps waking, as in Montaigne's description of a sleepwalking, fever-wracked humanity (*Essais* 2.12.342, 307).

Chabot's first book culminates in an imaginative impasse. Why, then, logically speaking, does he follow up with another? Or—to put the problem in the terms used by Laugaa in his concluding remarks on Cyrano de Bergerac's *L'Autre Monde*—how can one conceive of a world where contradictions are fecund rather than fatal (24)? Chabot's following book, *La Province lunaire*, suggests an answer. Though similarly bound for an Eldorado which its inventor has never seen, Chabot's adventurers in *La Province lunaire* (the descendants of the builders of Babel and the survivors of Atlantis in search of a mythical land conjoining the paradise losts and Happy Isles of antiquity with the solar cities of the future) seem quite indifferent to the indications of impasse tacit here as in Chabot's previous incursion into "LA LIGNE BRISÉE DU LYRISME BAROQUE" (145, 162, 126). In effect, what Montaigne says of the sceptical Pyrrhonians is also true of Chabot's moonbound protagonists—"tout leur est un" (*Essais* 2.12.222). If you tell them that snow is black, they tell you that it is white. If you tell them it is neither, they maintain it is both; and so on. Near the end of *L'Eldorado dans les glaces*, a polar light entrances Chabot's avatar into a dream that similarly marries "la neige d'une redoutable blancheur" with its opposite, "noir" (190, 191). But whereas in *L'Eldorado* the self-cancelling contradiction suggests a dead end, of sameness and indifference, in *La Province lunaire* the image of a universal blank is said to be a fecund one. Dreams are no more an "absence," insists Chabot's present narrator, than white is colourless, since, just as white contains every colour, so, too, are dreams the repositories of all "forces" (*La Province* 268). Like the "cabinet de curiosités de quelque savant de l'âge baroque" which the travellers encounter on their northwestern errand, the utopian fabulist's fiction is only limited, it seems, by the extent or scope of his invention. Chabot illustrates at length, listing, improvisationally, some of the contents of his cabinet of curios: a necklace made of ermine teeth; balloons shriveled like old dung; boxes of fireworks; a round table for spirit rapping; a branding iron; clothes-brushes in a pair of lambskin boots; a book of instructions for the voyager who wanders into the secret empires of the dead; a broken portable solar dial-plate that dilates the time; some used tobacco chew; a broken mirror belonging to a horoscope machine; litres of alcohol denatured to kill insects; a marble goddess wearing a bronze wig; a magic clock-lantern irradiating time in space; strange shells from the West Indies; and so on and so forth—"ça n'en finissait pas," Chabot's narrator interjects (204–05).

True to the imaginative scepticism and hellish subjectivity basic to his enterprise, the harlequin virtuoso intent on celebrating the baroque imaginary he sees as the wellspring of Québec culture (Chabot's third and latest novel is appropriately entitled *La Tête des eaux* [1997]) reverses positions and comes full circle. If the mind is its own place, it is free to "make a Heav'n of Hell, a Hell of Heav'n," as Milton's Satan would have it (*Paradise Lost* 1.255). Where Chabot saw black, he now sees white, and where he once implied a theological order of values, he now implies a secular one. A source of wonder, the "cosmos" (as the author of *La Province lunaire* affirms with Renaissance sages) is in man, the Little World, or nowhere ("nulle part") (235).

Chabot's work thus betrays a substantial ambivalence. On the one hand, as the bit of narrative from Bergerac's *L'Autre monde* that served as our starting-point suggests, utopia is where the secular mind of the imaginative Québec writer is most at home. Fittingly, then, Chabot's aerial acrobat in *La Province lunaire* never entirely leaves the ground. Assisted by the uncertain light of the moon, he only seems to fly. On the other hand, though, the marriage of Québec's folklore with "a cosmopolitan literary strain" so brilliantly achieved in Chabot's first novel (Sénécal 85–93)[2] tends to foster the sense of placelessness, timelessness, and thus of sameness associated with the genre of utopia as a whole. Followed as it is by a reference to the freezing of which Chabot's previous Romantic protagonists are victims, an ironic allusion in his *La Tête des eaux*—which otherwise confines itself more narrowly to Québec lyricism and folklore—suggests the author's abiding awareness of the perils that adhere to his allegiance to the mind's country. The allusion is to the hero of Thomas De Quincey's *Confessions of an Opium-Eater* (1822), who dreams of making his home in snowbound Québec (*La Tête des eaux* 40). "Tout est dans la tête ... tout se situe à l'étage du cerveau, voyageries autant que sauvageries," Chabot would seem to repeat (*L'Eldorado* 24). As such, however, one voyage is as good as another. There is no reason to read on. Who has seen one city of utopia has seen them all.

NOTES

1. André J. Sénécal's study of Chabot's *L'Eldorado dans les glaces* from the perspective of fantastic literature includes an extended consideration of his use of the "*doppelgänger* motif" (85). "Chabot's original invention," rightly notes Sénécal, "resists cause-and-effect analysis" (86).

2. Though Sénécal reads this marriage as evidence of Chabot's success, the aesthetic criteria that he uses are, of course, different from my own (92). The fantastic "depends on the postponement of an answer" to the questions about ultimate reliability and reality the author's various narrators raise: "Chabot freezes time ..." (87, 90). This freezing can also be perceived in Chabot's characteristic move away, temporally and spatially, from ville Kébec, the seat of political power and ambition, into a mythical past that abides in Québec's folklore, notably in that of the Abitibi region that he has spent some time researching.

WORKS CITED

Blake, William. *The Complete Poetry and Prose of William Blake*. Ed. David Erdman with a commentary by Harold Bloom. Berkeley and Los Angeles: University of California Press, 1982.

Carlyle, Thomas. *On Heroes, Hero-Worship, and the Heroic in History*. Ed. Archibald MacMechan. Boston: Athenaeum, 1902.

——. *Sartor Resartus*. Ed. with an introduction by Kerry McSweeney and Peter Sabor. Oxford: Oxford University Press, 1987.

Chabot, Denys. *L'Eldorado dans les glaces*. Montréal: Éditions Hurtubise HMH, 1978.

——. *La Province lunaire*. LaSalle, Québec: Éditions Hurtubise HMH, 1981.

——. *La Tête des eaux*. Montréal: XYZ, 1997.

Cyrano de Bergerac. *Voyages dans la lune (L'Autre Monde ou les États et Empires de la Lune)*. Ed. with an introduction by Maurice Laugaa. Paris: Garnier-Flammarion, 1970.

Dante Alighieri. *The Divine Comedy*. Transl. John Aitken Carlyle, Thomas Okey, and Philip H. Wickstead. New York: Modern Library, 1932.

Montaigne, Michel de. *Essais*. Ed. Pierre Michel with prefaces by André Gide, Albert Thibaudet, and Maurice Merleau-Ponty. 3 vols. Paris: Gallimard, 1965.

——. *The Essayes of Michael Lord of Montaigne*. Transl. John Florio. 3 vols. London, Edinburgh, Glasgow, New York and Toronto: Henry Frowde, 1904.

Nelligan, Émile. *Poésies*. Ed. with a preface by Louis Dantin. Québec: Éditions du Boréal, 1996.

Sénécal, André J. "The Use of the Fantastic in Denys Chabot's *L'Eldorado dans les glaces*." *Canadian Literature* 104 (1985): 85–93.

The Ordinary and the Fabulous: Canadian Fantasy Literature for Children

JUDITH SALTMAN

THE FOLLOWING IS A SURVEY of Canadian fantasy literature for children in English and its major subgenres and trends viewed in the international context of nineteenth-century juvenile fantasy. Definitions and categories are, of course, constricting, especially in the case of fantasy, which is marked by an ineffable sense of otherness and magic. Nevertheless, fantasy leaves its mark, much as that quintessential fantasy hero Harry Potter is branded on his forehead with the lightning bolt of defiant magic. In fact, the literary form of fantasy, in its historical shape as a genre of children's literature, is recognized precisely by its inclusion of an element of otherness, magic, or wonder, something beyond the quotidian. The roots of fantasy lie deep in the oral tradition of folklore, legend, and mythology; it is often fueled by archetype and dream. Like the earliest myths and human stories, from the *Odyssey* and Gilgamesh epics onward, the fantasy narrative often echoes the monomyth of the hero's quest, including journey and pilgrimage, trials and tests, honour and betrayal, drama and tragedy. In setting, plot, or character, it is a threshold literature, exploring the boundaries of the possible and finding mystery in the ordinary and the fabulous alike.

Fantasy crosses boundaries of readership as well. Unlike the sharply divided territories of realistic fiction for children and adults, where we are unlikely ever to find an eleven-year-old reading John Updike, fantasy's appeal spans age groups, from child through young adult to adult reader. In his essay "On Three Ways of Writing for Children," C. S. Lewis writes, "I am almost inclined to set it up as a canon that a children's story which is enjoyed only by children is a bad children's story. ... This canon seems to me most obviously true of that particular type of children's story which is dearest to my own taste, the fantasy or fairy tale" (210). Lewis and J. R. R. Tolkien also remind us that fairy tales, which they subsume under the fantasy genre, are natural and life-long reading tastes. In his "On Fairy-Stories," Tolkien comments on fairy-stories and fantasy: "Only some children, and some adults, have any special taste for them.... It is a taste, too, that would not appear ... very early in childhood ... [and] it is certainly one that does not decrease but increases with age, if it is innate" (35).

Fantasy is perhaps the only genre to find children and adults reading the same book, as more recently witnessed by the popularity of J. K. Rowling's *Harry Potter and the Philosopher's Stone* (1997) and, on a subtler and less marketed level, without the baggage of wizards, enchantments, and dragons, that of Philip Pullman's *Northern Lights* (1995). Their deeply moral and philosophical expressions in mythopoeic form appeal to a particular temperament found in all age groups.

E. M. Forster tells us in *Aspects of the Novel* (1927) that the fantastic "demands an additional adjustment because of the oddness of its method or subject matter—like a sideshow in an exhibition where you have to pay sixpence as well as the original fee" (160). Fantasy requires Coleridge's "willing suspension of disbelief ... which constitutes poetic faith" (169). According to Tolkien, fantasy must command that literary or "Secondary Belief" by offering a fully credible inner logic ("On Fairy-Stories" 36). He states that the power of the fairy-story (and, by extension, fantasy) lies in its ability to command belief through the creation of "a quality of strangeness and wonder" shaped by logic, law, and prohibition: "To make a Secondary World inside which the green sun will be credible, commanding Secondary Belief, will probably require labour and thought, and will certainly demand a special skill, a kind of elvish craft" (44, 45). He goes on to define the central literary and emotional effect of fantasy as "a catch of the breath, a beat and lifting of the heart..." (60). That is, fantasy is not escapist in a negative sense; rather, it offers the reader an encouraging refreshment of the spirit. Tolkien's paradigm of fantasy as Recovery,

Escape, and Consolation applies as deeply to children's as to adult fantasy (43).

A short summary of the development of children's fantasy from the Victorian age to the present day provides a useful backdrop to Canadian fantasy. Fantasy dominated nineteenth-century British children's literature. It was the forming spirit of early-nineteenth-century folklore scholarship that acted as a harbinger for the revolutionary writing of Victorian fantasy for children, writing that left behind the didactic and cautionary moral tales for children that had preceded it. Hans Christian Andersen and the Grimm Brothers influenced the development of the literary fairy tale and the first fantasies—from John Ruskin's Germanic *The King of the Golden River* (1851) to Lewis Carroll's *Alice's Adventures in Wonderland* (1865), with its imaginative amalgam of nonsense, wit, and elegant dream fantasy. Oscar Wilde's ironic and poignant literary fairy tales in *The Happy Prince and Other Tales* (1888) looked back at Andersen in their bittersweet tone. George MacDonald's *At the Back of the North Wind* (1871) and *Princess and the Goblin* books (1872) further shaped the development of children's fantasy through their mythic and archetypal quests and high moral concepts.

At the turn of the century, Rudyard Kipling continued Carroll's linguistic play in his *Just So Stories* (1902) and introduced heroic animal fantasy in *The Jungle Book* (1894), while Edith Nesbit introduced the topic of time travel with deep social conscience in *Harding's Luck* (1909). Nesbit also developed the subgenre of the light, witty fantasy in which magic goes haplessly wrong with hilarious consequences in *The Five Children and It* (1902). She set a standard for the misunderstood magic tradition that continued through Edward Eager's *Half-Magic* series (1954).

Kenneth Grahame refined Kipling's animal fantasy in his Edwardian *The Wind in the Willows* (1908), in which he melded the themes of the love of the magical world of nature and the pleasure of the wild with the domestic friendship of animals whose "society" resembles a gentleman's social club. J. M. Barrie's *Peter Pan* (first published as *Peter and Wendy* [1911]) was even more quintessentially Edwardian, a story of secret gardens and other worlds, where childhood adventures and play borrow from the high melodrama of the Victorian *Penny Dreadfuls*—the sensationalized boy's magazines of Barrie's own childhood—idealized to the point of sentimentality. The sentimental nursery fantasy written for two levels of adult and child reader continued in A. A. Milne's *Winnie the Pooh* stories, *Winnie-the-Pooh* (1926) and *The House at Pooh Corner* (1928), with their linguistic play and warm, witty parables of animated animal toys.

Following the Edwardian period, fantasy slowly diverged into two strains of writing for children: low fantasy and high fantasy. Low fantasy is usually set in this world. Characters, incidents, and quite often physical laws of reality may be altered and exaggerated for humorous effect. High or epic fantasy is often for older child readers, teenagers, and adults, and incorporates elements of Tolkien's Secondary Reality, the concept of the created "other-world" (Tolkien 39–40). High fantasy traditionally presents the ongoing, epic battle of good versus evil within the construct of a mythic, folkloric, or feudal world.

Through the twentieth century, low fantasy developed within such subgenres as the tales of personified toys and inanimate objects, as found in Rumer Godden's *The Doll's House* (1947) and Lynne Reid Banks's *The Indian in the Cupboard* series (1980). Following in the traditions of Carlo Collodi's *The Adventures of Pinocchio* (1892) and Hans Christian Andersen, stories in this subgenre focus on the fascination with the miniature and the mystery of life quickening as toys come alive. Also within the Low Fantasy category, there developed a light, comic fantasy of exaggerated character traits, stretched physical laws, and nonsense extending to sharp satire. Examples include Astrid Lindgren's story of a heroically strong, self-possessed, folkloric girl in *Pippi Longstocking* (1950) and Mary Norton's saga of miniature people who hide among the floorboards in *The Borrowers* (1952). Both take place in this world, the primary real world, only slightly skewed from our perceived reality.

Turning to high fantasy—the secondary realities of other worlds with their compelling inner logic, invented geography, language, history, and mythology—this form gave us J. R. R. Tolkien's Middle Earth in *The Hobbit; or, There and Back Again* (1937) and *The Lord of the Rings* (1954–55), C. S. Lewis's land of Narnia in *The Lion, the Witch and the Wardrobe* (1950) and the remaining *Narnia Chronicles*, and Ursula LeGuin's archipelago world of Earthsea in *A Wizard of Earthsea* (1968). These mythopoeic and inventively thrilling narratives explore the presence of magic in worlds rich in the ongoing battle of good versus evil. Such fantasies are layered with folk and mythic imagery, and possess a serious belief in the moral quest of human life, its acts of choice, failure, and courage. They owe much in particular to Celtic and Norse folklore and mythology, and the Arthurian Matter of Britain.

A new kind of epic fantasy, which is set not in a secondary reality but in this primary world, developed in the mid-twentieth century in works by such writers as Susan Cooper in her *Dark is Rising* series (1973), and Alan Garner in *Elidor* (1965) and *The Owl Service* (1967). The child and adolescent characters may travel through a rent in the cloth from this world to another Secondary World (as in Narnia), or the forces of the other world, powerful, mythic, and often treacherous, may move into ours. Indeed, parallel worlds may commingle, as in Rowling's *Harry Potter* series, in which the separate but sliding worlds of human Muggles and of supernatural witches and wizards jostle comically, uncomfortably, and at times tragically. Or the fabric of our world may be subtly altered to create a historical reality that never existed. For example, Philip Pullman's faux Victorian *Northern Lights*, which combines the obsessive Arctic exploration of the era, a new alignment of church, state, and academe, an eerie quest for the human soul, and an investigation into the nature of god.

Another subgenre of fantasy, which Sheila Egoff terms "Enchanted Realism" (99), is somewhat similar to magic realism in its this-worldly setting, but also introduces a delicately transformed reality and a focus on the mysteries of time and human consciousness across generations. Natalie Babbitt's *Tuck Everlasting* (1975), a morality play on eternal life, is a fine example.

Yet another subgenre is time-travel fantasy, sometimes referred to as time-slip or past time fantasy. Quite sophisticated, this hybrid of historical fiction and fantasy offers narratives of children moving across a threshold of time into the past through the magical aid of a talisman or ritual, or through the power of psychic displacement. Philippa Pearce's *Tom's Midnight Garden* (1958) and Lucy Boston's *The Children of Green Knowe* series (1954) both use old houses and magic gardens as settings in which lonely, displaced children find friendship and solace in the past. Understanding of mutability and loss is strong in these time-travel stories.

Animal fantasy continued to change over the twentieth century, with some stories becoming more sharply satirical in the Aesopian tradition of illuminating human flaws and foibles. Some works are sombre and misanthropic, such as Richard Adams's *Watership Down* (1972), or bleakly ironic, as in the case of Russell Hoban's *The Mouse and His Child* (1967).

By contrast, other authors moved to a younger, gentler, but equally serious focus on the natural world as magical and radiant, as evinced in E. B. White's classic barnyard fable *Charlotte's Web* (1967).

The late twentieth century saw supernatural and horror elements from adult fantasy and popular culture enter children's fantasy. The ghost story has always been a standard of children's literature, at times reaching a subtle and even comic level, as in Penelope Lively's *The Ghost of Thomas Kempe* (1986). Experimental, atmospheric fantasies have evolved beyond simple ghost or supernatural motifs, which are more sophisticated and dark in tone, including elements of ESP, horror, and witchcraft. In this new style of psychological fantasy, psychic and supernatural powers replace the old-fashioned, traditional magic and Arthurian Matter in the struggle between good and evil. Margaret Mahy's witchcraft thriller *The Changeover* (1981) is a prime example.

Science fiction is considered by some to be a subgenre of fantasy. Speculative fiction that addresses the big questions of the future of society, technology, and the environment also appeals to children, particularly during the period of cognitive growth at puberty. The hard science fiction and the space opera of the early twentieth century have shifted over time to soft science fiction focusing on more sociological and psychological dimensions. From Jules Verne's Victorian science fiction adventures, such as *Twenty Thousand Leagues under the Sea* (1873), which both children and adults enjoyed, to Madeleine L'Engle's didactic and magical *A Wrinkle in Time* (1962) and more recent science fiction, the tone and imagery has become progressively darker and more realistic. Science fiction for children today is less adventure than struggle, less utopian than dystopian, following in this emphasis themes in adult science fiction of environmental degradation, societal collapse, totalitarian government, amoral scientific experimentation, and dangerous technology.

Where does Canadian fantasy fit into this scheme of international trends and patterns? It entered the game very late by comparison with British, American, and Australian fantasy writing for children. Canadian writing for children in general was strongly realistic or historical from its beginnings in the late nineteenth century. Canada did not seem to offer potential fantasists a tradition of magic analogous to the bottomless well of Arthurian and Celtic lore that had sustained the development of British fantasy. Canadian children's literature continued to chronicle the ordinary rather than the fabulous until the sixties and seventies, when a small number of writers began exploring different forms of fantasy. Interestingly, the most successful of these fantasies were reality-based.

Canadian fantasists for children before the seventies did not reinterpret or appropriate the oral tradition of this new land, so different from the European model. They appeared to experience the enormity and alien otherness of the Canadian landscape as inhospitable to envisioning fantasy, particularly Secondary Realities. Only one early writer of note attempted to consider the power of Native lore and the challenge of a Canadian landscape. In the fifties, before the concepts of cultural appropriation came into use, Catherine Anthony Clark, in *The Golden Pine Cone* (1950) and other works, attempted to shape a new Canadian genre by mingling First Nations imagery and legend with the British Columbia wilderness. It would be another thirty years before other writers followed her lead.

A young writer in the sixties, Ruth Nichols, wrote Tolkien and Lewis-style quest fantasies with recognizably Canadian settings—Vancouver and Ontario's Georgian Bay area give way to Secondary Realities in her books *A Walk Out of the World* (1969) and *The Marrow of the World* (1972).

In the seventies and eighties, Canadian fantasists for children seemed more comfortable with the ordinary than the fabulous, ignoring what Tolkien has called the elvish craft of creating secondary worlds or realities. Instead, they focused on this world, the primary and often recognizably Canadian world, both contemporary and historical. Janet Lunn, Kit Pearson, and Margaret Buffie, for example, all wrote breakthrough Canadian time-travel fantasies in which pubescent and adolescent girls, fueled by generational conflict and the misery of dislocation, slip into the past or observe its unfolding as mute witness. Janet Lunn's *The Root Cellar* (1981) is also strong historical fiction: her protagonist ventures through the horror-filled wasteland of the American Civil War before returning to contemporary southern Ontario with a newfound solacing perspective to soothe her divided heart and family. Kit Pearson, in *A Handful of Time* (1987), and Margaret Buffie, in *Who Is Frances Rain?* (1987), work with the device of the talisman—an old pocket watch, a pair of spectacles—to give their protagonists actual revelations of family histories and generational tragedy as they observe (rather than participate in) the past. Margaret Laurence's miniature *The Olden Days Coat* (1979) also brings a girl to her grandmother's childhood through gentle and delicate magic.

In the nineties, time-travel fantasy embraced less personal or individual pasts. Instead, larger themes of social injustice and historical tragedy entered the subgenre. Julie Lawson's *White Jade Tiger* (1993) explores the cruel treatment of Chinese labourers on the Canadian railway; Kevin Major's *Blood Red Ochre*, the political genocide of the Beothuk people of Newfoundland.

Also in the nineties, several fantasists sent their characters into the mythological and ancient past of Celtic legend and early Irish history. The most successful of these has been O. R. Melling in her *Chronicles of Faerie*. In *The Hunter's Moon* (1993) and *The Summer King* (1999), Melling propels her adolescent girls, visiting Ireland from Canada, into a maelstrom of faerie magic, lore, and legend. The haunted and glittering underworld of the ancient Celtic faerie realm draws the girls into heroic quest, romance, and transformation of self as myth and history are retold and re-envisioned.

Welwyn Wilton Katz explores the obsessive righting of ancient wrongs and the pain of culture clash against the backdrop of Canadian history and place in the exceptional *Out of the Dark* (1995). Set in Newfoundland's Viking settlement at L'Anse aux Meadows, this dark and riveting tale of guilt and revenge brings together Norse sagas, the first Viking settlers to Canada, and contemporary family tragedy.

Classic high fantasy of the epic kind has been less successful in Canada than has that of time-travel. More success has been found in experimentation. A handful of fantasists moved in the eighties and nineties in the direction of the experimental and psychological new fantasy. Michael Bedard and Katz, for example, are eclectic in their approaches, blending time-travel with the ghost story and horror with young adult realism. In *A Darker Magic* (1987) and *Painted Devil* (1994), Bedard depicts credible realistic home lives and teenage concerns, into which setting he subtly introduces Mephistophelian magicians and puppeteers searching for human souls. The ensuing struggle of good versus evil does not involve swords, wizardry, or traditional magic. Their place has been usurped by extra-sensory perception, supernatural power, human moral choice, and the light of everyday as weapons in the battle against the dark.

Katz is also a practitioner of the new psychic fantasy. She synthesizes contemporary young adult issues with Arthurian Matter in *The Third Magic* (1988), an ambitious epic drama in which a science fiction world of gender magic and war provides the setting for a re-enactment of the Arthurian romance.

Several fantasists use postmodern approaches to deconstruct traditional fantasy conventions. Sarah Ellis and Priscilla Galloway alter folklore and fantasy motifs, settings, or characters to destabilize readers' expectations of the genre. Ellis's short-story collection *Back of Beyond* (1996) introduces fairy tale characters, from the helpful Selkie to malign spirits, into the precarious lives of modern teenagers. Galloway, in *Truly Grim Tales* (1995), drastically alters the classic stories to illuminate their thematic inner core. In both Ellis and Galloway, surrealism casts an eerie light.

Canadian animal fantasy for children has had few adherents and little achievement until recent years, although the first animal fantasy appeared very early in Canadian publishing, in 1900. *Mooswa and Others of the Boundaries*, by W. A. Fraser, derives from Kipling's heroic animal clan fantasies but utilizes anthropomorphized Canadian wildlife—including the moose, the bear, the fox, the wolf, and the wolverine. Despite the attempts of such considerable talents as Margaret Laurence (her animal fantasy, *Jason's Quest*, is surprisingly flat), it was not until the nineties that strong animal fantasy appeared. Kenneth Oppel, in *Silverwing* (1997) and its sequel *Sunwing* (1999), creates a convincing world of bat emotions, physiological life, communication, history, and mythology. Since Adams could create a full fantasy world for rabbits in *Watership Down*, it should be no surprise that, given Oppel's livelier material, his works are equally fascinating. The young bat's quest for a home and his lost father becomes an odyssey of spiritual dimension as well as an adventurous high fantasy as he heroically leads the bats in a battle against evil.

Light, comic fantasy set in the real world with a slight cast of inventive exaggeration or satire has only one big-name practitioner. Mordecai Richler's *Jacob Two-Two* series (1975), of slapstick and farcical romp, pits children against cruel and avaricious adult caricatures. More notable in emotional depth, plot twists, and clever premise is Richard Scrimger's *The Nose from Jupiter* (1998) and its sequel, in which a tiny alien flies his spaceship from Jupiter into the nose of an otherwise average Canadian thirteen-year-old boy.

Canadian science fiction for children has one grand master—Monica Hughes. Hughes's world-renowned work is deeply influenced by Canadian landscape and cultural diversity, whether it is set on Earth in the Arctic, in

Alberta after future ecological disaster, or on a barren, wilderness lighthouse planet in space, as in *The Keeper of the Isis Light* (1980) and its sequels. Hughes's stories are philosophical wrestlings with scientific concepts and sociological issues ranging from intolerance and bigotry and the clash of cultures to the misuse of technology and the abuse of the environment. All her narratives are driven by adventure as well as thought, and are tempered by careful consideration of the earth's future.

It has been a long journey for Canadian fantasy, with missteps and trials upon its path. Original talents have emerged, demonstrating invention and vision. They have not always been successful at creating that convincing inner fantasy logic that Tolkien required. Canadian fantasy for children, however, in its delicate balance of the ordinary and the fabulous, does convince at its emotional core. Indeed, it illuminates the ordinary, casting light on its innate mystical force and power, and simultaneously articulates and renders comprehensible the fabulous, that which is other and transcendent. For fantasy can bring these two seeming opposites together in a new continuum, a refreshed reality. Using metaphors of magic and parables of quest and discovery, Canadian juvenile fantasy explores for young people newly on their own paths the adventurous and spiritual dimensions of human life which have always been the matter of fantasy.

WORKS CITED

Adams, Richard. *Watership Down.* New York: Macmillan, 1972.

Andersen, Hans Christian. *Wonderful Stories for Children.* London: Chapman & Hall, 1846.

Babbitt, Natalie. *Tuck Everlasting.* New York: Farrar, 1975.

Banks, Lynne Reid. *The Indian in the Cupboard.* London: Dent, 1980.

Barrie, J. M. *Peter and Wendy.* London: Hodder & Stoughton, 1911.

Bedard, Michael. *A Darker Magic.* Don Mills: Collier, 1987.

——. *Painted Devil.* Toronto: Lester, 1994.

Boston, Lucy. *The Children of Green Knowe.* London: Faber & Faber, 1954.

Buffie, Margaret. *Who Is Frances Rain?* Toronto: Kids Can Press, 1987.

Carroll, Lewis. *Alice's Adventures in Wonderland.* London: Macmillan & Co., 1865.

Clark, Catherine Anthony. *The Golden Pine Cone.* Toronto: Macmillan, 1950.

Coleridge, Samuel Taylor. *Biographia Literaria.* 1817. London: J. M. Dent, 1975.

Collodi, Carlo, pseud. *The Adventures of Pinocchio.* Translated from the Italian by M. A. Murray. London: T. Fisher Unwin, 1892.

Cooper, Susan. *The Dark Is Rising.* New York: Atheneum, 1973.

Eager, Edward. *Half-Magic.* New York: Harcourt, 1954.

Egoff, Sheila. *Thursday's Child: Trends and Patterns in Contemporary Children's Literature.* Chicago: American Library Association, 1981.

Ellis, Sarah. *Back of Beyond.* Toronto: Douglas & McIntyre, 1996.

Forster, E. M. *Aspects of the Novel.* 1927. New York: Harcourt, Brace & World, 1954.

Fraser, William Alexander. *Mooswa and Others of the Boundaries.* Toronto: Briggs, 1900.

Galloway, Priscilla. *Truly Grim Tales.* Toronto: Lester, 1995.

Garner, Alan. *Elidor.* London: Collins, 1965.

——. *The Owl Service.* London: Collins, 1967.

Godden, Rumer. *The Doll's House.* London: Michael Joseph, 1947.

Grahame, Kenneth. *The Wind in the Willows.* London: Methuen, 1908.

Grimm, Jakob, and Wilhelm Grimm. *German Popular Stories.* Translated by Edward Taylor. London: C. Baldwyn, 1823.

Hoban, Russell. *The Mouse and His Child.* New York: Harper, 1967.

Hughes, Monica. *The Keeper of the Isis Light.* Toronto: Nelson, 1980.

Katz, Welwyn Wilton. *Out of the Dark.* Toronto: Groundwood, 1995.

——. *The Third Magic.* Vancouver: Douglas & McIntyre, 1988.

Kipling, Rudyard. *The Jungle Book.* London: Macmillan & Co., 1894.

——. *Just So Stories.* London: Macmillan, 1902.

Laurence, Margaret. *Jason's Quest.* Toronto: McClelland & Stewart, 1971.

——. *The Olden Days Coat.* Toronto: McClelland & Stewart, 1979.

Lawson, Julie. *White Jade Tiger.* Victoria: Beach Holme, 1993.

LeGuin, Ursula. *A Wizard of Earthsea.* Berkeley: Parnassus, 1968.

L'Engle, Madeline. *A Wrinkle in Time.* New York: Farrar, 1962.

Lewis, C. S. *The Lion, the Witch and the Wardrobe.* London: Geoffrey Bles, 1950.

——. "On Three Ways of Writing for Children." 1952. In Sheila Egoff, G. T. Stubbs, and L. F. Ashley, eds., *Only Connect: Readings on Children's Literature,* 207–20. Toronto: Oxford University Press, 1969.

Lindgren, Astrid. *Pippi Longstocking.* Translated by Florence Lamborn. New York: Viking, 1950.

Lively, Penelope. *The Ghost of Thomas Kempe.* Bath: Chivers Press, 1986.

Lunn, Janet. *The Root Cellar.* Toronto: Lester & Orpen Dennys, 1981.

MacDonald, George. *At the Back of the North Wind.* London: Strahan & Co., 1871.

——. *The Princess and the Goblin.* London and Philadelphia: Lippincott, 1872.
Mahy, Margaret. *The Changeover.* London: Dent, 1981.
Major, Kevin. *Blood Red Ochre.* Toronto: Doubleday, 1989.
Melling, O. R. *The Hunter's Moon.* Toronto: HarperCollins, 1993.
——. *The Summer King.* Markham: Viking, 1999.
Milne, A. A. *The House at Pooh Corner.* London: Methuen, 1928.
——. *Winnie-the-Pooh.* London: Methuen, 1926.
Nesbit, Edith. *The Five Children and It.* London: T. Fisher Unwin, 1902.
——. *Harding's Luck.* London: Hodder & Stoughton, 1909.
Nichols, Ruth. *The Marrow of the World.* Toronto: Macmillan, 1972.
——. *A Walk Out of the World.* Don Mills: Longman, 1969.
Norton, Mary. *The Borrowers.* London: J. M. Dent, 1952.
Oppel, Kenneth. *Silverwing.* Toronto: HarperCollins, 1997.
——. *Sunwing.* Toronto: HarperCollins, 1999.
Pearce, Philippa. *Tom's Midnight Garden.* London: Oxford University Press, 1958.
Pearson, Kit. *A Handful of Time.* Markham: Viking, 1987.
Pullman, Philip. *Northern Lights.* London: Scholastic, 1995.
Richler, Mordecai. *Jacob Two-Two Meets the Hooded Fang.* Toronto: McClelland & Stewart, 1975.
Rowling, J. K. *Harry Potter and the Philosopher's Stone.* London: Bloomsbury, 1997.
Ruskin, John. *The King of the Golden River.* London: Smith, Elder & Co., 1851.
Scrimger, Richard. *The Nose from Jupiter.* Toronto: Tundra, 1998.
Tolkien, J. R. R. *The Hobbit; or, There and Back Again.* London: Allen & Unwin, 1937.
——. *The Lord of the Rings.* London: Allen & Unwin, 1954–55.
——. "On Fairy-Stories." In *Tree and Leaf,* 11–70. London: Unwin Books, 1964.
Verne, Jules. *Twenty Thousand Leagues under the Sea.* London: S. Low, Marston, Low & Sear, 1873.
White, E. B. *Charlotte's Web.* New York: Harper, 1967.
Wilde, Oscar. *The Happy Prince and Other Tales.* London: David Nutt, 1888.